LECTURES
ON CONTEMPORARY
SYNTACTIC THEORIES

CSLI
Lecture Notes
Number 3

LECTURES
ON CONTEMPORARY
SYNTACTIC THEORIES

AN INTRODUCTION TO GOVERNMENT-BINDING THEORY, GENERALIZED PHRASE STRUCTURE GRAMMAR, AND LEXICAL-FUNCTIONAL GRAMMAR

Peter Sells

Postscript by Thomas Wasow

CENTER FOR THE STUDY
OF LANGUAGE
AND INFORMATION

CSLI was founded early in 1983 by researchers from Stanford University, SRI International, and Xerox PARC to further research and development of integrated theories of language, information, and computation. CSLI headquarters and the publication offices are located at the Stanford site.

CSLI/SRI International   **CSLI/Stanford**   **CSLI/Xerox PARC**
333 Ravenswood Avenue   Ventura Hall   3333 Coyote Hill Road
Menlo Park, CA 94025   Stanford, CA 94305   Palo Alto, CA 94304

Library of Congress Cataloging-in-Publication Data

Sells, Peter.
  Lectures on contemporary syntactic theories.

  (CSLI lecture notes ; no. 3)
Bibliography: p.
Includes indexes.

  1. Grammar, Comparative and general–Syntax.
2. Government-binding theory (Linguistics) 3. Gener-
alized phrase structure grammar. 4. Lexical-function-
al grammar. 5. Generative grammar. I. Title. II.
Series.
P291.S36   1987   415   87–10243
ISBN 0–937073–13–X
ISBN 0–937073–14–8 (pbk.)

Author's Preface

This second printing incorporates several minor changes of text and references, but does not differ in any substantial way from its predecessor. There has been some minor reformatting, and indexes of names and subjects have been added. The changes that have been made are due in large part to the comments I have received from many people over the past year; my thanks to them all.

In the Spring of 1985, I gave a series of lectures on contemporary syntactic theories at the University of California, Santa Cruz, covering Government-Binding Theory, Generalized Phrase Structure Grammar, and Lexical-Functional Grammar. The material presented here is based on my notes from those lectures. I have tried to provide enough background so that the non-linguist might understand the concepts and motivations in each of the theories. To that end, I include a short introductory chapter. In addition, Tom Wasow has generously provided a Postscript to my own presentation which gives a more general historical and methodological overview.

I should emphasize that the three theories discussed here by no means exhaust the inventory of syntactic theories deserving the label 'contemporary'; rather, these are the ones of which I have enough knowledge to be able to discuss them in a serious way. I have not made any effort to compare analyses of particular constructions; such an enterprise would require another separate book in itself. Rather, I have tried to present the most important aspects of each of the theories. I have also limited myself (except where forced by expository obligations) to discussion of purely syntactic aspects of these theories.

Syntactic theories change rather rapidly, and nothing presented here represents the current state of the art within any theory; moreover, I have not attempted to provide definitive analyses, but rather representative ones. The version of Government-Binding Theory presented here is roughly that in Chomsky (1981) and Chomsky (1982), and does not incorporate recent developments documented in Chomsky (1986a, 1986b). The version of Generalized Phrase Structure Grammar is that given in Gazdar, Klein, Pullum, and Sag (1985), and does not include recent developments stemming out of the work of Pollard (1984). Finally, the version of Lexical-Functional Grammar is based on that presented in Kaplan and Bresnan (1982), with some more recent modifications added. In each case, I have chosen the particular formulation of the theory that seems to me to be most internally consistent and accessible to the non-specialist. I have not provided extensive references, though it has been my intention that from the references I do provide, the reader will be able to work back to a wider literature.

I would like to thank everyone connected with the Syntax Research Center at Santa Cruz for their hospitality and kindness, especially Victoria Liptak, who organized the lecture series. The presentation of the material here has benefited greatly from comments on an earlier draft by Joan Bresnan, Carol Cleland, Edit Doron, Ron Kaplan, David Perlmutter, Geoffrey Pullum, Ivan Sag, Tim Stowell, Tom Wasow, and Annie Zaenen, though I remain solely responsible for all errors, inconsistencies and misstatements that persist. The writing and preparation of this work would have been much more arduous without the support of Geoffrey Pullum, Ivan Sag, and Tom Wasow, and without the aid of Masayo Iida and Dikran Karagueuzian, who, in their own ways, suffered uncomplainingly in their dealings with an impatient author. I would also like to thank Emma Pease for her work on my final draft, to bring it into its present form.

The published version of these notes was prepared at The Center for the Study of Language and Information, and was made possible by a gift from the System Development Foundation.

–Stanford
February, 1987

Contents

Author's Preface

Chapter 1 *Basic Concepts of Syntax* **1**

1. Syntactic Competence   2
    1.1 Grammaticality   3
    1.2 Universal Properties of Language   4
    1.3 Data   6
2. Constituency   9
    2.1 Tree Diagrams   10
    2.2 Labelled Bracketing   11
3. Phrase Structure Rules   11
4. The Lexicon   13
    4.1 Lexical Insertion   13
    4.2 Subcategorization   14
5. Transformations   15

Chapter 2 *Government-Binding Theory*   **19**

1. X′-Theory   27
    1.1 The X′-Scheme   27
    1.2 Subcategorization   31
2. Projection Principle   33
3. θ-Theory   35
    3.1 θ-Roles   35
    3.2 θ-Criterion   37
4. C-Command and Government   38
5. Move-α 42
    5.1 Trace Theory and Empty Categories   42
    5.2 Coindexing   44
    5.3 Landing Sites   46
    5.4 Subjacency   48
6. Case Theory   52
7. Summary of Types of Movement and
   Complement Structures   57
8. Empty Category Principle (ECP)   62
9. Binding and NP-types   67
    9.1 Binding Theory and the Typology of
       Empty Categories   67

9.2 Control   73

Chapter 3   *Generalized Phrase Structure Grammar*   77

1. Features and Syntactic Categories   80
    1.1 X′-Theory   81
    1.2 Categories   82
    1.3 Features   83
2. ID/LP Format   84
    2.1 ID/LP   85
    2.2 Heads and Subcategorization   86
3. Rules   89
    3.1 Lexical and Non-Lexical ID-Rules   89
    3.2 Metarules   90
4. Sketch of Semantics   97
5. Projecting From Rules To Trees   100
    5.1 Feature Cooccurrence Restrictions   102
    5.2 Feature Specification Defaults   103
    5.3 Head Feature Convention   105
    5.4 Foot Feature Principle   107
    5.5 Control Agreement Principle   112
    5.6 Linear Precedence Statements   117
6. Unbounded Dependencies and Coordination   119
    6.1 Unbounded Dependencies   119
    6.2 Coordinate Structures   127

Chapter 4   *Lexical-Functional Grammar*   135

1. Constituent Structures   138
    1.1 Phrase Structure   138
    1.2 Functional Annotations   140
2. Functional Structures   144
    2.1 Properties of F-Structure   144
    2.2 Well-Formedness Conditions on F-Structures   146
    2.3 From C-Structures to F-Structures   147
3. The Lexicon   154
    3.1 Types of Grammatical Function   155
    3.2 Subcategorization   156
    3.3 Some Sample Lexical Entries   158
    3.4 Lexical Rules   160
4. Control and Binding   164
    4.1 Functional Control   165

4.2 Anaphoric Control   171
4.3 Anaphoric Binding   174
5. Long-Distance Dependencies and Coordination   179
    5.1 Long-Distance Dependencies   179
    5.2 Coordination   186

Chapter 5   *Postscript*
            by Thomas Wasow   193

            List of Abbreviations   207
            References   209
            Index of Names   217
            Index of Subjects   219

Chapter 1

Basic Concepts of Syntax

The different syntactic theories that I will describe here have a shared ancestry and a common core domain of concepts and terminology. This chapter will provide a backdrop against which the remaining chapters will be set, and will cover the basic vocabulary and the shared assumptions that are basic to contemporary syntactic theory.

In fact, for many readers of this book, the very idea of syntax as it is conceived of here may be somewhat unusual; the various rules of syntax—or of grammar—that we remember from high school are usually of a pre-scriptive nature. Probably the most salient and common is the supposed prohibition against splitting the infinitive: against saying, for example, *to boldly go* rather than *to go boldly*. The factors that govern the distribution of these two alternatives are partly historical and, in our current society, partly sociological. From the point of view of syntax—and from this point on I use both the terms 'syntax' and 'grammar' in a technical sense—forces of history and sociology are largely irrelevant. For syntax concerns itself not with the distinction between a possible phrase in English such as *to go boldly* and a passable (if somehow dispreferred) variant; syntax concerns itself with the possible and the *im*possible phrases of English, or of any other human language for that matter. The key datum in syntax is a difference that a native speaker will assent to, that some sentence A is possible while sentence B is under no stretch of the imagination acceptable as a sentence of the language in question. If one is developing a theory of gravity, the key datum is that things fall and very rarely rise. The difference between possible and impossible sentences is in principle no different from the point of view of constructing a theory to explain some observed behavior as the difference between attraction to a large body and repulsion from it, and in practice that linguistic difference is at least as hard to discern as is 'pure fall,' with all external effects and disturbances removed. In the following section, I would like to elucidate the nature of syntactic data as conceived by practitioners of the theories to be described below.

However, before moving on, I would not like to leave the reader with the impression that the study of syntax is of necessity divorced from perhaps more tangible considerations of history, sociology, and whatever else contributes to human experience. Ultimately, when we know much more about all these things, syntax will have its place in larger theories of human action and human interaction; until then, it is probably wise, and from my current exegetical point of view essential, to leave such larger considerations out of mind. One of the compelling things about syntax is that while the study of it is a highly abstract theoretical enterprise, syntacticians are discovering and refining their understanding of phenomena that are arguably quite real.

1. Syntactic Competence

The beginning point of the syntactic enterprise as conceived of currently is the question "What do we know when we know a language (say English)?" The answer given by Noam Chomsky in his book *Syntactic Structures,* published in 1957, brought about a whole new discipline within the larger field of linguistics; his answer was that what we know is a collection of words and rules with which we *generate* strings of those words which we call sentences of our language. Any string of words that cannot be produced in this way is not a sentence of the language. Moreover, while there are only a finite number of elements in this collection, say several thousand words and no more than a few hundred rules, they will generate an infinite number of sentences, some of them very long. This will happen as some of the rules will be recursive, i.e., they apply to their own output to produce the same structure over again. For example, any linguist will tell you that *George thinks that it never rains in Tulsa* is a sentence of English, and that we can continue to produce new sentences of English by embedding that under the sequence *George thinks that* .... We will end up with sentences of the form *George thinks that George thinks that ... George thinks that it never rains in Tulsa*; if we collect all of these sentences we will have a boring, somewhat useless, but nevertheless syntactically impeccable subset of English.[1] These will all be, then, *grammatical* sentences. The subfield

---

[1] It is important to note that it is the *structure* that is generated over and over here; with a few more words we could add to our set structurally identical

of linguistics that takes this point of view, that what is important is this conception of generating sentences, is known as *Generative Grammar*.

1.1. Grammaticality

Language ultimately expresses a relation between sound at one end of the linguistic spectrum and meaning at the other. I produce sounds—or, in the present context, graphic symbols—which you perceive and derive some meaning from. Somewhere in the middle of this process lies syntax. It is a fact of English, for instance, that the sequence *The women sold the paintings* can convey a certain meaning that *The women the paintings sold* can not. Two points are relevant here: one, it is not the case that we couldn't guess what this last example would mean—what it should mean is relatively clear; the point is, one is not speaking English if one chooses to convey that meaning in that way. Secondly, there are many languages of the world in which the word-for-word translation of the second example is indeed a grammatical (and in some cases the only grammatical) way of arranging the words in question to convey the meaning in question. Thus, there is nothing inherent in the message conveyed that could explain the impossibility of that sequence as being a sentence of English.

In *Syntactic Structures*, Chomsky gave the now-famous example (1) to illustrate the importance of investigating syntax independently (in part) of other considerations:

(1)   Colorless green ideas sleep furiously.

This is meaningless in any usual sense yet, again, syntactically impeccable. In contrast, (2) is as senseless, yet also syntactically deviant:

(2)   *Furiously sleep ideas green colorless.

The asterisk (*) preceding the example indicates that it is syntactically ill-formed; thus our rules for English should be set up so as to produce (1) but not (2). We see the syntactic distinction again if we replace the words in these examples with others so that the whole thing makes sense, as in (3).

(3)   a.   Revolutionary new ideas appear infrequently.

       b.   *Infrequently appear ideas new revolutionary.

---

but rather more useful sentences like *George thinks that Max said that Betty believes that it never rains in Tulsa.*

In these examples, I have replaced some words with other words belonging to the same part of speech—or, as I shall say here, in more usual linguistic usage—belonging to the same *syntactic category*. In fact, this switch indicates another aspect of syntax that Chomsky emphasized—the structure of sentences. For the real syntactic truth underlying the contrasts in grammaticality seen above is that while some sequences of the form

Adjective-Adjective-Noun-Verb-Adverb

are syntactically well-formed in English, sequences of the form

Adverb-Verb-Noun-Adjective-Adjective

are not. Plugging in certain combinations of words will also lead to sentences that are meaningful in the former case, but this is not a relevant consideration if we are just concerned with syntactic well-formedness. A more subtle grammatical (i.e., syntactic) contrast is seen in the examples in (4):

(4)   a.   The book seems interesting.

   b.   *The child seems sleeping.

Again, it is obvious what (4)b means; but again it is not English (the closest acceptable example is *The child seems to be sleeping*).

Although I have spoken here of strings of words, the most important aspect of the syntax is its structure, and not simply the strings. I will discuss the concept of structure in more detail in the following section.

1.2. Universal Properties of Language

I have so far talked mainly about data from English; yet what I have said would hold, other things being equal, for any other human language too. Thus it is a fact of English sentence structure that it has the basic order subject-verb-object (*The man read the book*), while Welsh, for instance, has verb-subject-object (*Gwelodd – y dyn – y llyfr*), and Japanese has subject-object-verb (*Sono otoko ga – hon o – yonda*).

When someone knows a language, any language, that person is considered to possess a certain competence such that they can distinguish between grammatical and ungrammatical sequences of words in that language. Actually, we must be a bit more precise here, and note that we are talking about the grammaticality of sequences of words *qua* sentences.

For example, the sequence *the man the woman was accidentally* is not a grammatical sentence, but it can be part of a grammatical sentence: *Ferdinand rescued the man the woman was accidentally chained to.* (Anyone still having difficulty should imagine a *that* between *man* and *the woman*.)

Digressing briefly, I should point out that I will use the words 'word' and 'sentence' without providing a definition of either. These particular terms appear to resist all scrutiny, and while I know of countless definitions and counter-definitions in the literature, I know of none that accord with intuition in all cases. Yet in the case of sentences, which is what we are primarily interested in here, we can be sure that we are restricting ourselves in our syntactic work to a subset of English sentences. While we might not be able to claim (as no one can at present) to have an understanding of all of English, we can claim to have an understanding of some of it.

So, while studying and making hypotheses about the syntax of, say, English or Irish, we must be careful to keep in mind a range of potential variation. It is a goal of syntactic theory to provide a descriptive space within which the range of variation that we find among languages is precisely captured. That is, we would like to have a theory which is flexible enough to allow us to characterize all the fine variation we find, while still not allowing us to even consider certain possibilities; to choose a common example illustrating the last desideratum here, there are no languages in which questions are formed from normal sentences by reversing all the words in the sentence, as if (3)b were an interrogative form of (3)a.

Ultimately, knowledge of this sort would lead us to various new reseach areas concerned with the mind—we might ask questions like "What can we find out about the computational procedures and capacities of the brain given that we know that it never has to deal with operations reversing all linguistic symbols in a given sequence?" or "How is it possible that language is learned?" This latter question is considered very important and has been very influential in shaping research programs in syntax. Chomsky certainly conceives of linguistics (i.e., syntax) as a part of cognitive psychology in that ultimately we are probing properties of the mind. There is a large and healthy sub-discipline of Psycholinguistics which relates our knowledge of the mind and of language.

Again, it is not necessary to go into detail on these matters here, for the matters of syntax that I will discuss below are (or can be considered) largely independent of psycholinguistic concerns; the only point is that 'universal' in the sense that it will be used in this work refers to properties ultimately attributed to mental phenomena, rather than, say, social ones. There is a wide range of variation among linguists as to how psychologically real they conceive their syntactic theories to be, and in a presentation like this I think it is better to err on the side of caution. So when I speak of syntactic explanation I will initially be speaking of a system of description that covers the most facts with the minimum number of independent assumptions and postulations. I leave it up to personal preference whether a theory of syntax is to be viewed as a direct account of our linguistic knowledge, or as a description of a system whose behavior models our linguistic behavior.

1.3. Data

In this subsection I would like to address two matters, one of substance in the theoretical sense and one of substance in the material sense. Each distinction of syntactic structure that we find is the result of a little experiment—we find our native speaker of Irish or Hopi or whatever we want, and we try to tap that person's sense of grammaticality of certain strings of words. Linguists refer to these judgements as *intuitions*. Intuitions are, unfortunately, not presented to us in any obvious way, and often they are not simple matters of 'ungrammatical' (*) versus 'OK.' Consider the examples in (5): how do we describe a book belonging to Martha and me?

(5)   a.   Martha and my book

     b.   Martha's and my book

     c.   Martha and me's book

     d.   Martha and I's book

There are many more possibilities here. We may also have some prescriptive idea of how to say this. My sense, for what it is worth, is that (d) is not acceptable and that all of the others are clumsy but I could imagine producing them. From these facts alone, then, we don't know exactly how to describe the rules for putting together English noun phrases (for that is what these examples are; a noun phrase usually contains a noun and maybe some modifying adjectives and determiners). Yet some things seem clearly no good—for example, *Martha's and me book* is surely impossible, and should be excluded. So even this apparently failing little experiment can give us some useful data.

    Fuzziness of intuitions is noise in the data to the syntactician, and one must simply find ways to deal with it. Linguists live with this fuzziness and try to stick with clear cases as much as possible; and as intuitions are not something the normal speaker of English has any conception of, linguists have to learn to tap into their intuitions. Linguists are in a sense language-experts, for they, if anyone, have some idea of what is English and what isn't. Consequently, it is quite possible that some of the judgements of grammaticality that I will indicate in the following chapters, while accepted by a body of professional linguists, will seem opaque and perhaps perverse to the reader. I shall therefore take a little more space below in elucidating the notion of intuitions.

First, let me try a little experiment on your intuitions. Imagine that I'm asking questions about a movie that you saw and the man who directed it.

(6) a.   Which movie did you meet the man that directed?

     b.   Which man did you see the movie that directed?

Both of the sentences in (6) are ungrammatical,[2] yet one can still sense a contrast—(b) is somehow *worse* than (a). You will probably experience a structural effect in (b)—it seems to want to have the interpretation where the movie directed the man, which is silly given our real-world knowledge. I would note that although this is a feature of the interpretation of the example, it is nonetheless a syntactic feature, for it derives from a decision about what should be the subject and what should be the object of the verb *direct*.

There are two further points about intuitions that I would like to make; the first concerns the relationship between intuitions of grammaticality and our actual linguistic usage. It is not a claim of theoretical syntax that people actually speak all the time in fully grammatical sentences—clearly this is not so; there are innumerable mental and physical obstacles to be overcome in any given speech-situation. Does this undermine the foundation upon which the study of syntax is based?—not in the least, for what is important is that once the rigors of actually producing speech are abstracted away from, one can get fairly reliable data about what is and what is

---

[2] It is a strange quirk of linguistic terminology that leads me to be able to speak of 'ungrammatical sentence,' for these should be mutually incompatible terms. It is, of course, a potentially significant fact that English (or any other language to the best of my knowledge) does not provide a word meaning 'thing that would be a sentence if only it weren't ungrammatical.' As this is even more unwieldy than 'ungrammatical sentence,' I shall be sloppy and stick to the shorter phrase.

not English. Using a close analogy, philosophers and semanticists concern themselves a lot with truth-conditions when talking about meaning. Thus one would normally use the sentence *It is raining in Tulsa* if indeed it were true that it was raining in Tulsa, and any native speaker would assent to this. Yet it is not a semantic fact of any human language that its speakers (always) speak the truth; again, quite clearly they do not. (This is not to deny that there is in general some communicative utility to speaking the truth, and usually people do; big liars are people who tell big lies, not who lie with every utterance. Similarly, most utterances are grammatical, especially in careful styles.)

The last point about intuitions is more of a caveat. The intuitions we have are intuitions relative to a structure assigned to the example under consideration. Given enough imagination and time, it is probable that most of the sequences of words deemed ungrammatical in this work could be found to be acceptable. For example, any linguist will tell you that (7) is ungrammatical:

(7)   *Reagan thinks bananas.

Why? For the verb *think* takes as its complement (i.e., the sequence that follows it) something that is of a sentential, or clausal, nature, as in *Reagan thinks that it never rains in Tulsa.* Yet we have apparently given *thinks* a direct object noun phrase, as if it were *Reagan sells bananas.* Assigned this syntactic structure, the example is ungrammatical because it has failed to conform to the rules of English.

Now the string *Reagan thinks bananas* is in fact acceptable, as will be apparent in (8):

(8)   What is Kissinger's favorite fruit?
         —Reagan thinks bananas.

We understand this with the clausal complement, as our rules say we must; the interpretation of the example is something like *Reagan thinks (that) bananas (are Kissinger's favourite fruit),* with the parenthesized words omitted. In confirming that the complement of *think* really must be a sentence, this again demonstrates the importance of investigating the structure assigned rather than the string.

At the beginning of this subsection I said I would talk about the theoretical and material substance of judgements and example sentences and phrases. All of the above has been the theoretical part; now I will say a few words about material substance.

Example sentences in syntax are used to make specific points of theoretical relevance, though the same sentence may of course be used to demonstrate different points. In general, examples are constructed by the linguist, often on the spur of the moment (an ability to produce relevant examples quickly is a definite asset), and become data objects through publication in the literature and subsequent discussion and analysis. For example, it is part of many people's syntactic training to learn about the 'sonata-sentences' and to understand why they are important. (Their importance is too much buried in complex theoretical issues for me to display it here.) Consequently, most of the examples here will probably strike the reader as unimaginative at best; this is precisely what they are, for again we are not concerned with usage, but with underlying knowledge. In fact, the different theories described below use slightly different styles of example, and I have done my best to make each chapter representative in that regard too—though I defer to my reader a theory of what those differences indicate.

2. Constituency

I have been speaking of the structure assigned to a string of words; one thing that is clear is that the job of syntax is not simply to characterize strings of English, but also to assign them an appropriate structure. Exactly how one goes about deciding what structure is correct in any particular case is a very complex matter that I could not describe here. And in the context of the present discussion of syntactic theories, this matter is again not crucially relevant, for there is a fair amount of agreement on what structures to assign, in general. Differences of opinion arise, though, over what information those structures carry and how the theory relates occurring structures in the language to non-occurring ones.

Pieces of syntax that are constructed out of smaller pieces of syntax are called *constituents*. For example, the noun phrase *several smelly fish* is a constituent, consisting of a determiner, an adjective, and a noun. Another constituent is the verb phrase (a phrase usually containing a verb and some other stuff) *bothered Nigel*. Combining these two constituents, we can get a sentence, whose minimal constituent structure is shown in (9):

(9)

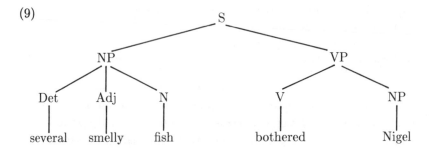

The sentence (S) consists of a noun phrase (NP) and a verb phrase (VP).[3] Rules which affect noun phrases will, under ideal circumstances, affect the NP *several smelly fish* or the NP *Nigel* equally. On the other hand, we expect to find no rules that affect the sequence *fish bothered,* for that is not a constituent. In fact, if we did encounter such a rule, that would count as evidence for the hypothesis that these things really did form a constituent, perhaps contradicting other observations.

Often it is convenient to suppress the internal structure of a constituent, where it is not relevant to the point at hand, and this is represented in the following way:

2.1. Tree Diagrams

The structure shown in (9) is known as a tree diagram, or more usually simply a *tree* that represents the syntactic structure of the sentence or phrase in question. Various important technical terms are stated in terms of tree-geometry (continuing with (9) as an example), such as:

---

[3] Many terms used in syntax have standard abbreviations; linguists, for example, nearly always speak of "an NP" rather than "a noun phrase." It is also a common practice to introduce abbreviations for names of theories and principles which are used over and over again. The non-linguist might find this a little disturbing, and so I have provided at the end of this work an appendix of the abbreviations used throughout.

- A sentence of the language is a string assigned a syntactic structure that is *rooted* in the category S (i.e., S is the topmost category label). There may be additional occurrences of S within the entire S.

- The *node* of the tree labelled S *dominates* everything else in the tree. S *immediately dominates* NP and VP. The relation of domination is very important in that lots of syntactic rules and operations refer to it.

- The node S is the *mother* of NP and VP, and NP and VP are *sisters* (i.e., NP and VP have the same mother). Note that N and V are not sisters.

- A *constituent* is any section of tree that has a single mother.

These are some of the basic features of syntactic trees.

2.2. Labelled Bracketing

Sometimes it is convenient, and sometimes it is more revealing, to use a different representation of constituency. This involves the *labelled bracketing* representation, which encodes the same information as a tree but presents it linearly. The labelled bracketing of the example (9) is shown in (10):

(10) $[_S [_{NP} [_{Det}$ several$][_{Adj}$ smelly$][_N$ fish$]] [_{VP} [_V$ bothered$][_{NP}$ Nigel$]]]$

These representations will undoubtedly be quite hard to follow at first for those readers unfamiliar with them, but are very commonly used in syntactic description, and I mention them for that reason. Where possible, I will use trees in the rest of this work, but sometimes the labelled bracketing has much more utility, and in those cases I will use it.

3. Phrase Structure Rules

Trees represent the structure of phrases and sentences of the language. The next question is then, Where do the trees come from? That is, how does our syntactic theory tell us which structures are well-formed and which are not? The basic answer to this question is that we specify a set of rules which *generate* trees; our knowledge of syntax consists in a knowledge of such rules. For what we have seen so far, the *phrase structure rules* (PS-rules) shown in (11) will generate the tree under consideration.

(11) a.   S   →   NP VP

   b.   NP   →   Det Adj N

   c.   VP   →   V NP

Technically, the arrow means 'rewrites as' (i.e., if you have an S, you can 'rewrite it as' NP and VP). For purposes here, we can interpret the arrow as 'expands as' (i.e., 'dominates in the tree').

There are two variations on the little system in (11) that I wish to consider here; the first introduces recursion and the second introduces optionality. Some verbs, like *think* as discussed above, do not take NPs as their object (as specified by rule (11)c), but rather sentences (Ss). If we add to our little grammar the rule in (12), the size of the set of trees generated becomes potentially infinite.

(12)   VP   →   V S

For now this rule can 'feed' (11)a, and we will generate Ss within Ss, and we now have a system that generates as many objects as we could possibly want. (Of course, the hard work still remains—we have to get the rules to generate exactly the right structures, not simply any old structures.) This is an important step towards capturing the nature of the flexiblity and creativity of language.

The notion of optionality is perhaps less impressive. Consider the first set of rules in (11). While an English NP is grammatical if it contains a determiner, an adjective, and a noun, this is not the only option. In fact, just having a noun would suffice (as in *Fish bother Nigel*), and so we will want to make the determiner and adjective optional. Similarly, within the VP, some verbs can get by without an object (e.g., *sneeze*), and so we should make the NP optional. In English, neither category on the right-hand side of the S-rule is optional, but in other languages the NP is arguably optional (e.g., Italian *verrò* 'I will come'). So we can revise the rules in (11) to those in (13), according to the variation we find in English, and we use parentheses to indicate an optional constituent:

(13) a.   S   →   NP VP

   b.   NP   →   (Det) (Adj) N

   c.   VP   →   V (NP)

This gives an overview of the way we produce trees; but sentences are trees with words on the bottom, and so the next step is to get the words in.

4. The Lexicon

Part of our linguistic knowledge involves knowledge of a large number of words, which constitute our vocabulary, or the *lexicon* as linguists have it. In general, the elements of the lexicon are what we might think of as words, although different syntactic theories have slightly different conceptions of what a 'lexical item' is, and so it is not always safe to think of the lexicon as just a stock of words. In particular, the lexicon of a generative grammar may contain a listing of various affixes, such as the *-s* verbal affix in English (the affix that distinguishes *the sheep walks* from *the sheep walk*). The study of word-formation, e.g., 'verb+*s*,' is known as *morphology*, for it relates to the form of words. The study of *phonology* is the study of the way things sound; thus it is a fact of English morphology that the 3rd-person singular present tense affix is *-s*, and a fact of English phonology that it is pronounced 's' in some environments and 'z' in others (compare the last sound in *stinks* with that in *stings*).

4.1. Lexical Insertion

When lexical entries of the appropriate category are inserted onto the bottom of a tree, we then have a sentence. Lexical entries, like *fish* and *tall* and *suddenly*, are known as *terminal symbols*; the tree stops there, in a sense. Categories like V and N and Adj are known as *preterminals*. We can express lexical insertion in our PS-rule format as below in (14); I also introduce a bit more notation: curly brackets indicate a choice point. So (14)a says that V can immediately dominate *sneeze* or *sleep* or *cook*, etc.; and I use A for 'adjective,' which is the more usual notation.

(14) a. V → { *sneeze, sleep, cook, tell, ...* }

   b. N → { *fish, man, despair, bathtub, ...* }

   c. A → { *smelly, tall, confident, fake, ...* }

Nothing prevents what looks like the same word from appearing in different categories—so *sneeze, sleep,* and *cook* are all nouns as well as verbs. In such cases, it is safest simply to consider that we have two different, though related, lexical items that happen to sound the same.

4.2. Subcategorization

Lexical entries carry lots of different information about lexical items—
think of the average entry in a good dictionary. For example, the entry
of the lexical item *give* will contain the information that it belongs to the
syntactic category of verb, that it is pronounced in a certain way, that its
past tense form is irregular (*gave* not **gived*), what it means, and so on.
I will cover some of these kinds of information in the following chapters.
One very important piece of information that some lexical items carry is
the information linguists call *subcategorization*. The simplest illustration
of this is the difference between a transitive and an intransitive verb; a
transitive verb must have an object in order to be grammatical, and an
intransitive verb cannot have such an object. This is illustrated in the
examples in (15).

(15) a.   Caesar died.

b.   *Caesar produced.

c.   *Caesar died four children.

d.   Caesar produced four children.

The rules we have given so far, if augmented with the appropriate lexical items, would generate all four of these examples. What we need to do
is to divide the class of verbs into *subcategories,* such as the intransitives,
the transitives, etc.; we must add into the lexical entry for *die* the restriction that it can *only* be inserted into a syntactic structure with no object
following the V, and the opposite for *produce*. (Again, verbs may belong to
more than one subcategory, and commonly do—*eat* is a popular example
of a verb that may be either transitive or intransitive.)

Some sample lexical entries of verbs are shown in (16), followed by
some example verb-phrases.

(16)   die, V, _

sneeze, V, _

eat, V, _

eat, V, _ NP   *eat fried shrimp*

produce, V, _ NP   *produce four children*

devour, V, _ NP   *devour the meatball*

give, V, _ NP PP   *give a cookie to Sam*

think, V, _ S   *think that Max likes fish*

tell, V, _ NP S   *tell Susie that elephants fly*

The sixth line here, for instance, says that *devour* is a verb, and that it must appear in the environment (the ' _ ') immediately preceding an NP. We say that it *subcategorizes for* the NP, and the last part of the entry (following the second comma) is called the *subcategorization frame*. As another example, the seventh line says that *give* subcategorizes for a noun phrase (NP) and a prepositional phrase (PP), in that order.

5. Transformations

In *Syntactic Structures*, Chomsky gave various arguments to show that PS-rules alone were not adequate to give a reasonable description of English, and by extension, any human language. I will not go into these arguments here, for they will arise naturally in the chapter on Generalized Phrase Structure Grammar, which *is* a theory of syntax that tries to use only (mechanisms equivalent to) phrase structure rules. The fact of history is that, from the early 1960s until the 1980s, the dominant theory of grammar was Transformational Grammar, developed originally by Chomsky. A transformational grammar takes a lexicon and PS-rules and augments the system with *transformations,* which take structures created by PS-rules and transform them into new structures.

For example, questions[4] in English are different from normal sentences in that (a) a *wh*-word or -phrase (such as *who, how many fish,* etc.) appears initially, (b) some position within the clause (the 'body' of the structure) is missing a phrase where you would expect one in a normal sentence, and (c) an auxiliary verb (*do*) appears in the structure. Thus, in a certain sense, (17)b is a 'question-version' of (17)a:

(17) a.   The police want to arrest that man.

b.   Which man do the police want to arrest?

What happens with the auxiliary is not uniform in all cases, and I will switch examples slightly to control for it; in embedded questions in English, nothing corresponding to part (c) above happens. The hypothesis of transformational grammar is that (18)b is derived by letting PS-rules and the lexicon generate (18)a, with a transformation ('Question Formation') altering the structure so that the *wh*-phrase is initial within its S, which I indicate by square brackets.

---

[4] Excluding 'yes-no' questions like *Did Max fall?*.

(18) a.   Maxine wonders [the police want to arrest which man]

    b.   Maxine wonders [which man the police want to arrest]

I will not go into detail about the formulation of transformations here, as there is nothing resembling them in the contemporary theories. A first approximation to 'Question Formation' would be (19).

(19)   Any structure that can be analyzed

$$[_S \text{ X—}wh\text{-NP—Y}]$$

is transformed into

$$[_S \ wh\text{-NP—X—Y}]$$

In (19), X and Y are variables over any sequence of structure, possibly null; so the transformation simply finds a *wh*-phrase somewhere in the structure and puts it at the front.

The classical transformational grammar developed in the 1950s and 1960s was built around this basic scheme; PS-rules and the lexicon create *deep structures,* which are then (possibly) transformed into *surface structures,* which are the output of the grammar. For example, (18)a is the deep structure of (18)b. With an active sentence like *The police arrested that man,* the deep and surface structures will be identical, while its passive counterpart will have the deep structure of the active version, and the Passive transformation will derive from this the surface structure *That man was arrested by the police.* Classical transformational grammar embraced a whole set of transformations, applying in a cyclical order, such as those just discussed, and others such as 'Raising,' '*There*-Insertion,' and 'Relativization' (to produce such pairs as *It seems that Harold is asleep/Harold seems to be asleep, A pig was rooting in the bushes/There was a pig rooting in the bushes,* and relative clauses like *the continent that Columbus discovered*).

Everyone is agreed that simple PS-rules as I gave them above are not adequate to the task of natural language syntax, and that the work done by transformations must be done somehow. The framework of Transformational Grammar is the common ancestry which the three theories to be described here share, and each preserves different aspects (possibly very few) of that framework in attempting to go beyond it. Moreover, Transformational Grammar produced a massive body of data and set certain standards of adequacy with respect to that data that any contemporary theory must match. For the interested reader, Newmeyer (1980) gives an excellent historical account of the developments that took place in generative grammar from 1955 up to 1980, and Newmeyer (1983) presents an overview of the assumptions and concepts of generative grammar.

Chapter 2

Government-Binding Theory

Government-Binding Theory (GB) was developed initially by Chomsky and is in a sense the immediate descendant of Transformational Grammar. In fact, one feature of Government-Binding Theory that distinguishes it from the other theories presented here is that it makes use of transformational operations. However, the 'transformational' nature of these operations is not their most important aspect, and little rests on it. So while there is a direct historical chain from Transformational Grammar to Government-Binding Theory (GB), many of the ideas of GB either alter or in some cases turn around completely their apparent counterparts in earlier theories.

Similarly, much of the terminology that remains from Transformational Grammar (TG) has been revised in Government-Binding Theory. In Chapter 1 I discussed how TG posited two levels of analysis, deep- and surface-structure. As the range of the theory increased during the 1970s, two other levels of representation were brought in; these are now (usually) called *phonetic form* and *logical form*. The levels which persisted from Transformational Grammar (TG) have been renamed *d-structure* and *s-structure*, for they play roles similar but not identical to the TG notions of deep- and surface-structures. The overall organization of the GB grammar is shown in (1). I give below an example that demonstrates each level.

(1)

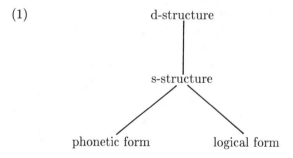

Again, to save confusion with other uses, phonetic form and logical form are usually referred to as PF and LF respectively. PF ('phonetic form') is the level representing the actual string that is the output of the grammar at the 'sound' end; LF ('logical form') is the corresponding level at the 'meaning' end. The properties of PF have not been the focus of much attention in GB, and so I shall say little about them, and concentrate on the other three levels and the relationships among them.

We can now begin to look at those relationships. The TG rule for expanding S (sentence) that came to be widely accepted was slightly more complicated than I have so far suggested, namely:

(2)   S   →   NP Aux VP

In this rule, the new category Aux dominates material carrying information about such things as tense, aspect, verb agreement, and modality in the clause (often carried in English by a 'modal' verb like *might* or *could*). (There has in fact been a long debate over whether there is evidence of syntactic constituency of Aux and VP, though I will not go into the issues here.) Even if there is no modal, information about tense appears under Aux, and these elements are inserted into the tree from the lexicon; for example, the 'underlying' structure of (3)a is shown in (3)b:

(3)   a.   They fired Mary.

      b.   They PAST fire Mary.

In GB, the node Aux is called INFL (for 'inflection'). (3)b would be the structure manipulated by transformations (note too that the lexicon must include elements like PAST, which (arguably) never occur in English as separate words). In GB, (3)b would be both the d- and s-structure of the sentence, for no transformations apply to it. Between s-structure and PF the PAST element is joined with the verb, and is 'spelled-out' as the -*ed* ending on the verb.[1] Here is a case, then, where the s-structure of an example and its PF representation are different. Other typical operations in this part of the grammar are the rule of Auxiliary Reduction (*He is* ⇒ *He's*, etc.) and subject-verb agreement (**Lucy sing* vs. *Lucy sings*). Both

---

[1] In LGB, this operation is called 'Rule R.' Throughout this chapter, 'LGB' refers to Chomsky (1981).

of these are syntactically conditioned in the sense that their s-structure representation will contain the information necessary to their operation, but that operation itself (e.g., the 'spelling-out') takes place in the PF part of the grammar.

The levels of d- and s-structure are related by the transformational operation of Move-α. Here α is understood to be a variable over syntactic categories, and the fundamental idea is that a structure may be altered in any way by 'moving anything anywhere'; independent principles will dictate just what can move and where it can move to, allowing the transformation itself to be stated in a maximally general way. Another way of thinking of it (one that is historically accurate) is that many of the transformations proposed within TG have been factored into elementary operations, one of which is Move-α, which expresses the 'movement' part of a relation between two structures.

For example, passive sentences are derived via Move-α as illustrated in (4) and (5), *Mary was fired* (ignore for now the *e* and the subscript *i* symbols that appear in the trees—they will be explained later):

(4)   d-structure

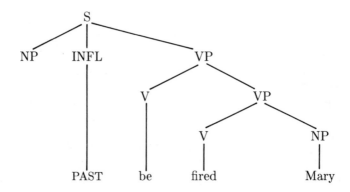

(5)   s-structure

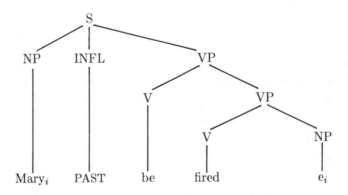

One motivation for this analysis is that we need to ensure that Mary in this example is interpreted as the object upon which the action was performed, that she was the one who got fired, not who did the firing. By having *Mary* in the position of the object of the verb at d-structure, this NP is assigned the status of the semantic object in exactly the same way as in (3)b; however this is actually done for (3)b will carry over directly to the present passive example.

A very important aspect of GB is that it assumes that there are no construction-specific rules, and this is an important departure from TG; while TG has rules (transformations) of Passive, and Question Formation, GB eschews this point of view. So, for example, Passive essentially moves objects to make them subjects; it does not move objects and make them prepositional objects. Exactly the wrong thing to do, as far as GB is concerned, is to set up a rule, which you call Passive, which says to make an object a subject. The GB point of view is not that movement to the subject must be specified, but rather that movement to any other position must be prevented. Thus the GB analysis of passive is that Move-α moves anything anywhere, and that other independent (universal) principles and constraints rule the example out unless the movement happens to be from object to subject position. So passive is the epiphenomenal result of the interaction of various aspects of the grammar, these aspects being direct functions of properties of Universal Grammar (see below). What we find in Universal Grammar, then, is not a rule of Passive, but rather more abstract things like constraints on movement applying across the language as a whole.

Completing the picture, LF encodes information relevant to the semantic interpretation of the example in question—in particular, such matters as quantifier scope and the scope of question-words are dealt with at this level. As illustration, the sentence *Two languages are spoken by most people* has two LFs, as seen in (6):

(6)   a.   [$_S$ Two languages are spoken by [$_{NP}$ most people]]

      b.   [$_{NP}$ most people$_i$] [$_S$ two languages are spoken by e$_i$]

The representations are intended to bear a similarity to the representations used in first-order logic, in which left-right order indicates the relative scope of quantifiers. The first LF represents the interpretation where everyone who knows two languages knows the same two languages; the second interpretation is where maybe each knows different languages. The first LF comes from leaving the s-structure alone, the second from applying Move-α to it, moving the NP *most people* to a position outside the original S (known as the 'wide-scope' interpretation for that NP). So the same transformational rule, Move-α, relates the levels d- and s-structure and the levels s-structure and LF. LF itself feeds into the semantic part of the language faculty, though there is no uniform consensus among practitioners of GB as to what the nature of that part is.

While GB conceives of the relations between d- and s-structure and s-structure and LF as matters of syntax, I will alter the current usage slightly, as a certain unclarity often arises in that usage. When speaking of something that happens in the mapping from d- to s-structure, I shall say that it happens *in the syntax*; for between s-structure and LF, I shall say *in LF*. When speaking of operations that are defined on the levels themselves, rather than the mapping between them, I shall say *at s-structure*, and *at LF*.

It is an important and potentially distinguishing feature of GB that it maintains that such interpretive mechanisms as quantifier scope are governed by the same principles of grammar (e.g., Move-α) that govern the form of such constructions as Passive (whose form differs visibly from the corresponding active) or interrogatives. GB proposes that the grammar itself consists of a series of 'modules' that contain constraints[2] and princi-

---

[2] I come to the notion of a 'constraint' shortly.

ples which govern the well-formedness of the output. Such constraints as we might find supporting evidence for on the basis of overt movement of constituents, as in the case of Passive, will also be expected to apply (in the unmarked case) to these more abstract cases of movement (movement in LF, as in (6)b), such as the assignment of quantifier scope. (By 'abstract' here I refer to the fact that the two different interpretations of the sentence *Two languages are spoken by most people* are not distinguished by any overt marking in the output string itself.)

The organization of the GB grammar, with all its different components, is shown in Figure 1. During the course of this chapter, I will illustrate each of these parts of the overall theory.

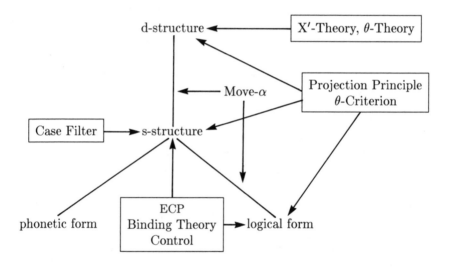

Figure 1.   Government-Binding Theory

Before getting into more detail, I would like to touch on some rather broader points, which again might be viewed as potentially distinguishing features of GB.

Syntax and Universal Grammar

What is it that we are trying to describe when we are doing syntax? All theories are very much concerned with 'the big picture,' that is, with a characterization of what it is to be the syntax of a human language. The point of view of practitioners of GB is that the human mind comes with quite a lot of linguistic knowledge 'wired in,' and that experience with one particular language or another is a kind of fine-tuning within that predetermined range. The endowment of a language faculty is known as UG (for 'Universal Grammar'). Now let me not mislead here: it is certainly *not* a particular feature of GB that it concerns itself ultimately with the study of UG, for I think that all contemporary syntacticians believe that we have some kind of endowment of this nature; but what differ across the theories (and of course across syntacticians) are (a), what the nature of the information UG supplies is and (b), how much we can infer about the properties of UG from studying properties of individual languages.

The fundamental grammatical notion in GB is that of a constraint. The working assumption is that everything is possible and that gaps in the data reflect the operation of some constraint;[3] this assumption is not peculiar to GB, and many theories adopt it in some form. In fact, the constraints will be so strong as to limit very severely the actually realized possibilities. A constraint is something which is part of the grammar which disallows certain logical possibilities in the data. As an example, in studying the syntax of a certain construction in a certain language, we typically find ourselves wanting to say something like 'Move-α moves NPs unless they are in a certain structural position.' This would be stated in the grammar by letting Move-α apply with full generality and then ruling out (i.e., deeming ungrammatical) those examples where the moved NP had started out in the offending position. Again, this conception is not particular to GB. What is perhaps more particular to GB is the inference from this to UG. At this level, the logic goes as follows: our syntactician here has just proposed a constraint on the application of Move-α that is crucial to the proper description of the phenomena under consideration. How might speakers of the language become sensitive to this constraint?—Well, hardly through exposure to the relevant data, for all the relevant data is *un*-grammatical and therefore unavailable. (Even if it occurs, it will hardly come with a 'flag' indicating that it is in fact ungrammatical.) Yet if speakers know the constraint (though not consciously, of course), and they cannot learn it,

---

[3] In addition, the idea that each rule or principle should be as simple as possible motivates this view; complexity in the data is taken to reflect complex interactions of simple (i.e., overgeneral) principles, rather than complex principles.

then the only other option is that it is part of the very nature of language itself, i.e., given to us in UG.

Next, suppose we look at another language and find a similar constraint—the NP cannot be moved from some specific, but different, structural position.[4] For this, GB invokes the notion of a *parameter*. What UG specifies is something like 'A constituent cannot be moved from position X,' where X is a variable over a range of specified values (typically, some small number of values $X_1, \ldots, X_n$). So once one example with movement from position X_1 is encountered, the language-learner knows that the language is a language with X_2 as the value for this parameter (i.e., that movement is possible from position X_1, and not possible from X_2). Cross-linguistic variation is thus conceived of in terms of parameterized variation, the idea being that setting all the switches in UG one way gets you French and another way gets you Chinese.

Given this conception, there is every reason to expect that the effects of parameter-setting will show up in different constructions in the grammar; for example, the effects of setting the parameter hypothesized in the previous paragraph to X_2 would mean that every construction that is analysed by movement would lack movement from the X_2 position.

Related to this overall outlook is the matter of the range of data assumed to be the domain of syntax. Language-particular details of description typically go uncharted in GB, for there is no obvious way in which their study would yield interesting hypotheses about the nature of UG; for example, the Rule R which puts together elements of INFL and the verb is at best tricky to state (and some would argue impossible). There is no statement or definition of the operation of Rule R in LGB (Chomsky (1981)), for it is presumably considered that nothing would be gained by such a statement—for instance, the rule obeys none of the constraints that apply to Move-α, and so Rule R is taken to be a rule of a rather different character than the members of the family characterized by Move-α. As another example, it is a fact of English that the word *aren't* can only appear with the subject *I* if the sentence is inverted (i.e., the auxiliary verb precedes the subject). So we have *Aren't I the one?* but not **I aren't the one*. It again seems unlikely that GB will ever want to say anything about this fact (Generalized Phrase Structure Grammar, in contrast, describes

---

[4] This is a slightly artificial example, in that the usual case is that, say, movement in language A takes place from a subset of the positions allowed in language B; cf., the discussion of English and Italian in Section 5.4.

this fact and uses it to motivate a particular feature (see Chap. 3, Sec. 3.2)).

These are, of course, matters of philosophy in a certain sense. Chomsky once said in a class lecture (I'm sure he's said it many times) that it would be a mistake to come up with a grammar of English full of lots of rules and little riders that got all the facts right, down to every detail. The reason it would be wrong is not that it would not be an honorable scientific endeavor, but rather that you'd be so bogged down in little details that you'd find nothing of sufficient generality that would lead you to make hypotheses about UG. I will say no more about this except to note that not everyone shares this point of view.

1. X′-Theory

X′-Theory (pronounced 'X-bar Theory'[5]) was developed in the 1970s and plays an important role in GB. The idea is that when one looks at the structures internal to different phrases in a language, one typically finds a similar pattern within each. For example, in English the verb precedes its object and a preposition precedes its object; in Japanese exactly the opposite situation is the case (hence, Japanese has *post*positions). By abstracting away from particulars of one syntactic category or another, we can talk about a language-wide template for characterizing phrasal and sentential structure. This is X′-theory.

1.1. The X′-Scheme

A fundamental and central concept in all contemporary syntax is the concept of a *head*. The head of a linguistic unit is that part of the unit that gives its essential character. In the present context, the head of an NP is the noun; it is in virtue of the fact that it is headed by a noun that the phrase is a noun phrase. Similarly, a verb heads a VP, and so on for adjectives (I will use the category symbol A for adjective) and prepositions (category P). The phrase is said to be a *projection* of the head. Standardly, two levels of

---

[5] The name here derives from the original formulation of the theory, in which the notation was $\overline{X}$. However, overbars are also used in a different way (meaning set-complement) in other parts of the GB grammar, and so I will use prime-notation for X′-Theory in an attempt to avoid confusion.

projection are countenanced; the phrasal level (e.g., NP) is assumed to be related to its head by an intermediate, semi-phrasal, level.

The X'-scheme for English proposed by GB is shown in its bare outlines in (7). The phrasal level is characterized by being a second-order projection of the head, i.e., X''; this is equivalent to the notation XP (second-order (phrasal) projection of any head), and I will use the latter in general throughout. The highest level of projection is called the *maximal projection*; hence AP is the maximal projection of A, etc.

(7)

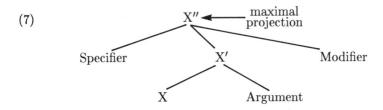

(I should note that there are many different versions of this scheme to be found in the literature; I am choosing what is the simplest for expository purposes, without claiming that it is the absolute best for English.) The categories that are sisters to the head (often called the 'lexical head') in the syntactic structure are its *arguments*; *arguments* are those constituents that a head subcategorizes for, the prototypical argument being the object of a verb. At the higher levels of structure come *modifiers*, and *specifiers*. Specifiers are things like determiners in NPs and degree modifiers (like *very*) in APs. Things are not entirely cut-and-dried; the distinction between modifiers and arguments is notoriously difficult in certain cases, for instance. And the position of modifiers is somewhat variable in English—so many adjectives, for example, precede the noun (e.g., *happy man*), while *asleep* follows the noun (**asleep man*). This is not problematic for GB, as what is important from (7) is the hierarchical structure; this is factored out from, and hence theoretically separate from, the relative order of constituents. Order is fixed by other principles of the grammar, such as Case assignment. So, ultimately, one might hope to abstract slightly further than in (7), and just have the information that arguments are sisters of the head and that modifiers and specifiers are sisters of X'. Then any further ordering restrictions would be stated independently.

Some sample instantiations of the X'-scheme are shown below:

(8)

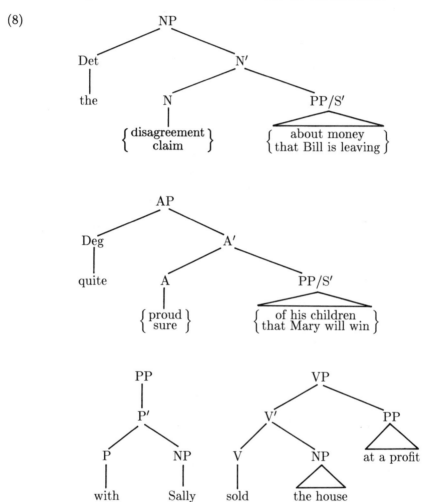

I should note that in practice (as a typographical convention) it is usual to leave out the intermediate levels of structure if they do not branch; so for example the usual way of representing a PP would just have PP immediately dominating P and NP.

Next we come to the structure of sentences. INFL is taken to be the head of S, and in many versions of GB S is taken to be the intermediate projection, the maximal projection being called (for historical reasons) S′. This is an unfortunate clash of terminology, for we should really be talking about INFL′ and INFL″. However, S and S′ are what one finds in the literature, and I shall use these. A sample S′-structure is shown in (9):

(9)

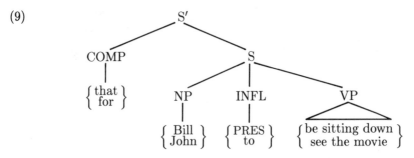

The specifier of S′ is COMP (for 'complementizer'), which dominates the presentential material like *that* and *for*. If the complementizer is *that* the clause must be tensed; if the complementizer is *for*, the clause is untensed. Untensed clauses are called *infinitives*. For purposes of exposition, I will take the particle *to* to be of category INFL. (There has been and still is a lot of debate about the relationships between S′ and COMP and S and INFL; in Chomsky's more recent work (e.g., Chomsky (1986a)), he takes COMP to be the head of S′ and INFL to be the head of S. Stowell (1981) presents evidence for this view.)

The X′-equivalences are summarized in Table 1:

Table 1
X′-Equivalences

X	X′	X″
N	N′	NP
V	V′	VP
A	A′	AP
P	P′	PP
INFL	S	S′

In addition, the categories N, V, A, and P are assumed to be defined in terms of two two-valued features, N (nominal category) and V (verbal category). This is shown in Table 2:

Table 2

Categorial Features

	[+N]	[−N]
[+V]	A	V
[−V]	N	P

This classification allows the statement of generalizations across categories; for example, [+N] categories appear as the complement of *consider*, so we have *consider Bill sick/ a fool* but not **consider Bill under the table/ singing*.

These X'-structures (partly) characterize well-formedness at d-structure. GB, in another departure from classical TG, has few or no phrase-structure rules, just the X' template. The idea is that any structure can be built out of any categories, but only those conforming to (7) will be well-formed; so if for instance, an A heads an NP, that will simply be ruled out at d-structure (or ruled out 'in the base'). Phrase structures, like entire constructions, are viewed as arising out of complex interactions of different principles, and are not assumed to be generated in any traditional way (i.e., by a set of rewriting rules as illustrated in Chap. 1). (In fact, it is not even clear if GB is a 'generative grammar' any more, but I will not dwell on this issue.)

1.2. Subcategorization

In the late 1970s it was realized that there was a large redundancy in the system of phrase structure rules and subcategorization frames; for example, the information that a transitive verb is followed by an NP object was encoded both into the rule expanding VP *and* in the subcategorization frame of the verb. The GB view on this is that it is another reason for thinking that PS-rules are simply not appropriate theoretical devices, and the burden of the work has been shifted to the subcategorization frames of heads.

As an illustration, it is fairly uncontroversial that any maximal projection (that is, AP, NP, PP, S', or VP) can be the argument to a head, in principle. Typically, different heads select different elements from the set of maximal projections as their arguments. The verb *kick* selects NP, *think* S' (as in *think that tea is ready*), *wax* AP (as in *to wax lyrical*), and so on. Often there are idiosyncracies—so the verb *discuss* looks like a verb that should take an S' argument, but it only takes NP (as in *We discussed the problem* but not *We discussed that there was a problem*). Using terminology adopted in Chomsky (1986a) (proposed in Pesetsky (1982)), we can say that each verb *c-selects* ('c' for 'category') a certain subset of the range of maximal projections.

The subcategorization is then used as a filter on randomly generated phrase structures in the following sense: if we try, for example, to do lexical insertion of *discuss* in a structure where it is sister to an AP, that structure with that head will be ruled out, for its subcategorization requires NP.

Another important feature of GB is the relation between subcategorization and the appearance of subjects. The subject NP (in English) does not appear sister to the head of the VP and therefore cannot be subcategorized by that head. The domain of subcategorization is limited to the domain of the maximal projection containing the head, and it is really this notion of the domain within the maximal projection, rather than the notion of being a sister, which is important here. Given the X'-theory assumed, the subject is not within the domain of the verb as the maximal projection of the verb is VP. This leads to many important predictions about differences in syntactic behavior of subject and non-subjects (the latter being the class of things subcategorized for). The relevant phenomena here are usually, and slightly misleadingly, called 'subject/object' asymmetries. Ultimately all of these reduce in GB to the fact that the subject is *external* to the VP (see (9)).[6]

It is not a necessary feature of X'-theory that it be set up this way; for instance, in Generalized Phrase Structure Grammar, V is the head of S and so the subject is, in a certain sense, in the domain of the verb. But in GB much rests on setting up the theory this way, and the indirect relation between the verb and its subject is a crucial aspect of the overall theory; this will be present in any analysis.[7] Finally, I should make a point about

---

[6] An alternative view is that the subject is out of the domain of the verb due to it being to the left rather than the right (in English). Work by Kayne (especially "Connectedness," Chap. 8 of Kayne (1984)), among others, explores this as a means of deriving subject/object asymmetries.

[7] For example, in the Celtic languages, the order of constituents is verb-subject-object; the GB account of this is to propose a d-structure like English,

my usage of the terms 'subject' and 'object'; in GB, these are not primitive notions, but are assumed to be structurally defined. The subject is the NP immediately dominated by S, and the object is the NP immediately dominated by VP (technically, this should be V'). This is usually represented by the notations [NP,S] and [NP,VP] respectively. I will continue to use the terms 'subject' and 'object' in this chapter, understanding them as abbreviations for the structural definitions. So in the case of a passive construction, for example, we say that the d-structure object moves to become the s-structure subject.

2. Projection Principle

What I discussed under the heading of 'subcategorization' in the previous section about the way the syntax respected lexical selection was really part of a more general principle about the relation between the requirements of lexical items and the syntax which fills those requirements. An overarching constraint on syntactic representation in GB is the *Projection Principle*, which is given in its initial form in (10).[8]

(10)   Projection Principle
         Representations at each syntactic level are projected from the lexicon, in that they observe the subcategorization properties of lexical items.

The Projection Principle is a fundamental tenet of GB; it is responsible for many deductions that lead to hypotheses that are distinctive features of the theory. For example, it states a constraint on the mapping between d- and s-structure and LF to the effect that if there is an NP-position in a certain structural configuration at one level, that NP-position must be present at all levels. (Though, as we will see, that position may be *empty* in the sense that it dominates no lexical item.) Certain transformations in TG had exactly the property that the Projection Principle rules out, and so these transformations have no analogs in GB. For instance, a transformation

---

with the verb moving out of the VP to an initial position at s-structure. For discussion of such an analysis, see Sproat (1985).

[8] This is Chomsky's formulation (LGB, 29). Later, he revises it to include thematic structure as well (LGB, 38ff), and this revised version is now the accepted formulation; see Section 3.2.

which takes a deep-structure subject and makes it into a surface-structure object has enjoyed much support over the years—but this is ruled out in GB, for the idea of the Projection Principle is that if the object is there at one level, it must be there at all levels.

While this expresses the basic intuition, there is more to say here. In a passive construction the d-structure object can move to the subject position; the subject position is there by an extension to the Projection Principle, discussed shortly below. The object position is there as the verb subcategorizes for it. In the case of a subject moving to object position, we will see below in Section 3.2 that nothing can sanction a comparable empty object position, and hence the movement cannot take place. Returning to the case of legal movement as in passive, the d-structure subject position is empty, and after movement the s-structure object position is occupied by an empty category (see Section 5.1); the Binding Theory will determine what type of empty category this is. The empty category will need to be there to satisfy thematic requirements (see Section 3). However, for our current concerns, what is most relevant is that the Projection Principle forces the existence within the theory of empty categories, for otherwise, any kind of movement structure would violate the Principle.

The conception of syntactic structure that comes out of the Projection Principle is that some position will exist in syntactic structure just in case some lexical item requires it to exist. In such cases, the lexical item is said to *license* the category in the structure. Not everything can be licensed via the Projection Principle, and recently there has been much emphasis on, and study of, this concept of licensing,[9] such that one really can end up with a theory in which each bit of structure is there because some other bit of structure requires it to be there, or else the second is dependent on the first for its own well-formedness.

Note that this leaves a problem with subjects—subjects are not subcategorized, so why do they appear at all? The solution given in Chomsky (1982) is to add in a second clause to the Projection Principle (giving the *Extended Projection Principle*) which simply adds that all clauses have subjects. The more recent work on licensing has looked for ways to derive this as a consequence of other requirements rather than leaving it as a bald stipulation.

There will be more to say about the effects of the Projection Principle after the discussion of θ-theory.

---

[9] See, for discussion and references, Chomsky (1986a).

3. θ-Theory

The theory of θ-roles (or 'thematic relations' as they are more generally known) was developed in the 1960s and 1970s (though it has antecedents in the work of ancient grammarians) but has only been brought into syntactic description in a general way in recent years. While subcategorization in its core conception provides information about the syntactic form of arguments, θ-roles provide essentially semantic information. For example, while the verb *find* subcategorizes for an NP, it has two θ-roles: Agent and Theme (or Agent and Patient in some terminology); these are notionally the one responsible for the action and the thing upon which the action is performed, respectively. These properties are written into the lexical entries of heads, and are known as the *argument structure* of the head; each syntactic argument of the head will receive one θ-role.

3.1. θ-roles

Many different theories make reference to θ-roles (under one name or another) yet there is unfortunately no presently available theory of what the range of possible roles is and how you might tell in a given context which one you're dealing with; one must, for the present, rely on intuition in large part. There are some aspects of semantic interpretation that are apparently sensitive to thematic relations and these too can be used as heuristics.[10]

There is presumably some relatively small finite number of θ-roles from which heads will pick a few for their argument structure; here I will just look at the argument structure of verbs. It is unusual to find a verb with more than three basic arguments, though others may be added by various word-formation processes. Some sample lexical entries are shown in (11); note that while verbs do not subcategorize for subjects, they may assign θ-roles to them (I use 'may' here as there are in fact verbs with 'non-thematic' subjects, which do not receive a θ-role). Often the subject is the Agent argument, but not always. For example, in *Bill received the package*, *Bill* is arguably the Goal argument. The θ-role assigned to the subject needs to be distinguished in some way, and I have followed the convention of Williams (1981) in underlining (though I am not presenting Williams' particular views on the whole topic of θ-roles). I represent

---

[10] See Jackendoff (1972) for a classic discussion of such phenomena, following work by Gruber (1965).

subcategorization (categorial-selection) in angle-brackets and the argument structure (semantic-selection) in parentheses.[11]

(11) a.   sneeze, V, (Agent)

   b.   devour, V, <NP>, (Agent, Theme)

   c.   donate, V, <NP, PP>, (Agent, Theme, Goal)

Each θ-role is assigned by a head within its domain (e.g., within VP for a verb) with the exception of the underlined argument, if there is one. This is known as the *external* argument; the others are *internal* arguments. The external θ-role is taken by many to be 'compositional,' in the sense that its nature is determined not just by the verb but by the whole verb-phrase. I will not dwell on details here, for they are not important to the matter at hand; what is important is that some sort of thematic argument position for the subject must be encoded into the lexical entry of the verb.

   The assignment of θ-roles to internal arguments is known as *direct* assignment; the external θ-role is *indirectly* assigned, the process mediated by VP. θ-roles are assigned at d-structure. (12) indicates the assignment with a simple transitive verb.

(12) θ-role Assignment

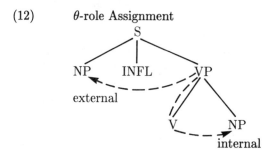

Nothing that I have mentioned so far ensures that there is a match between the number of places in the argument structure of a head and the number of phrases around to host the θ-roles assigned by that head. This is taken care of by the θ-Criterion, which is our next topic.

---

[11] The parenthesized terms are those used in Chomsky (1986a). The angle-bracket notation for subcategorization is something that I have invented for expository convenience.

3.2. θ-Criterion

The idea behind the θ-Criterion is that if the syntax is to be a 'projection' of lexical properties, as is the GB conception, then there should be a requirement to the effect that each head gets exactly the number of arguments that are lexically specified for it. Moreover, each such argument should be assigned exactly one θ-role, and hence, in a sense, have a unique function in any given syntactic structure.

While θ-roles are assigned at d-structure, the θ-Criterion applies at all levels (LGB, 112ff), ensuring that heads and their arguments are in suitable configurations. In its simplest form, the θ-Criterion says:

(13) θ-Criterion
         Each argument bears one and only one θ-role, and each θ-role is assigned to one and only one argument.

Finally, there must be a principle that relates subcategorization and the assignment of θ-roles (usually called 'θ-marking'). This principle makes the two subsystems interact in very important ways.

(14)   If α subcategorizes the position occupied by β,
         then α θ-marks β.

Note that subcategorization is for a position, e.g., an NP, while θ-marking is to the lexical content dominated by that position (i.e., its 'semantic' content).[12] The requirement in (14) is built into the revised Projection Principle (LGB, 38); that principle is also revised to say that it is thematic requirements that are projected at each level. This interacts with (14) to ensure that both thematic and subcategorization requirements are projected at each level.[13]

The requirement that subcategorization entails θ-marking provides a very strong restriction on the mapping between levels (i.e., the mapping mediated by Move-α), for movement can never take place from one subcategorized position to another. This is impossible as the argument that

---

[12] Actually, in LGB Chomsky defines θ-marking as to both positions and to the material that they dominate, but we need not worry what any implications this might have.

[13] The revised Projection Principle requires the existence of thematic subjects, for these are lexically required by predicates. However, the 'extended' part of the principle is still necessary to ensure the presence of subjects that are non-thematic (such as the empty d-structure subject position in a passive sentence).

moved would have two θ-roles, in violation of the θ-Criterion; for it would get one θ-role in its pre-movement subcategorized position, and another in its post-movement subcategorized position. I will discuss the positions that are *open* for movement (positions to which movement may take place) in the subsection below on 'Landing Sites.'

It is important to note that different tokens of the same θ-role are distinct from the point of view of the θ-Criterion. If there were a case where, say, some NP moved from a position assigned a Theme role to another position assigned a Theme role, this would violate the θ-Criterion, for these would be Themes assigned by different heads. In fact, some people like to think of θ-roles as relative to a head, and so will talk about "Theme of this occurrence of the verb *slice*," etc.

To complete the survey of well-formedness at d-structure, one last point is that d-structure is conceived of as a 'pure' representation of argument structures, and that θ-roles are assigned to arguments at this level. All the thematically relevant configurations will then be present at d-structure. Along with this, a d-structure satisfying the subcategorization and X' requirements will be well-formed.

4. C-Command and Government

Many processes in syntax are known to be local, in that they only make reference to relatively small sections of tree-structures at any one time. For example, I have used above the notion of 'domain' of a head, namely its containing maximal projection, in the description of subcategorization and θ-marking. *Government* is a fundamental concept in GB that is used to get at this notion of a local domain; following quite traditional usage, the idea is that some category β is in the domain of some other category (typically a head) α just in case α *governs* β. Thus we require that subcategorization and internal θ-marking are satisfied *under government*; a verb cannot subcategorize for an NP in another clause, for instance.

The relation of government is defined in terms of a more primitive notion, that of *c-command*, which states a relation defined on tree-structures ('c' for 'constituent'). Originally motivated by studies on anaphora[14] and other types of structural dependency, the notion of c-command now enjoys wide acceptance and will be found, in one guise or another, in many

---

[14]   A survey of the data supporting the notion of c-command can be found in Reinhart (1983).

different syntactic (and in some cases semantic) theories. The notion of c-command expresses something like the notion of that subpart of a tree which a given category α is hierarchically superior to.[15]

There are several different definitions of c-command that have been proposed in the GB literature, motivated by different empirical concerns, to the point at which a valid and interesting topic for a research paper might be (in fact, has been) a survey and critical evaluation of the different versions. Here I will present two different definitions, both of which have been proposed to deal with topics that I will discuss; it is sometimes suggested that some components of the theory will use one definition and others the other (or variations thereon).

(15)   **C-Command** (preliminary definition)
   α c-commands β iff
   every branching node dominating α dominates β.

This is the definition originally proposed by Reinhart, but currently the revised definition in (16) is more widely used.

(16)   **C-Command** (revised definition)
   α c-commands β iff
   every maximal projection dominating α dominates β.

Note that these are alternative definitions, not two clauses of the same definition. The first definition is often known as the 'strong' definition of c-command, and the second as the 'weaker,' as it allows more cases. Most of the appeals to c-command that I will make below will be to the latter, revised definition, and I present the former just to give the idea upon which the current formulation is based.

These different definitions can be illustrated in the simple tree in (17):

(17)

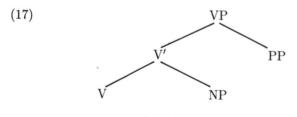

---

[15] As c-command can be mutual, it would be more accurate to say 'not inferior' rather than 'superior.'

Under definition (15), V c-commands NP but not PP; under (16), V c-commands both NP and PP. Note that in the latter case, c-command cannot go upwards through a maximal projection, for then a maximal projection would dominate α (e.g., the verb) without it also dominating β. So, for example, a verb cannot c-command its subject, which is outside the VP, under the latter definition; however, with the former definition, this is possible if the VP does not branch, as in the structure in (18):

(18)

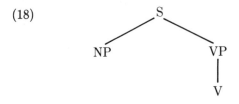

This should be enough to illustrate what c-command is about. *Government* is a localized version of c-command; while c-command may hold between α and some β that is arbitrarily far down in a tree, government is defined over a much 'flatter' domain.

(19)   Government
         α governs β iff:
         (a) α c-commands β, and
         (b) α is an X^0, i.e., $\alpha \in \{N, V, P, A, INFL\}$, and
         (c) every maximal projection dominating β dominates α.

So government is in a sense a special version of c-command;[16] the governor must be one of the five X' head categories, and no maximal projections may intervene between it and the governee: this last requirement comes from clause (c). If a maximal projection did intervene, there would be a maximal projection (namely, the intervening one) dominating β but not α, in violation of (c). In the literature, this is summarized as 'maximal projections are barriers to government.' Government is essentially restricted to the sisterhood relation, with one important exception. This is in the case of verbs which take clausal complements (clausal arguments); in GB theory,

---

[16] With the revised definition of c-command, government is roughly a case of mutual c-command.

some take S′ complements while others take S (e.g., examples (50)a and (50)c below). As S is not a maximal projection, a verb taking an S complement will govern the subject NP of that S (though not relevant for our concerns here, it also governs the INFL and VP of the S). In the case of an S′ complement, the verb will govern nothing in that complement, for the S′ is a barrier to government. The possibilities are illustrated in (20). (More recently, Chomsky, and others, have suggested that COMP might be governed by the higher verb in such structures; see, e.g., Chomsky (1986a, 1986b).) However, no version of the definition of government would allow the subject NP in (20)b to be so governed.) It is in exactly the case of an S-complement that the relation of government departs from the sisterhood relation.

(20) a.

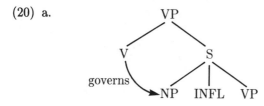

b.

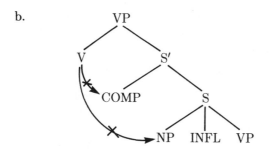

Government and c-command are used in the definitions of other principles and constraints; for example, by the end of this chapter, the reader will have seen that it is in the configuration of government that the following happen (some of these concepts have not been presented yet):

- subcategorization is satisfied

- internal θ-role assignment takes place
- Case assignment takes place
- the Empty Category Principle (in part) is satisfied

In addition, government is important for dictating the distribution of the empty category PRO, and both government and c-command play a crucial role in the statement of the Binding Theory.

5. Move-α

The relation between levels of representation is mediated by the transformational operation, Move-α ("Move anything anywhere"). As we have seen, θ-theory and Projection Principle restrict many logically possible cases of movement. In this present section, I would like to cover three main points: what happens when Move-α occurs, where Move-α may move a category to, and what structural constraints apply to restrict the application of Move-α. In among these, I will discuss the notation of coindexing and its place in the grammar.

5.1. Trace Theory and Empty Categories

Given the Projection Principle, once some syntactic position exists, it must always have existed and must always continue to exist, within the context of a deriviation (a 'derivation' in this usage is one d-structure—s-structure—LF sequence). This entails the existence of *empty categories*; an *empty category* is typically an empty NP position that has been vacated by Move-α. Such empty categories are called *traces*, and traces come in two varieties, as I will outline shortly. In addition, GB recognizes two more empty categories that are essentially pronouns. These four types of empty category will be discussed in detail in the section on the Binding Theory.

In the late 1970s, Chomsky proposed that there were two basic types of transformational movement, which at that time were called 'NP-movement' and '*wh*-movement.' As the names indicate,[17] the former affects only NPs, and the latter only phrases with *wh*-morphology (a class not restricted to

---

[17] The presentation here is not strictly correct, for cases of 'NP-movement' of non-NPs have been suggested (e.g., in Stowell (1981)), and GB posits the existence of abstract *wh*-elements which have no morphology at all. However, these are beyond the range of the presentation here.

NPs). I will continue to use these names as sub-instances of Move-α, for the sake of clarity.

A typical case of NP-movement is what we find in a passive construction. The GB analysis of passive is that a d-structure object moves to become an s-structure subject. I indicate this in the strings in (21); *-en* indicates the passive morphology on the verb (i.e., the fact that the verb is a passive participle).

(21)

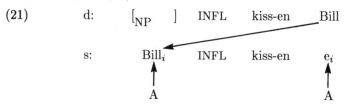

(I will discuss the meaning of the A notations below.) The verb *kiss* is a transitive verb that assigns two θ-roles. The analysis of the passive morphology is that it attaches to the verb and causes the external θ-role to be suppressed.[18] This allows subject position to be empty at d-structure, for no θ-role is assigned to it. However, the syntactic position will exist, due to the Extended Projection Principle ("all clauses have subjects"). Move-α may apply, moving the object into this subject position, without violating the θ-Criterion; this is why the external θ-role must be suppressed. The movement will leave behind an empty category, which I will refer to as *NP-trace*.

Let me comment some more on the notation and introduce some new terms. The trace of movement is coindexed with the NP that moved, to indicate that movement has occurred. When Move-α applies, it always creates indices in this way. The pair (more generally, the n-tuple) of NP_i and e_i are known as a *chain*, and the θ-Criterion is revised to apply to chains: All θ-roles are assigned to chains, and each *chain* has exactly one θ-role. The chain is represented thus: (Bill, e).

Continuing, it is useful to have terminology to distinguish positions that are assigned θ-roles from those that are not. Those that are, are called 'θ-positions'; those that are not are called '$\bar{\theta}$-positions' (known as

---

[18] As we will see below in Section 7, the passive morpheme takes away the ability of the verb to assign Case, forcing movement. The suppression of the external θ-role is a precondition for this movement, as explained here.

'theta-bar' positions). (Here the overbar is the set-complement overbar, and is not the same concept as the 'bar' in 'X-bar theory.' For that reason, I used primes in the X′ discussion, and will continue to reserve the overbar for contexts where it approximates to set-complement.) One of the characteristics of NP-movement is that it is movement from a θ- to a $\bar{\theta}$-position.

In addition, a similar distinction is used for structural positions; the theory distinguishes the 'core' grammatical positions where subject, object, indirect object etc. are located, from more 'peripheral' positions such as the clause-external position COMP. These are known as A- and $\bar{\mathrm{A}}$-positions, respectively ('A' for 'argument'). The distinction here is left rather up to intuition, but a fruitful way to conceive of it is that A-positions are those positions to which a θ-role *may* be assigned, given some suitable head; the rest are $\bar{\mathrm{A}}$. Both positions involved in the passive example are then A-positions, as indicated in (21).

The case of *wh*-movement is again movement from a θ-position to a $\bar{\theta}$-position, as in fact all movement must be—for some item to be in a position in d-structure, that must be a position assigned a θ-role, so the only way to satisfy the θ-Criterion is if movement is restricted to movement to a $\bar{\theta}$-position. Moreover, movement will always start out from an A-position, for only A-positions are filled at d-structure (though in some cases they are 'filled' with an empty category). With *wh*-movement, we have movement to COMP, and so the movement is distinguished from NP-movement in that this time we have movement to an $\bar{\mathrm{A}}$-position. A sample *wh*-movement case (the embedded question *who Bill saw*) is shown in (22).

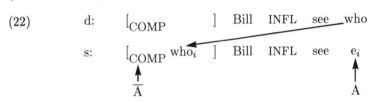

This kind of movement, *wh*-movement, will leave behind an empty category that I will refer to as *wh-trace* (many GB practitioners refer to this as 'variable').

5.2. Coindexing

Coindexing is used to represent many important relations in GB. There are three coindexing mechanisms that will be important in the present discussion, which I will introduce here without too much comment; the only relatively novel coindexing is that given in (23)a below, which is responsible for subject-verb agreement. AGR is the 'agreement' component in INFL.

(23)   **Coindexing**
(a) Coindex [NP,S] and AGR at d-structure.
(b) Move-α creates and preserves indices.
(c) Freely index all A-positions at s-structure.

Clause (c) ensures that all A-positions have an index at s-structure;[19] this will be relevant for the Binding Theory. We have seen clause (b) above; so at s-structure, all A-positions will have received an index, and those $\overline{\text{A}}$-positions to which movement has taken place will have an index. I assume here that the free indexing in (c) does not reindex NPs indexed by Move-α, though it would be quite possible to alter the theory slightly to allow for this, if any motivation were found.

Clause (a) is of a rather different nature, in that it indicates not a purely formal relation but in fact one that has overt realization, as agreement on the verb.

The category INFL is assumed to be a complex bundle of information, and in particular it contains tense and agreement information. Every d-structure has the following schematic form:

(24)

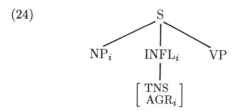

The rule coindexes the subject NP and AGR, and by convention INFL shares that index. Two points to note: one, it is the NP *position* that is indexed—the position (as in the case of passive) may be empty at d-structure; and two, while only tensed clauses show agreement in English,

---

[19] The exclusion of $\overline{\text{A}}$-positions is motivated by some very interesting and important facts, but it would not be appropriate to go into them here. For discussion, see Chomsky (1982, 59ff).

there are languages—such as Portuguese—in which infinitive (non-tensed) clauses show agreement with their subjects, motivating the distinction between TNS and AGR.

5.3. Landing Sites

As we have seen, only certain positions are available for movement to take place to—these are known as 'Landing Sites'; the main discussion of these can be found in Baltin (1982). One potential Landing Site is the subject position, just in case it is a $\bar{\theta}$-position; this is straightforward. On the other hand, movement to COMP is often taken to involve a slightly different operation, known as *adjunction* (I will say more about movement to COMP presently). Adjunction of β to α creates a new instance of α which immediately dominates α and β. For example, another instance of adjunction occurs in the movement of a quantified NP in LF; this involves adjunction of the phrase to S:

(25)   s: $[_S$ an oak$_i$ INFL grow from every acorn$_j]$

LF: $[_S$ every acorn$_j$ $[_S$ an oak$_i$ INFL grow from e$_j]]$

In this example, *every acorn* has undergone this operation, which is known as QR (for 'Quantifier Raising'). (According to one's theory of quantification, one may want some NPs to undergo QR obligatorily, some optionally, and some not at all; that is not important here.) It is a general property of adjunction that it appears to violate the Projection Principle, in that it creates positions out of nowhere; however, the Projection Principle does not say anything about non-subcategorized positions, and so adjoined positions are outside of its purview.

Other instances of Move-α in LF involve '*wh*-construal,' which moves to COMP all *wh*-phrases that have not been moved in the syntax; this is again motivated by interpretive considerations—*wh*-phrases have 'scope' just like quantified NPs. In English, one *wh*-phrase must be in COMP at s-structure (movement in the syntax); GB assumes, following earlier work in TG, that the rest in a multiple interrogation (e.g., *Who gave what to whom?*) move in LF.[20] This time, Move-α adjoins the *wh*-phrase to COMP; we can assume

---

[20] This may be analyzed as a parameter of variation. Some languages, such as Chinese and Japanese, have no movement of *wh*-phrases in the syntax,

that all movement to COMP is adjunction, with the first movement being a trivial kind of adjunction, in that COMP may not be branching. Consider the following derivation (of *Who ate what?*); I have assumed adjunction to the left in this case, following LGB (p. 232):

(26)   d: $[_{S'}[_{COMP}\ ][who\ INFL\ eat\ what]]$

          s: $[_{S'}[_{COMP}\ who_i][e_i\ INFL\ eat\ what]]$

          LF: $[_{S'}[_{COMP}\ what_j\ [_{COMP}\ who_i]][e_i\ INFL\ eat\ e_j]]$

We have now seen the cases of movement listed below, to which I add one final case (adjunction to VP); note that all are $\overline{A}$-movement except the first.

The set of possible movements is:
- movement to [NP, S] position (NP-movement)
- adjunction to COMP (*wh*-movement/*wh*-construal)
- adjunction to S (QR)
- adjunction to VP

The typical example of adjunction to VP involves the 'post-verbal' subject that we find in Italian and Spanish, among many other languages. Thus we find alternate word-orders as illustrated in (27) (Italian):

(27) a.   Molti studenti telefonano.   'Many students telephone.'

       b.   Telefonano molti studenti.

       c. $[_S\ e_i\ [_{VP}\ [_{VP}\ telefonano][_{NP}\ molti\ studenti]_i]]$

The structure of (b) is shown in (c) (ignoring INFL); the [NP, S] subject moves and adjoins to VP.

This concludes what I will say about Landing Sites; many of the examples discussed here will come up again.

---

and all move in LF (see Huang (1982)). English moves one. Some East European languages, such as Polish, Rumanian, and Serbo-Croatian, appear to move all *wh*-phrases to COMP in the syntax, but this is a matter of some controversy.

5.4. Subjacency

The notion of *subjacency* is relatively old, having been around for 15 years
or so, and deriving in part from earlier work. This topic is often currently
referred to as 'bounding theory.' Most languages display what syntacticians call *island constraints*, a name which derives from restrictions on the
operation of transformations: certain constructions are syntactic 'islands'
in the sense that it is impossible for a transformation to apply between a
position outside them and one inside them. In the present circumstance,
what we are dealing with are restrictions on the application of Move-α.
Subjacency provides such restrictions, by requiring that each application
of Move-α not operate over too large a distance; though applications of
Move-α may iterate, so the movement is a series of smaller hops. The idea
of subjacency is that domains of rule application must be relatively close to
each other—not as close as *ad*jacent, but rather one step removed, hence
*sub*jacent. Subjacency may be stated in the following way, though much of
the work is embedded in the notion of *bounding node*.

(28)   Subjacency
        Any application of Move-α may not cross
        more than one *bounding node*.

An interesting analysis of movement constraints, which also illustrates
the idea of parametric variation again, is due to Rizzi (1982).[21] If we take
the bounding nodes for English to be NP and S, we can explain the following
typical facts. First, 'long-distance' movement out of a complement clause
is possible:

(29)   the man who$_i$ [$_S$ I think [$_{S'}$ that [$_S$ you said

        [$_{S'}$ that [$_S$ you had seen e$_i$]]]]]

The analysis of this relative clause is that the *wh*-phrase *who* moves
from its d-structure position indicated by e to the COMP at the top. This
cannot be in one swoop, due to subjacency, but must proceed 'COMP-to-
COMP' as indicated, in order that each step respect subjacency; in GB, the

---

[21] See Rizzi's paper "Violations of the *Wh*-Island Constraint and the Subjacency Condition," Rizzi (1982, Chap. 2).

moving phrase literally hops through each COMP. (Some linguists refer to this as the 'pit-stop' property.) COMP is the only position which allows itself to be hopped through, and hopping is not prevented by the presence of the complementizer *that*.

(A historical note: in the 1970s, there was a big theoretical debate over whether movement hopped like this or took place in one swoop. More recently, morphological evidence (see, e.g., Goldberg (1985) and Zaenen (1983), and references therein) has been found that suggests that this basic view of hopping is correct. However, other theoretical outlooks and considerations have now led to a quite common conception that not just every intervening COMP might be affected by—and therefore show signs of—movement (or the counterpart of movement in other theories), but that in fact every intervening *node* is so affected, in that it bears information of the movement that has taken place over it. Thus many linguists (GB[22] and non-GB alike) favor a view in which there is some kind of abstract 'path' between the two positions related by movement (e.g., between *who* and *e* in (29)).)

In contrast to (29), movement (to form, in these examples, a relative clause) cannot take place out of a relative clause, or an embedded question; this is shown below, and is predicted if NP and S are bounding nodes.

(30)   *the man who$_i$ [$_S$ I identified [$_{NP}$ the dog
        [$_{S'}$ which$_j$ [$_S$ e$_j$ bit e$_i$]]]]

(31)   *the man who$_i$ [$_S$ I wonder
        [$_{S'}$ which woman$_j$ [$_S$ e$_i$ married e$_j$]]]

In each case, the lowest COMP is filled by a *wh*-phrase, and is not available as a temporary stopping-point for *who* (though I will not go into details, the difference in allowing hopping between *wh*-phrases in COMP

---

[22] See Kayne (1984, Chap. 8 ("Connectedness")) and Pesetsky (1982).

and *that* is that the latter is not indexed). Other cases confirm that NP is a bounding node:

(32)   *the man who$_i$ [$_S$ I started [$_{NP}$ the rumor

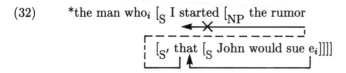

We can again explain the ungrammaticality by blocking movement in one swoop across NP and S or two Ss.

Now in the work cited, Rizzi was trying to explain a difference between English and Italian. For while movement out of an NP is generally bad in Italian just like English, movement out of an embedded question (cf., the English (31)) is good in Italian (34):

(33)   *questo incarico, che$_i$ non sapevi   la novità
            this   task   which$_i$ [$_S$ I didn't know [$_{NP}$ the news

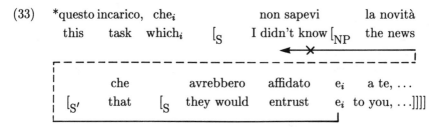

(34)   il incarico che$_i$ non sapevi
           the   task   which$_i$ [$_S$ I didn't know

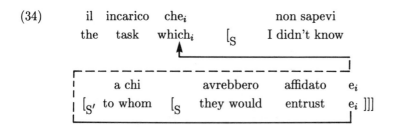

To account for the difference between the two languages, Rizzi proposed that the bounding nodes are parameterized, and that Italian chooses NP and S′ while English chooses NP and S. This will predict that movement out of NPs containing S's is impossible, while movement out of embedded questions, which are S's, will be acceptable in Italian; in this latter case, the movement (in (34)) crosses two S-nodes, but only one S'.

As I have noted above, GB treats naturally any parallels that might be found between movement in the syntax, of the kind I have just discussed, and movement in LF. In this regard, some Japanese data brought to light in recent years provide intriguing evidence. In Japanese, all *wh*-phrases stay in their d-structure position in the syntax, though the clause is marked by a final particle indicating that it is interrogative (*ka* in the examples below). A simple Japanese embedded question has the form indicated in the bracketed part of (35).

(35)   Boku-wa [$_{S'}$ dare-ga   kuru ka] sirimasen.
        I-topic   who-subj come   Q   know-not
        'I don't know who will come.'

'Q' indicates the interrogative marker, and *ga* is (for our purposes) the subject marker. Now *wh*-phrases may appear inside of relative clauses, which, given the hypothesis that there is movement in LF, would lead to the conclusion that subjacency is not operative in Japanese.

(36)   [$_{NP}$ [$_{S'}$ dono   kyoozyu-ga   suisen siteiru $_{S'}$] hito $_{NP}$]-ga
                which professor-subj recommend   person-subj

                saiyoosare   soo desu ka.
                employed   likely be Q

There is no translation of this into English that is not awkward. The best we can do is something like "Which professor's recommended person is most likely to get the job?" The sentence is literally "The person that which professor recommends is likely to get the job?" Now what makes this example interesting in the context of subjacency is the pattern of answers that are possible for it. For while it is normally possible to truncate answers in Japanese, as in English, it is only partly possible in response to (36). Some logically possible answers are given in (37):

(37) a.   Suzuki kyoozyu-ga   suisen siteiru hito   desu.
           Suzuki professor-subj recommend   person be
           'It's the person that Professor Suzuki recommends.'

     b.   *Suzuki kyoozyu desu.
           Suzuki professor be
           'It's Professor Suzuki.'

However, in these cases one must repeat (at least) the entire containing NP to give a good answer. Although a certain amount of inference is necessary to argue from the answers to questions to claims about syntactic structure, these facts strongly suggest a subjacency account. If subjacency is operative in Japanese, and applies in LF in this purely abstract way, as is the unmarked GB assumption, then the only way to respect subjacency (assuming bounding nodes of NP and S' or S[23]) would be to move the entire containing NP (the top line of (36)). The structure at LF is apparently reflected in the answer. The assumption is that the whole containing NP inherits the *wh*-feature from the contained *wh*-word, and is moved in LF.

To the extent that there exist strong parallels in between syntax and LF, this would support a GB-view that there is more than one structural level of syntax (specifically, that syntactic properties of LF and the mapping to it have 'overt' counterparts). Neither Generalized Phrase Structure Grammar nor Lexical-Functional Grammar acknowledge a level of interpretation like LF whose syntactic or configurational properties have analogs in the surface syntax, and, as this lack of such a level is axiomatic in both cases (though for different reasons), it might not be a trivial task to extend them accordingly.

6. Case Theory

We have so far seen what conditions apply at d-structure and what the mapping relation between d- and s-structure is, amongst other things. The remaining parts of the theory all characterize well-formedness at s-structure, or LF, or both. *Case Theory* is responsible for determining in large part the distribution of NPs, and possibly other maximal projections too. Here I will concentrate on NPs.

The notion of Case in GB is based on the traditional notion of case, which is manifested in many languages. English is rather impoverished in this regard, with only personal pronouns retaining case distinctions: for example, *they* is nominative, *them* accusative or objective, and *their* genitive. In GB, each NP must be assigned Case (the capitalization indicates that we are dealing with a technical notion of Case here), with the possible exception of some empty categories. If some NP fails to be assigned Case,

---

[23] It would require a much more thorough study than the few facts I have presented here to determine whether S or S' is the correct choice for Japanese.

or more strictly, fails to be in a position to which Case is assigned, then the structure is ruled ungrammatical. This is expressed in the *Case Filter*, given in (38):

(38)   Case Filter
          *NP, if NP has phonetic content and no Case.

This applies at s-structure;[24] having 'phonetic content' means having some physical realization, as opposed to being an empty category. Actually, in the general case, the Filter must apply to chains; each chain must have exactly one Case-marked position if it has NP as its first member. The Case Filter is like the θ-Criterion in that having two Cases is as bad as having none at all; there is quite a large similarity in the operation of the θ-Criterion and the Case Filter, and more recent work (Chomsky (1986a), following ideas in LGB) revises the θ-Criterion to subsume the Case Filter. However, it is important to understand what the Case Filter does, even if current formulations of the theory do that grammatical work in a slightly different way. The notion of Case assignment remains a central part of GB.

The basic instances of Case assignment (in English) are the following:

- if INFL contains TNS, Nominative Case is assigned to the [NP,S] position

- a verb assigns Accusative Case to [NP,VP]

- a preposition assigns Accusative or Oblique Case to [NP,PP]

- nouns and adjectives ([+N] categories) do not assign Case

- Case is assigned under government with the exception of Genitive

- Genitive Case is assigned in the structure $[_{NP} \ - \ X]$.

The category INFL assigns Case to the subject under government if it is tensed; the infinitival INFL *to* does not assign Case. Verbs and prepositions assign Case to their objects; in English, it is the same Case, but typically, prepositions assign some kind of oblique Case, such as Dative.[25] With Genitive, there is no assigner; rather it is a property of the structure, as in *John's book*, *Lucy's betraying Maud*, etc. Exactly which Case is assigned

---

[24] There is some debate in the GB literature as to whether the Case Filter applies at s-structure, PF, or LF; I will assume that it is s-structure.

[25] As discussed in the following section, verbs and prepositions also assign Case across an S boundary to an NP, so long as government holds.

is not a matter of much importance in GB; it is the fact of having *a* Case that is significant.

In English, Case is further restricted to be assigned under *adjacency*, for in general, nothing may intervene between a Case assigner and its assignee. (I will discuss some counterexamples below.) The basic picture of Case assignment is shown in (39):

(39)

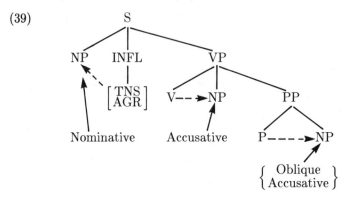

The idea of an adjacency condition is to account for facts like the following:

(40) a. I like flowers very much.

   b. *I like very much flowers.

   c. I smell gas very strongly.

   d. *I smell very strongly gas.

   e. I believe very strongly that you will win.

   f. I gave the book to Bill.

   g. *I gave to Bill the book.

Examples (b) and (d) and (g) indicate that nothing may intervene between a verb and its NP argument; (e) and (f) show that this does not hold of other arguments, such as S' and PP. The requirements of Case as outlined above will account for this; S' and PP do not need Case.

The adjacency condition on Case assignment is also assumed to be a parameter; for example, the French translation of (40)b, *J'aime beaucoup les fleurs*, is grammatical (see Stowell (1981) for more discussion).

Two obvious kinds of counterexample appear against the adjacency idea for English. One is the class of 'ditransitive' verbs, as exemplified by something like *We sent Mary the letter*; I will return to this shortly. The other kind involves the fact that if the NP is 'heavy,' linguistically speaking, it may (and may be preferred to) follow other things in the VP:

(41)   I gave to Bill [my last copy of the third-quarter report].

Although I will not go into details, there is an analysis of these examples in which Move-α has applied to adjoin the NP to the VP, leaving a trace adjacent to the verb which is assigned Case. Chomsky (1982, 47ff) presents evidence that movement has occurred here. It is worth noting too that this rule does not apply out of PP (*I talked about to Sue my latest ideas on physical fitness*); given some further constraint to the effect that the shift rule applies within the domain of the Case assigner, this would be predicted: in moving out of the PP into the VP, the NP has passed out of the (government) domain of its Case assigner, which is the preposition in this case.

With the ditransitives, there is more of a problem.[26] It may just be prudent to add to the grammar some additional way of assigning Case in just these configurations (e.g., Case may be a property of the structure, as with Genitive); for the sake of discussion, let me assume that this is so. What the GB analysis now predicts is that, however the second NP does get Case, it does not get it from the verb, and again there seems to be evidence for this. We will come to this below.

Another important function of Case Theory is to force movement. For example, in passive, the NP moves from object- to subject-position; but nothing that I discussed above forces this movement to happen. Yet the movement is obligatory—otherwise English would allow sentences of the form *There was arrested John*. The analysis of the passive morpheme *-en* is that it has two effects: it takes away the verb's ability to assign Case, and also the ability to assign an external θ-role. The Case Filter now renders movement apparently obligatory—for if the NP remains in object position, it will violate the Case Filter at s-structure. Movement must be to subject position, for this is the only free position for movement, and in that position Case is assigned, so all is well. In general, cases of NP-movement (of overt NPs) are instances of movement in order to get Case. On a more

---

[26] For discussion of these constructions, see Kayne (1984, Chaps. 7 and 9 ("Unambiguous Paths" and "Datives in French and English")) and Stowell (1981).

general level, it is very much part of GB to handle obligatoriness in this way—obligatory application of some operation is explained by positing a principle that is violated by the pre-application structure but satisfied by the post-application structure.

Returning to the ditransitives, if only the first NP gets Case from the verb, then only it should be forced to move in passive. That is, the GB analysis predicts that only the immediately post-verbal NP should be allowed in the passive construction, and this is so:

(42) a.   We gave Mary the envelope.

     b.   *We gave the envelope Mary.

     c.   Mary was given the envelope.

     d.   *The envelope was given Mary.

The first two examples show that it is the Goal argument that must follow the verb in this construction; and the latter two show that only this NP passivizes.

I will conclude this section with an illustrative example from (Mandarin) Chinese, which will show the potential interaction between θ-role assignment and Case assignment; I will also introduce the idea of a *directionality* of assignment. The basic generalization about the order of arguments of the verb in Chinese (i.e., only those constituents assigned a θ-role by the verb) is shown in (43), ignoring INFL:

(43) $[_S$ NP $[_{VP}$ PP V NP$]]$

We are only concerned with order within the VP here. Arguments except the direct object NP precede the verb, with one additional wrinkle; sometimes the direct object may appear as the object of a preposition, *ba*, in which case it precedes the verb. The GB analysis of this is as follows:

- at d-structure, θ-role assignment is from right-to-left (i.e., the VP is head-final)

- at s-structure, Case is assigned from left-to-right.

Directionality is a parameter along with adjacency (I do not know enough about Chinese to state whether adjacency is relevant in that language or not for Case assignment). All subcategorized arguments must be to the left of the verb at d-structure. To get Case, an NP argument must move to the right of the verb, adjoining to VP; only NPs need Case so only NPs move. (To be fully correct, we should also require that PPs and the like *resist* Case, to prevent them from moving arbitrarily. Such proposals have been made in the GB literature; see e.g., Stowell (1981).) However, the NP need not move if it can get Case in some other way; the analysis of the *ba* would be that it is semantically inert and just functions as a Case assigner, and so *ba*-NP sequences would appear preverbally.

7. Summary of Types of Movement and Complement Structures

This would be a good point to summarize the kinds of movement that are allowed in GB. The simplest is perhaps the *wh*-movement kind, that is, movement to an $\overline{\text{A}}$-position. This type of movement has the following abstract properties:

(44) $\overline{\text{A}}$-movement:
         Movement from a position that is assigned both a θ-role and Case; the movement creates an adjoined position, which is an $\overline{\text{A}}$-position, and lacks a θ-role and Case. The resulting chain (α, e) receives exactly one θ-role and one Case, both assigned to the empty category created by movement.

Examples of this kind of movement are, in English, overt *wh*-movement in the syntax, as in questions and relative clauses; and in LF, QR and *wh*-construal. In each case movement is forced by some external principle—say the necessities of interpretation in the case of a quantified NP, or by an additional requirement that a question in English is only well-formed if it has one *wh*-phrase in COMP.

The other kind of movement, A-movement, is movement forced by the Case Filter, and so affects only NPs. It has the following abstract properties:

(45)   A-movement:
         Movement from a position assigned a θ-role but no Case; the NP must move to get Case, and so must move to a position that has Case but no θ-role. The only possible candidate here is subject position, which is an A-position. The resulting chain (α, e) receives exactly one θ-role and one Case, the former assigned to the empty category created by movement, and the latter to α.

The effect of the passive morpheme *-en* can now be fully demonstrated. Attachment of the morpheme affects a verb's properties in the way seen in (46).

(46) a.   kiss, V, <NP>, (Agent, Theme), assigns Accusative Case

  b.   kiss-en, V, <NP>, (Theme), assigns no Case

(The form *kiss-en* turns into *kissed* in PF.) The fundamental property of passive is that the verb loses its ability to assign Case (not having this ability is the theoretical reconstruction within GB of the notion of 'intransitive verb'). It still subcategorizes for an NP and assigns an internal θ-role. Concomitant with the loss of Case, the external θ-role must be suppressed, for otherwise movement will take place to a θ-position. For independent reasons, namely the Binding Theory (see Sec. 9 below), movement cannot pass out of the clause in these cases, so movement must be to the local subject position if it is to be possible at all.

The other construction where we have NP-movement, in English, is the so-called 'Subject-to-Subject Raising' construction. This terminology derives from the original transformational analysis which related examples like (a) and (b) below by moving the embedded subject up to the subject position of the main clause (and performed a few operations on tense, etc., at the same time).

(47) a.   It seems that Max is sick.

  b. Max_i seems e_i to be sick.

This is A-movement and so the GB account forces the following conclusions: the position of e in (47)b must be a Caseless position, and the subject position of *seems* must be a $\bar{\theta}$-position. This latter conclusion is confirmed by (47)a; the 'non-referential' *it* is one of two NPs that are stipulated not to require a θ-role. (The other NP is *there* as in *There is a woman in the room.*) So what we want to say for *seem* is that it takes one argument, some kind of proposition. The difference between (47)a and (47)b is reduced to the category of the complement; in (a) it is S', in (b) it is S. I will explain below how this works. The actual implementation of this in LGB is to say that *seem* takes an S' complement but allows the S' node to be deleted, leaving an S complement. So the following might be the lexical entry for *seem*:

(48)   seem, V, <S' $\Rightarrow$ S>, (Proposition)

I have again invented notation to indicate the S'-deletion property; the material within the angle-brackets says that the verb subcategorizes for an S' that may be 'pruned' to an S.

Now, as I mentioned above, the Binding Theory only permits NP-movement to take place within the clause. As 'clause' is identified with the maximal projection S', movement will be allowed just in case S'-deletion takes place. The account of raising, then, is as shown in (49):

(49)

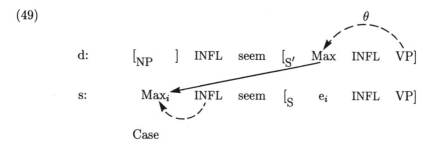

Here movement is forced again; the NP *Max* must move in order to get Case, for *seem* does not assign Case. The θ-role of the subject is determined entirely by the lower VP, and may even be non-thematic with respect to that, as in *It seems to be raining* or *There seems to be a fly in the soup*.

In contrast to this raising operation, GB posits no movement in the corresponding 'Subject-to-Object Raising' construction; in the classical TG analysis, a raising transformation of the general type just discussed would relate the first two examples in (50), the movement this time being to object position.

(50) a.   I believe [$_{S'}$ that Mary is a genius].

b.   I believe Mary$_i$ [$_S$ e$_i$ to be a genius].

c.   I believe [$_S$ Mary to be a genius].

Note that (b) is not acceptable in GB, for movement cannot take place to object position, due to the θ-Criterion. Yet there is a clear sense in these structures in which *Mary* acts simultaneously like the subject of the lower clause and object of the higher clause. GB again employs the mechanism of S'-deletion in these cases, assigning the s-structure (50)c. The lexical entry for *believe* is as follows:

(51)   believe, V, <S' ⇒ S>, (<u>Agent</u>, Proposition),
          assigns Accusative Case

The verb does not subcategorize for an NP argument, but does have the ability to assign Case. Given the definition of government, a verb governs across an S boundary but not S'. Hence *believe* can assign Case to the lower subject; this is known as *Exceptional Case Marking*:

(52)   s: I   INFL   believe   [$_S$ Mary   INFL   VP]

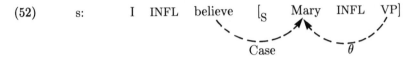

Case   θ

Thematically, *Mary* is the subject of the lower S, for it gets its θ-role from the embedded VP; yet it is Case-marked by the higher verb, and so in that sense is its object.

In these cases of S'-deletion, the only option if deletion does not apply is to have a tensed clause as complement, and no raising structures will be possible. I will not go through the details of this. The advantage of this analysis is that two subcategorization frames are not necessary; both Generalized Phrase Structure Grammar and Lexical-Functional Grammar would posit two different subcategorization frames for these verbs, say S' or the sequence NP VP for the examples in (50). GB proponents would regard such 'surfacy' analyses of the syntax as being too superficial to uncover the underlying unity of the two cases.

Continuing with the *believe* example, there are other examples which look superficially similar, as in (53).

(53) a.   The men prefer the women to cook.

     b.   John wants Bill to win.

These verbs have demonstrably different properties; for example, the NP following *believe* passivizes, while that following *want* (or *prefer*) does not:

(54) a.   Mary is believed to be a genius.

     b.   *Bill is wanted to win.

In GB, the difference between the two verbs in (54) is that *want* does not allow S′-deletion; passive is NP-movement, which we know can cross S but not S′. If this is so, then a question arises as to how the postverbal NPs in (53) get Case, for government cannot cross the S′ boundary. With verbs like *want*, a *for* complementizer appears if the complement clause is separated from the verb, and it is this that is responsible for the Case to the subject (*for* is a prepositional complementizer and hence can assign Case like other prepositions):

(55) a.   *John wants very much Bill to win.

   b.   John wants very much for Bill to win.

Case is assigned, under government and adjacency, as shown in (56):

(56)

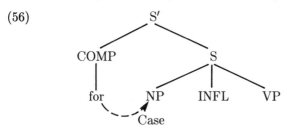

In case the *for* is adjacent to the verb, there is a deletion rule which removes it (some dialects allow things like *I'd prefer for you to go now*); if there is no adjacency, the *for* stays. As an additional piece of evidence, Chomsky notes that the rule shifting heavy NPs applies with *believe* but not *want*,[27] which would follow (with a few other assumptions) from the fact that the NP was shifting out of a non-maximal S in the one case but a maximal S′ in the other:

(57) a.   They'd believe to be foolish any candidate who would take the trouble to run in every primary.

   b.   *They'd want to win any candidate who would take the trouble to run in every primary.

Again, these facts would be potentially problematic for any theory that assigned a simple NP VP sequence in both cases.

---

[27] This observation is originally due to Paul Postal.

8. Empty Category Principle (ECP)

The ECP is a well-formedness condition applying to empty categories created by movement (i.e., the two kinds of trace), and it is this principle that is responsible for many of the subject/object asymmetries that GB predicts.[28] The main idea behind the ECP is that subject position is not in the domain of any lexical head (i.e., one of the categories defined by the features [N] and [V]) and that this is an important difference; while other A-positions are governed by a lexical head, the subject position, if governed at all, is governed by INFL. The ECP is formulated so that government by INFL alone is not enough to license the existence of an empty category; INFL is not a *proper governor*.

(58)   Empty Category Principle
         A trace must be properly governed.

         Proper Government:
         α properly governs β iff
         (a) α governs β and α is lexical (N, V, A, or P), or
         (b) α locally $\overline{\text{A}}$-binds β.

The first clause here is the 'core' case, with the empty category properly governed by a lexical head. The second clause is primarily for the case of subjects, and is best illustrated with an example. I will discuss what 'locally $\overline{\text{A}}$-binds' means below.

One of the main empirical motivations for the ECP was the following set of facts:

(59) a.   Who$_i$ do you think that Bill saw e$_i$?

     b.   Who$_i$ do you think Bill saw e$_i$?

     c.   *Who$_i$ do you think that e$_i$ left?

     d.   Who$_i$ do you think e$_i$ left?

The generalization here is that the complementizer may be optionally absent with movement from any non-subject position, but must be obligatorily absent with movement from a subject position. In the former

---

[28] I have assumed for the purposes of presentation that the ECP applies both at s-structure and LF, to emphasize the parallel constraints applying at both levels; many GB practitioners believe that it only applies at LF, for reasons that are too complicated to go into here.

examples, we have proper government by the verb, and the facts in the latter examples suggest that the complementizer is implicated in the proper
government of the subject. Let us look at the structure of (59)d first.

(60)

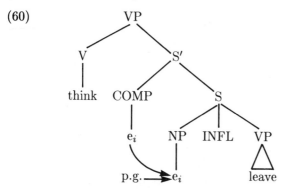

While INFL governs the subject position, it does not properly govern it,
for it is not a lexical category; rather, it is the empty category left behind in
COMP as the movement hopped through that is the proper governor. The
configuration shown is the configuration of binding[29] as required by clause
(b) of (58), and hence the subject empty category is properly governed.
The crucial difference between (59)d and (59)c is that in the bad example
COMP branches, as the *that* is in there already; this prevents a binding
relation. The internal structure of COMP in the bad case is:

(61)

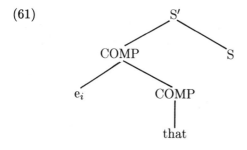

---

[29] The definition of binding is given in (71) below.

Now part of the definition of binding, which I will give in the next section, involves the notion of c-command; in the case where COMP branches, c-command will not hold between the empty category in COMP and the one in subject position, and so binding and hence proper government will not hold either. (59)c is therefore an ECP violation.

The requirement that the proper governor in these cases is a 'local $\overline{A}$-binder' prevents the *who* in (59)c from properly governing the subject empty category. For our purposes here we can understand 'local' to mean 'within the same S'.' An $\overline{A}$-binder of some category α is some category that is in an $\overline{A}$-position, is coindexed with α, and c-commands it. An extensive discussion of this kind of proper government can be found in Lasnik and Saito (1984).

There are many different ways within the GB framework that have been proposed to handle these data, and so what I have given is just an illustration of one possibility. Yet there is an interesting point to be made about the way the theory develops in response to these data. It is taken to be the case that (59)c is an ECP violation. Ultimately this reduces to a failure of c-command in (61). The strategy is then to *define* c-command in such a way as to make it fail in (61). Given the strong definition of c-command that I gave above, this is straightforward; COMP branches, and so the empty category cannot "see" out of it. With the weaker definition, things are not so clear, for the next maximal projection up is presumably the S'; in that case, we have to modify our understanding of the definition such that only heads c-command in their domain. This would mean that only the *that* would c-command the empty category in subject position, for it is the head (the head of COMP is the first thing that was there); but *that* is not a proper governor.

Similarly, although the prepositional complementizer *for* governs and assigns Case to subject position, it is not a proper governor as indicated by the contrast in (62):

(62) a.   *Who_i do you want for e_i to leave?

b. Who_i do you want e_i to leave?

Some typical ECP effects in LF are the ones relating to the phenomenon known as 'Superiority'; the generalization is that, given an s-structure with multiple *wh*-phrases, it is the leftmost ('superior') one that must move in the syntax:

(63) a.   Who saw what?

b.   *What did who see?

The account of these provides support for the idea that it is the head of COMP that governs subject position, irrespective of the branching of COMP. If we look at the LF in each case, we see that (63)b is an ECP violation.

(64) a. $[_{S'} \ [what_j \ [who_i]][_S \ e_i \ INFL \ see \ e_j]]$

b. $*[_{S'} \ [who_i \ [what_j]][_S \ e_i \ INFL \ see \ e_j]]$

In (64)a, *who* has moved in the syntax and therefore is the head of COMP, and remains so even when *what* adjoins in LF. Hence the subject empty category is properly governed from COMP and the object empty category by the verb. In (64)b the order of movement is the reverse; the subject empty category must be properly governed from COMP, but its potential governor is not the head of COMP, and so proper government fails. Again the object empty category is properly governed by the verb.

Evidence of this correlation between syntax and LF can be found in other languages. The following data and analysis are again from Rizzi,[30] extending some observations and proposals made by Kayne. In Italian, it appears that the so-called 'COMP-trace' effects such as we have just seen (in (59)) are not present.

(65) Chi_i credi   che e_i verrà?
         Who you-think that   will-come
         'Who do you think will come?'

However, if Italian did not obey the ECP, then the following facts of LF would be mysterious. The interpretation of an Italian sentence like (66) involves movement in LF:

(66)   Non pretendo che tu   arresti nessuno.
         NEG I-require that you arrest nobody

The quantifier *nessuno* may combine with the negation-marker *non*, so that the sentence is not interpreted as containing two independent negations. The analysis of this is to assume that *nessuno* moves in LF to the

---

[30] The reference here is to Rizzi's paper "Negation, *Wh*-Movement, and the Null Subject Parameter," Rizzi (1982, Chap. 4).

position of *non*. The sentence should then have the following wide-scope interpretation of *nessuno*, and indeed it does.

(67)   There is no person x such that I require that you arrest x.

This shows that *nessuno* can move from the object position. Given the grammaticality of (65), one would expect a similar wide-scope interpretation for *nessuno* in (68):

(68)   Non pretendo che nessuno ti   arresti.
        NEG I-require that nobody you arrest

However, this lacks the expected interpretation:

(69)   *There is no person x such that I require that x arrest you.

This fact suggests that the subject position is not properly governed. Rizzi hypothesized that in fact Italian was just like English with respect to proper government of the preverbal subject position, but that Italian allowed a second option: the subject may appear postverbally, on his analysis adjoined to the VP (cf., (27) above). The following data support this idea.

(70) a.   Non pretendo che nessuno sia arrestato.
           NEG I-require that nobody be arrested
     b.   Non pretendo che sia arrestato nessuno.
           NEG I-require that be arrested nobody

The latter example, only, allows the wide-scope interpretation for *nessuno*; thus proper government is satisfied in the postverbal position. Rizzi's analysis is that the subject moves from [NP,S] position to adjoin to the VP, where under the weaker definition of c-command the verb will govern, and being a lexical head properly govern, the adjoined position. Movement will therefore be possible from this position.

This account will also explain the grammaticality of (65); the movement will first be to the postverbal position, from where further movement will satisfy the ECP. The idea is that the 'COMP-trace' facts really stem from a prohibition against moving a subject NP over an immediately adjacent COMP (in fact, this is how the constraint was initially formulated in the TG system), but that Italian allows the subject to get to the postverbal position first, and from there further movement is possible.

More recently, confirming evidence for Rizzi's hypothesis has been found in data from dialects of Italian; the crucial cases are reported in Jaeggli (1984), Safir (1985), in which the reader may find further details and references.

9. Binding and NP-types

We finally come to the *Binding Theory*, which characterizes the interpretive relations between NPs, and covers, among other things, the distribution of pronouns and reflexive pronouns. In addition, it plays an important role in the distribution of empty categories.

As stated above in (23), indexing is free at s-structure; it is the Binding Theory that constrains the output of this operation. The definition of *binding* is as follows:

(71)   Binding
          α binds β iff
          (a) α c-commands β, and
          (b) α and β are coindexed.

I will not give examples of this here, as we will see many below.

9.1. Binding Theory and the Typology of Empty Categories

The statement of the Binding Theory partitions the class of NPs into different types and states binding conditions for each. The partitioning is effected by the two-valued features [anaphoric] and [pronominal]; intuitively, 'anaphors' are things that *must* have an antecedent, and 'pronominals' are those things that may have an antecedent. Personal pronouns are [−a, +p] in this system, while, and perhaps less obviously, reflexive pronouns are [+a, −p]. The other remaining (overt) NPs are [−a, −p], and are known as *R-expressions* ('R' for 'referential'). For reasons we will come to, there is no overt NP of the [+a, +p] type.

The unmarked hypothesis is that, if these features are motivated for overt NPs, they should also apply to categorize types of empty category. As noted above, GB recognizes four types of empty category, which correspond to the four possible feature/value-combinations. I list these in (72):

(72)   Types of Empty Category
          $[-a, -p]$ wh-trace (or 'variable')
          $[+a, -p]$ NP-trace
          $[-a, +p]$ pro ('little' or 'small' pro)
          $[+a, +p]$ PRO ('big' PRO)

The first three empty categories share distributional regularities with their overt counterparts, while PRO has a life of its own and its own special theory for relating PRO to its antecedent, the theory of *Control*. There has been some debate in the GB literature as to whether the lexicon should provide four empty categories specified as above, or whether it should provide just one, whose particular binding features would be recoverable (and uniquely predictable), in any given context. This latter view, which has been losing favor, is the so-called 'Functional Determination' of empty categories, about which I will say nothing more (there is a lot of discussion in LGB and Chomsky (1982)).

A rough generalization about pronouns and reflexive pronouns in English is that reflexives must find an antecedent within the same clause while pronouns cannot have an antecedent within that domain. The two types are in *complementary distribution*; some typical examples are given in (73). Coindexing indicates a coreferential interpretation; for instance, example (73)b below is grammatical so long as *him* is not *John*.

(73) a.   John$_i$ painted himself$_i$.

     b.   *John$_i$ painted him$_i$.

     c.   *Mary$_i$ recalled that John had painted herself$_i$.

     d.   Mary$_i$ recalled that John had painted her$_i$.

The entire range of data is much more complicated than these few simple examples show, but they give the general idea. The Binding Theory states the following:

(74)   Binding Theory
          Principle A: An anaphor ($[+a]$) is bound
                            in its Governing Category.

          Principle B: A pronominal ($[+p]$) is free
                            in its Governing Category.

          Principle C: An R-expression ($[-a, -p]$) is free.

Principle A says that anything that is [+a] must be bound within some specified local domain, known as the 'Governing Category'; I will discuss this presently. Principle B says that [+p] categories are free (i.e., not bound) in that same domain. Principle C says that R-expressions can never be bound. An important thing to note is that the Binding Theory only applies to A-binding (binding by a category in an A-position), and thus one can classify *wh*-traces as R-expressions without contradiction, for they are $\overline{\text{A}}$-bound.

Some of the examples here, especially those involving pronouns, may strike the reader as grammatical in certain contexts, or with certain intonations, even though I mark them ungrammatical. Principle B is quite weak in a certain sense, and many linguists believe that the facts of 'disjoint reference' for pronouns (such as example (73)b above) are not facts of syntax, but are pragmatically derived. On the other hand, many of the cases that look like counterexamples can themselves be argued to be instances where pragmatics overrides the grammar, and a proponent of this view would claim that it is correct to rule them ungrammatical *on the interpretation indicated*. This is the GB view, and it is not my place to defend it here (though I happen to subscribe to it). More importantly, it is essential to note that the effect of Principle B is not simply to derive disjoint reference for pronouns, but to classify types of NPs, which in turn generates many different predictions, most of which do not admit alternative pragmatic explanations.

The notion of the 'local domain' for certain binding processes is expressed in the Binding Theory in the *Governing Category*, which is a slight variation on the more traditional idea of a clause-nucleus.

(75)   Governing Category
        The Governing Category for β is the smallest NP or S
        containing β and a governor of β.

(The statement of the definition of Governing Category in LGB is somewhat more complicated than this in its final formulation, but the underlying concept is captured in (75).) I will comment on two aspects of this definition, the mention of NP as well as S, and the mention of a governor.

It has been known for quite a long time that the same kinds of syntactic processes apply within NPs and Ss. The simple facts of binding in (76) are just one instance of this (cf., (73)). The brackets indicate an NP contained within a larger NP.

(76) a.   Max$_i$'s painting of himself$_i$

     b.   *Max$_i$'s painting of him$_i$

     c.   *Mary$_i$'s recollection of [John's painting of herself$_i$]

     d.   Mary$_i$'s recollection of [John's painting of her$_i$]

Hence, NP is one of the relevant categories for defining a domain for binding.

The inclusion of a governor in the domain is necessary for the S'-deletion verbs like *believe* and *seem*. This can be illustrated with the examples in (77):

(77) a.   Max$_i$ believes [$_S$ himself$_i$ to be the candidate].

     b.   *Max$_i$ believes [$_S$ him$_i$ to be the candidate].

     c.   *Max$_i$ believes [$_{S'}$ that [$_S$ himself$_i$ is the candidate]].

     d.   Max$_i$ believes [$_{S'}$ that [$_S$ he$_i$ is the candidate]].

In (a), the reflexive must be bound in its Governing Category, according to Principle A. The governor of *himself* is the verb *believes*, and hence the Governing Category is the entire sentence. Similarly, a pronoun must be free in this domain, and so (b) is bad. When we switch to an S' complement, the pattern reverses as this time the governor of the subject position is the INFL of the lower clause, and so the Governing Category is the lower S. Thus, although the reflexive is bound in (c), it is not bound within its Governing Category (for its antecedent is outside of that domain); and the pronoun in (d), although bound, is free in its Governing Category.

A similar pattern to the reflexives holds for NP-trace, which is also [+a, −p] and therefore subject to Principle A.

(78) a.   Mary$_i$ was impressed e$_i$.

     b.   Mary$_i$ seems [$_S$ e$_i$ to be happy].

     c.   *Mary$_i$ seems [$_{S'}$ that [$_S$ e$_i$ is happy]].

In example (c), the empty category is governed by the lower INFL; hence the Governing Category is the lower S. Example (c) is then in violation of Principle A (and, as INFL is not a proper governor, the example also involves an ECP violation).

We have seen some examples of pronouns, subject to Principle B, in the preceding discussion; recall that pronouns are [−a, +p]. Some other relevant examples are shown in (79):

(79) a.   [Mary$_i$'s father] took her$_i$ to the movies.

b.   Mary$_i$ bought a present for [her$_i$ father].

In (a), the Governing Category for the pronoun is the whole clause, and while the antecedent *Mary* lies within that domain, *Mary* does not bind the pronoun, for it does not c-command it. Hence the pronoun is free and Principle B is satisfied. In (b), the Governing Category for the pronoun is the NP indicated by the bracketing (though I have not said enough about government within NP for this to be obvious to the reader), and again the structure respects Principle B.

The corresponding empty category, pro, does not appear in English. Exactly what properties determine its distribution are not clear, but the classic example of pro is the 'missing' subject that is allowed in many languages where the verb shows person/number inflection, such as the following Spanish examples:[31]

(80) a.   pro llegué   'I arrived.'

b.   pro llegaste   'You(sg.) arrived.'

c.   pro llegó   'He/she arrived.' etc.

In such examples, the missing subject shows all the interpretive properties of a regular pronoun, except that it is phonetically null. While pro is supposed to be absent in English, as English verb-inflection is so minimal, the presence of inflection cannot be the sole factor allowing the correct 'identification' of pro, for many highly inflecting languages fail to exhibit missing subjects, and others, such as Japanese, allow any verbal argument to be dropped even though there is no inflection whatsover. So the parameter that determines whether pro will be present in a given language or not has not really been fully isolated yet—though presumably the presence of informative verbal inflection will ultimately be part of that final determination.

---

[31] Recall that pro is an empty category and hence is not pronounced (or, has no phonetic matrix).

The prononimal pro may also be 'expletive' (semantically empty), just like overt pronouns (e.g., English *it*), as in:

(81) a.   pro$_i$ llegó Juan$_i$ 'Juan arrived.'

  b.   pro llueve   'It rains.'

  c.   pro parece que Juan está enfermo
      'It seems that Juan is sick.'

For (a), the nearest English example is something like *There arrived a man*; in the Spanish example *Juan* is within the VP and so does not bind pro, as it does not c-command it. Hence the pronoun (pro) is free in its Governing Category; pro is also free in (b) and (c) as it has no antecedent, and therefore is not bound.

Let us now look at $[-a, -p]$ categories. R-expressions and *wh*-traces, or variables, share the property that they must be A-free in any domain (Principle C). This is seen in the examples in (82).

(82) a.   *He$_i$ likes Max$_i$.

  b.   *Who$_i$ does he$_i$ like e$_i$?

  c.   *He$_i$ thinks that I like Max$_i$.

  d.   *Who$_i$ does he$_i$ think that I like e$_i$?

Examples (b) and (d) show the parallel data with empty categories for the overt categories in (a) and (c). In each case, the R-expression may not be A-bound within any domain. The empty categories are of course $\overline{\text{A}}$-bound, but this is outside of the realm of the Binding Theory. (The observant reader will have noticed that in (81)a, the pronominal pro A-binds the NP *Juan*, in violation of Principle C. Discussion of this problem can be found in Rizzi (1982) and Safir (1985).) If the c-command is broken, as in *His mother likes Max*, then coreference is correctly allowed; as before, if there is no c-command, there is no binding, and therefore despite the fact that the pronoun and *Max* will be coindexed, the pronoun does not bind *Max*.

Examples (b) and (d) above are known as examples of *Strong Crossover*. This name comes from the transformational account, where the movement of the *wh*-phrase 'crosses over' a coreferential pronoun as it moves into COMP. The GB analysis of this is that as the pronoun c-commands the *wh*-trace, the latter is A-bound, violating Principle C. Reversing the c-command relations, as in (83), gives a grammatical example:

(83)   Who$_i$ e$_i$ thinks that he$_i$ will win?

Here the empty category is correctly A-free (as it is $\overline{\text{A}}$-bound by *who*), and though this empty category A-binds the pronoun, the pronoun is A-free in its Governing Category, which is the lower clause.

Finally we come to PRO, the 'pronominal anaphor.' Due to its feature-specification of [+a, +p], PRO is subject to Principles A and B simultaneously, leading to an apparently paradoxical situation. Yet out of this another conclusion is possible: that PRO has no Governing Category; in lacking a Governing Category, it would effectively be immune from the dictates of the binding principles. In this way, GB derives the following statement:

(84)   PRO is ungoverned.

This is a statement about the distribution of PRO. It can only appear in ungoverned positions, for only in those will it lack a Governing Category, in virtue of lacking a governor. In any governed position, it will be required to be both bound and free in the same domain, which is not logically possible. There is one major position that is ungoverned—the subject position of an infinitival clause, as in examples like:

(85) a.   Mary hopes [$_{S'}$ PRO to win].

 b.   [$_{S'}$ PRO to err] is human.

While the tensed INFL governs (though it does not properly govern), the infinitival INFL *to* does not govern at all, allowing the appearance of PRO. The dominating clause must be S', to prevent potential government from outside. Note that the Binding Theory says nothing about the relation of PRO to its antecedent, but rather simply characterizes its distribution. The relation of PRO to its antecedent falls under the theory of *Control*.

As [+a, +p] categories must be ungoverned, by the Binding Theory, no overt category can have this specification; for an overt NP is subject to the Case Filter, but as Case is assigned under government, there is no possibility of satisfying both the Binding Theory and the Case Filter in this case.

Table 3 gives a summary of the Binding Theory and the types of NP. The Governing Category, where relevant, is indicated by unlabelled square brackets if it is not the matrix S.

9.2. Control

The theory of Control is not a homogenous one, in that it seems to involve information coming from syntax, semantics, and pragmatics. I will there-

Table 3
Summary of Binding Theory

NP -type	Binding Features	Binding Principle	
OVERT John	$-a,-p$	C	1. *He$_i$ likes John$_i$ 2. *He$_i$ thinks that I like John$_i$
him	$-a,+p$	B	1. *John$_i$ likes him$_i$ 2. John$_i$ thinks that [I like him$_i$] 3. *John$_i$ believes him$_i$ to be sick 4. John$_i$'s mother likes him$_i$ 5. His$_i$ mother likes John$_i$
himself	$+a,-p$	A	1. John$_i$ likes himself$_i$ 2. *John$_i$ thinks that [I like himself$_i$] 3. John$_i$ believes himself$_i$ to be sick 4. *John$_i$'s mother likes himself$_i$
EMPTY wh-trace	$-a,-p$	C	1. *Who$_i$ does he$_i$ like e$_i$? 2. *Who$_i$ does he$_i$ think that I like e$_i$?
pro	$-a,+p$	B	1. pro habla inglés 2. pro$_i$ llegó Juan$_i$ ayer
NP-trace	$+a,-p$	A	1. John$_i$ was seen e$_i$ 2. *John$_i$ thinks that [I was seen e$_i$] 3. John$_i$ seems [$_S$ e$_i$ to be here]
PRO	$+a,+p$	A/B	1. John$_i$ tried PRO$_i$ to sleep 2. John thinks that it is inadvisable PRO to sleep

fore say little about the theory itself, and limit myself to illustration of cases. The idea of classifying PRO as a pronominal anaphor stems in part from the fact that it can be interpreted either as one type or the other, as in:

(86) a.   John$_i$ decided PRO$_i$ to leave.

b.   Mary said that it is unnecessary PRO to cut the grass in winter.

In (a), PRO is subject to *obligatory* control, in that its antecedent must be the subject of the dominating clause. There is a class of predicates with this property, such as *decide*, *try*, etc.; PRO behaves like an anaphor when it is the subject of a clausal complement to such predicates. Other instances of PRO have *non-obligatory* control; in (86)b the interpretation can be that it is unnecessary for Mary to cut the grass, or for anyone salient in the discourse, or for the speaker, or for anyone in general. In such examples, PRO behaves like a pronoun. The 'anyone in general' interpretation is known as *arbitrary* control, as in *PRO to vote for Johnson is PRO to vote for war;* interestingly, in cases like this with multiple PROs, they are bound together in some way, for the interpretation of this example is like "in each case, for someone to vote for Johnson is for that same person to vote for war."

As I noted above, the clause dominating PRO must be S', to provide a barrier to external government. Control predicates like *try* show many superficial syntactic similarities with raising predicates like *seem*, but are also in many ways distinct. GB assigns the structures shown in (87):

(87) a.   Mary$_i$ seems [$_S$ e$_i$ to look happy]

b.   Mary$_i$ tried [$_{S'}$ [$_S$ PRO$_i$ to look happy]]

The control verbs also differ from the raising verbs in having a thematic subject; for example *try* assigns the Agent θ-role to its subject. From this, it follows that the subject of a control verb cannot be expletive (for expletives cannot bear θ-roles), as shown in (88); a similar pattern distinguishes *believe* and *persuade*.

(88) a.   It seems that Max is here.

b.   *It tries that Max is here.

c.   There seems to be a fly in the soup.

d.   *There tried to be a fly in the soup.

e.   Max believes it to be obvious that he will win.

f.   *Max persuaded it to be obvious that he will win.

Note that while traces appear in the tails of chains, PRO does not. So, for example, while (Mary, e) is a chain in (87)a, (87)b contains two chains, each with one member. This is necessary, due to the θ-Criterion, for both *Mary* and PRO are assigned θ-roles in (87)b. One diagnostic for PRO is that it must appear in structures where positing a trace would violate the θ-Criterion.

Where To Look Next

A more thorough introduction to GB (on historical lines) can be found in van Riemsdijk and Williams (1986). Possibly the most accessible of Chomsky's recent works is Chomsky (1982), which is a companion to the much fuller and denser presentation in Chomsky (1981). More recent developments in the theory are given in Chomsky (1986a), which also contains a certain amount of philosophical discussion. Chomsky (1986b) explores a radical alternative to the notion of Subjacency.

The work of Kayne and Rizzi has been very important in the development of GB; their papers are collected in Kayne (1984) and Rizzi (1982). Stowell (1981) contains the most detailed discussion of the program to eliminate phrase structure rules from the grammar. The extent to which movement in syntax is paralleled by movement in LF is discussed in Hornstein (1984) and May (1985).

The Japanese data in Section 5.4 comes from Nishigauchi (1984); see also Nishigauchi (to appear) and references there, and Huang (1982) for Chinese. The Chinese word order data alluded to at the end of Section 6 is discussed in Williams (1984) and in more detail in Huang (1982), Koopman (1984) and Travis (1984); Williams (1984) also presents a critical evaluation of Lexical-Functional Grammar from a GB perspective. On Control, see Manzini (1983). On pro, see Rizzi (1986).

Chapter 3

Generalized Phrase Structure Grammar

The theory of Generalized Phrase Structure Grammar (GPSG) developed out of work by Gerald Gazdar at the end of the 1970s, and while practically every detail of the theory has changed in the intervening period, the initial motivation of his original work is preserved. In the present chapter I will provide an overview of the version of GPSG laid out in Gazdar et al. (1985), hereafter 'GKPS.'

Generalized Phrase Structure Grammar is in a sense a very homogenous theory, in that it posits only one level of syntactic representation, surface structure, and, in its pure conception, only one kind of syntactic object, the phrase structure rule. What GPSG does is augment a phrase structure grammar in certain ways that still leave you with a phrase structure grammar, but one that can handle constructions previously thought to be describable only with the aid of transformations; most well-known is the analysis of '*wh*-movement' type constructions available within GPSG, which caught the attention of many linguists and led to a considerable amount of novel research within the GPSG framework.

Work in Generalized Phrase Structure Grammar has generally taken the idea of formalization quite seriously; consequently, GKPS is full of technical detail to a level almost unprecedented in contemporary grammatical theory. As such, the mathematical properties of GPSG grammars have been and are the focus of much attention, and their relation to a theory of parsing has also been the subject of much recent research. I shall say little about either of these things, except to note that the appearance of a grammatical formalism with relatively well-understood and mild generative power that could handle large chunks of natural languages has brought back to life what was a somewhat dormant area of enquiry: the study of the mathematical properties of human languages. GKPS only allows the system described context-free generative capacity, and as such (admittedly) cannot deal with certain known aspects of human language.

I would take us too far afield to consider the concept of context-freeness and its computational relevance; I simply note that context-free systems are limited in their descriptive power in a way that most linguists have believed is too restricting to deal with natural language syntax. What is interesting, though, is the fact that all of the constructions that have been shown to require greater power than context-freeness are somewhat unusual, and apparently not run-of-the-mill grammatical phenomena. Recently, there have been developments within the GPSG framework[1] that attempt to change it in certain ways to allow coverage of these previously problematic cases, though I shall not discuss them here.

While the emphasis in the development of transformational grammar into Government-Binding Theory was on constraining the transformational component, GPSG takes this emphasis to its conclusion and simply eliminates the transformational component. The claim is thereby advanced that one level of syntactic representation—namely, surface structure—will suffice; but it is important to note that sufficiency does not carry much weight as an argument in linguistics. The difference between the theories described here is not that one can do it one way or another, but that it is an advantage to do it one way: GPSG claims not only that it is possible to have just one level of syntactic representation, but also that in so doing it can solve several long-standing problems whose description required independent stipulations under the transformational grammar account. In its outlook on the architecture of the grammar, GPSG has inherited a tradition from formal language theory and, within the realm of generative grammar, from Montague Grammar. Every syntactic structure is directly paired with a semantic (model-theoretic) interpretation, and while in Montague Grammar syntax very much plays second fiddle, GPSG has explored the potential in the relation between syntax and semantics, in that the one may constrain and interact with the other, and recognizes several 'semantically-driven' syntactic processes.

As currently formulated, there are no phrase structure rules in a GPSG grammar, where we understand phrase structure rules as standing in a direct correspondence to pieces of tree. Rather, the grammar provides various constraints on what informational properties pieces of tree must encode, but does not go through the intermediary representation of phrase

---

[1] In particular, Pollard (1984) and subsequent work.

structure rules. GPSG does have rules, which only represent *immediate dominance*, and are called ID-rules;[2] these are related directly to trees by a *rule-to-tree* definition, which has a series of well-formedness conditions governing it. The overall picture of the grammar is shown in Figure 2, and I will devote most of this chapter to an explication of the different notions contained in it. In Figure 2, I use the term *tree* to refer to a surface structure paired with a semantic interpretation.

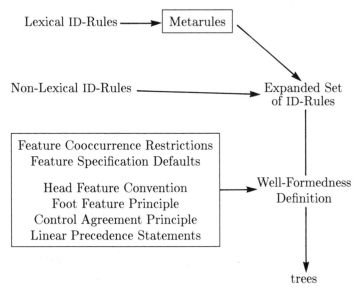

Figure 2.   Generalized Phrase Structure Grammar

Another formal point worth noting is that the grammatical information encoded by rules in GPSG is taken to be constraints on *node-admissibility*, rather than the traditional *rewrite* interpretation given to ordinary phrase structure rules. The difference can be shown with a simple example.

(1)   S   →   NP VP
           NP →   John / _ sleeps
           VP →   sleeps / John _

---

[2] See Section 2.

These are context-sensitive rules; interpreted as rewrite rules, they generate nothing, for once we have rewritten S as NP and VP, we can do no more. We can only rewrite NP in the context of *sleeps* and similarly for VP, but neither context is available. However, interpreted as admissibility conditions, the string *John sleeps* is admitted as an S, for under this interpretation we randomly generate trees and then 'check' them, and this string 'checks out.'

I will say little about Universal Grammar, that is, the general properties of the human language faculty, in this chapter; one reason is that GKPS is devoted to an analysis of English. Whatever universal features of language GPSG will ultimately propose (such as the various properties of the rule-to-tree definition), they will be couched in a rather different fashion than the way Government-Binding Theory states them. The GPSG view is that universals should follow from the very architecture of the theory; as an example, whereas Government-Binding Theory might say that it is a universal property of language that subcategorization is satisfied under government (i.e., in some local domain), GPSG would say that the very nature of the system (using something like phrase structure rules) forces this property, as such rules can only express local relations. Hence constraints, from a GPSG view, derive from the sheer impossibility of stating certain logically prior possibilities, given the primitives of the theory.

1. Features and Syntactic Categories

GPSG relies on being able to pass information around trees, and this information is encoded by means of syntactic features; GPSG is in fact a theory of how syntactic information "flows" within a structure. For example, there might be a feature specification on a given node that indicates that it has a TENSE feature with the value PAST, and an identical specification on the mother of this node. This is a situation where the information is taken to flow or pass from one to the other (the direction of this flow would be a matter for research). Intuitively, a feature (or more precisely, a feature-value pair) is a piece of linguistically significant information, and a feature often has linguistic realization; the feature of TENSE is realized in English as an *-s* on (third person) verb forms when its value is PRES (present), as in *She walks*, and is realized as *-ed* when the value is PAST, as in *She walked*. All syntactic theories use features—to differing degrees—but it is only recently that they have been put to any principled use, rather than simply used for diacritic effect in particular cases. In this section I will focus on various aspects of the GPSG approach to features—the X'-Theory of GKPS, the notion of 'syntactic category' that is adopted, and general properties of the set of features posited.

1.1. X'-Theory

The part of X'-Theory that defines a phrase as a projection of the features of a head is a central part of GPSG, for the information of what is the head determines much of the distribution of syntactic features. GPSG adopts a two-level X'-theory, and defines the major categories N, V, A and P in terms of the primitive features [N] and [V] (see Chap. 2, Table 2). At this point similarity with the Government-Binding Theory version of X'-theory stops; for GPSG proposes that the 'basic' X'-scheme is not to descend level by one, as in Government-Binding Theory, but rather to remain at the same level. This is dealt with by a default mechanism: unless otherwise indicated, the bar-level of a mother and the head daughter will be identical. We will see examples of this below. The motivation for this is essentially economy; GPSG proposes many more rules that do not obey the 'descend-one' idea than rules that do obey it.

A difference that is more immediately demonstrable is the fact that in GPSG S is a projection of V; this is not novel to GPSG but in fact dates back to the earliest work on X'-Theory. There are no abstract categories like INFL in a GPSG grammar as there is no level at which to represent them. Now it is well-attested that information that *ultimately* shows up on the verb must be present on the dominating S-node; for example, the verb *think* subcategorizes for a complement that is tensed:

(2)   a.   Lee thinks (that) Sandy is muscular.

  b.   *Lee thinks (for) Sandy to be muscular.

Information about the presence of tense must therefore pass between the inflection on the verb and the S-node. In Government-Binding Theory this is accomplished by assuming that the information flows up from INFL to its projection S in the syntax, before INFL is combined with the verb in PF. For theories which only allow fully inflected words to be inserted into trees, such an option is not available, and the information must flow directly from V to S. As it is relatively uncontroversial that information of this kind only passes up and down X'-projections, it follows that V must be the head of S in GPSG (given the assumption that words are fully inflected at the point of lexical insertion).

Now, from other considerations it is also desirable to have both VP and S′ be maximal projections (i.e., X″s); it is quite common to find rules that affect NP, VP, AP, PP and S′. In order to allow such generalizations to be captured, GPSG assigns the categories VP, S and S′ all to the same X′ level, namely the maximal projection of V. S is distinguished from VP by a SUBJ feature (for 'subject'), and S′ from S by a COMP (for 'complementizer') feature. Independent evidence for this categorization comes from coordination facts; for example, a widely-accepted constraint on coordination is that the coordinating categories must be of the same bar-level. Consider now the example in (3):

(3)   We expect $[_{VP}$ to be there by six] and $[_{S'}$ that we will be too late].

As no other category seems to coordinate with S′ under *expect* (e.g., *We expected a riot and that it would destroy the stadium*), the analysis that we could give for (3) is that *expect* subcategorizes for a complement that is a V^2. (It is usual to express bar-level in GPSG numerically.)

The X′-equivalences for these categories are shown in (4):

(4)   a. $V^2[-SUBJ][COMP\ NIL]$ = VP
      b. $V^2[+SUBJ][COMP\ NIL]$ = S
      c. $V^2[+SUBJ][COMP\ \alpha]$ = S′
           where $\alpha \in \{that,\ for,\ whether,\ if\}$.

1.2. Categories

A syntactic category in GPSG is taken to be a set of feature-value pairs. For example, the label NP (N^2) is taken to be an abbreviation for the set

$$\{<N,+>, <V,->, <BAR, 2>\}$$

where BAR is a feature just like anything else. (Some people find it mysterious that BAR should be a feature, but it is just another piece of information on a node.) The category N would have the same specification, except the value for BAR would be zero. (It is a little unfortunate that the features [N] and [V] are identical with the category names N (noun) and V (verb); I again refer the reader to Chap. 2, Table 2 for clarification.)

However, not every set of feature-value pairs is a possible syntactic category. Categories are taken to be partial functions from features to values. For example, the category NP applied to the feature V gives '−' as a value. Defining categories this way makes axiomatic the elementary observation that no syntactic category has different specifications for the same feature. For example, there are no NPs that bear both nominative and accusative case simultaneously; and

$$\{<N, +>, <V, ->, <BAR, 2>, <CASE, NOM>, <CASE, ACC>\}$$

is not a well-formed category for it is not a function; no function can deliver two values for the same argument.

Major categories are usually taken to be nouns, verbs, adjectives, and prepositions, and GPSG does not depart from this. The rest are known as *minor* categories: things like determiners, complementizers, particles, etc. Major categories participate in the X′-scheme while minor ones do not, and so minor categories can be defined in the following way:

(5)   A category C is a minor category iff C(BAR) is undefined.

That is, a minor category is one that (necessarily) lacks a value for BAR.

1.3. Features

Features in GPSG have two main properties—what kinds of values they take, and what distributional regularities they share with other features. Some features are *atom-valued*, and these are what for most readers will be the familiar case. As the name suggests, the values of such features are atomic, i.e., not susceptible to further analysis. Some sample features and value-sets are shown in (6).

(6)   PLU $+, -$

           BAR   0, 1, 2

           CASE   NOM, ACC, GEN, ...

           PFORM   *by, to, for*, ...

The traditional notion of singular and plural is reconstructed here in the binary-valued feature PLU (it is PLU rather than SING simply as a convention).[3] We have seen the BAR and CASE features above. The PFORM feature is a way of ensuring the right form for prepositions, and is in a sense a syntactic analog to θ-roles. Consider a verb like *give*; it subcategorizes for a PP that is headed by the preposition *to*:

(7)   I gave a book to/*for/*with/*towards Lee.

One way to get this is to assign a thematic role of Goal along with the subcategorization, and make sure that the Goal role is realized by the preposition *to*. Alternatively, one can subcategorize for a PP[PFORM *to*].

Other features in GPSG are *category-valued*; their values are not atomic, but are in fact categories. As an illustration, agreement (say, between a subject and a verb) is dealt with by means of a category-valued feature AGR, and encodes the information "I agree with a category of such-and-such a form," such as a 3rd-person, masculine, plural NP:

(8)   AGR   NP[3 M PL]

I will use [AGR NP[3 M PL]] as an abbreviation for the full specification, which is:

$$\{<AGR, \{<N, +>, <V, ->, <BAR, 2>, <NUM, 3>,$$

$$<GEND, MASC>, <PLU, +>\}>\}$$

in its full form. (I will use [SG] for $<PLU, ->$.)

Finally, any category can in principle label a node in a tree; for example,

$$\{<BAR, 2>\}$$

can label a node in English, and would correspond to the more familiar notation XP (i.e., maximal projection of any major category).

2. ID/LP Format

In the early conceptions of GPSG, the grammar consisted of a set of phrase structure rules, such as:

(9)   VP $\rightarrow$ V NP PP

---

[3] See Sag et al. (1985, 152ff) for more discussion of the feature SING.

Such rules encode two kinds of relation, those of *immediate dominance* and those of *linear precedence*; this particular rule says that VP immediately dominates V and NP and PP, and that the V precedes the NP which precedes the PP. In recent work, these two components are factored out, and phrase structure rules are not used at all. Dominance and precedence requirements are directly stated on nodes in the tree.

2.1. ID/LP

If we look at a set of phrase structure rules, such as those for English VPs given in (10), we notice a certain pattern in ordering of daughter constituents.

(10) a.   VP → V NP   *kiss the bride*

   b.   VP → V NP PP   *send the message to Kim*

   c.   VP → V NP S′   *tell the class that break is over*

   d.   VP → V NP VP   *expect results to be forthcoming*

In all cases, the NP immediately follows the verb, which is always initial in its phrase. Clearly any grammar that just lists these rules is missing something important about English. One could just as easily describe a grammar in which NP preceded the verb if there was also a VP complement, while NP was VP-final if the complement was S′. However, such languages probably do not occur.

Other instances where phrase structure rules seem to be inappropriate are cases where there are few, if any, ordering restrictions. Many languages have rather free constituent order (e.g., the major constituents of S can come in any order in Latin) and for a simple subject-verb-object sentence one finds oneself with six phrase structure rules. The idea of ID/LP format is that these problems are solved by factoring out information of *immediate dominance* (ID) and *linear precedence* (LP). The Latin example would now reduce to:

(11)   S   →   V, NP, NP

where the commas indicate that the categories are unordered with respect to each other. Similarly, the English rules above would now be expressed in the format:

(12) a.   VP → V, NP   *kiss the bride*

    b.   VP → V, NP, PP   *send the message to Kim*

    c.   VP → V, NP, S′   *tell the class that break is over*

    d.   VP → V, NP, VP   *expect results to be forthcoming*

    e.   V ≺ NP ≺ XP

This is not the actual GKPS formulation, which I have simplified a little to illustrate the point. The '≺' indicates the precedence relation in the LP-statement (12)e. I will elaborate in a later section on the actual ID-rules and LP-statements proposed for English.

2.2. Heads and Subcategorization

As I have hinted at above, many features are transmitted up and down X'-projections; for example, if a VP is marked as PAST, then the verb heading that VP will be too. The strategy for determining a head that was implicit in generative grammar until recently[4] was the following: look at a rule (like one in (12), or a corresponding tree fragment). Determine which daughter matches the mother in the features [N] and [V]—this is the head. Now copy over all features like person, number, gender, tense, etc., such that the features on the head and mother match.

A head is not defined in this way in GPSG. Essentially, GPSG accords no special role to the features [N] and [V], and copies them over as well. The head is indicated in a rule by the notation 'H,' as in (13).

(13)   VP → H

The idea is that this notation will express the same information (given the feature-passing conventions which I will present below) as the rule VP → V. The class of features that get copied over are called **HEAD** features, and I will say more about them in the section below on the Head Feature Convention. Given that BAR is classified as a **HEAD** feature, the H in (13) would actually be instantiated as a VP, and so we must override the operation of the feature-passing mechanisms with respect to BAR by explicitly mentioning its value. However, as we will see below, the zero bar-level is predictable from other information; that other information relates to subcategorization, which is our next topic.

---

[4] That is, until the appearance of Gazdar and Pullum (1981).

In Chapter 2, I noted that Government-Binding Theory proposed to eliminate the redundancy between phrase structure rules and subcategorization frames by dispensing with the former; in GPSG, the opposite tack has been taken, and verbs do not have a subcategorization frame as such. Rather, they have an indicator that points to the structures in which they occur. So a transitive verb will be marked in such a way as to ensure that it will only be inserted into subtrees that have an NP as sister to the verb. This is again implemented with a feature, SUBCAT, which takes integers as its values. So along with the rules given in (14) there will be the lexical entries in (15).

(14) a.   VP → H[1]

      b.   VP → H[2], NP

(15) a.   <$weep$, [[−N], [+V], [BAR 0], [SUBCAT 1]], {$wept$}, **weep′**>

      b.   <$devour$, [[−N], [+V], [BAR 0], [SUBCAT 2]], {}, **devour′**>

These entries also provide information about irregular morphology and a meaning (indicated by the boldface and prime[5]). The SUBCAT feature will ensure that the transitive verb *devour* will only appear in subtrees admitted by rule (14)b; given the view of syntactic categories taken here, failure to respect this feature-specification would be on a par with inserting a noun into a verb position, for example. It is of course possible for a verb to have multiple subcategorizations; each would correspond to a separate, but related, lexical entry.

One consequence of doing subcategorization this way is that it follows that a head can only subcategorize for its sisters; this gives the same results as the stipulation in Government-Binding Theory that subcategorization is satisfied under government, given the definition of c-command that makes reference to the first branching node (the 'stronger' definition). Note that this too entails that subjects are not subcategorized for in English. In this area GPSG may claim that it has accounted for subcategorization without having to stipulate that it must take place in a configuration of government. However, even the strong definition of government does not entirely coin-

---

[5] Note that this prime-notation does not mean the same as the X′-Theory prime-notation. I discuss meanings a little, in Section 4.

cide with the ID-rule system, for government may also go down through an S to a grand-daughter, and so the nature of the comparison is not clear. (This is a point on which Government-Binding Theory and GPSG differ—GPSG must view the sequence after 'object-raising' *believe* as NP VP;[6] for example, this NP corresponds to the subject of the related passive construction, and only sisters of the verb can have this property in GPSG. In Government-Binding Theory the complement must be an S, for no θ-role is assigned to the NP, so it cannot be a (subcategorized) sister of the verb.) Both theories differ from Lexical-Functional Grammar in not subcategorizing for subjects,[7] and this is due in each case to the idea that subcategorization must be satisfied in some local structural domain.

Note that complementizers too bear the SUBCAT feature; we might have the following rule and lexical item:[8]

(16) a.   S[COMP α] $\rightarrow$ {[SUBCAT α]}, H[COMP NIL]

     b.   <*that*, [SUBCAT *that*]>

The rule says that S with a certain value for COMP can dominate a category with a SUBCAT feature with the same value and an S (the head) without the specification of a complementizer (i.e., [COMP NIL]). Values for COMP are *for*, *that*, *if*, *whether* and NIL.

The notion of 'minor' category is now taken to pick out those categories lacking BAR but having SUBCAT, and the presence of SUBCAT is one way of getting at a wider notion of 'head' than that encoded by the H notation. For example, there are often cases where one wants to treat COMP as the head of S' for some syntactic purpose, such as passing features onto it, while retaining V as the 'ultimate' head. In such cases, the class of functional heads can be accessed by picking out those things with SUBCAT, while the strictly categorial heads will be those things that have both SUBCAT and BAR.

---

[6] As in *believe Kim to be singing*.

[7] Though this is perhaps not so clear in the case of GPSG, as the presence of the AGR feature (see Sec. 5.5 below) to handle subject-verb agreement has the effect of allowing subcategorization for subjects.

[8] Note that the range of values of SUBCAT is now integers plus various names like *that*, *for*, and so on.

3. Rules

Under the general heading of rules, I will discuss in more detail the particular ID-rules that are proposed for English, and then move to a discussion of *metarules*, which are useful ways of stating generalizations across large sets of rules. Metarules are operations on ID-rules that give back new ID-rules, and in this way expand the set of ID-rules. I shall refer to the ID-rules that are listed in the grammar as 'basic' ID-rules and those that are created by metarule as 'derived' rules.

3.1. Lexical and Non-Lexical ID-rules

The class of basic ID-rules partitions into two theoretical domains as far as other operations in the grammar are concerned. In this subsection I will just say what this distinction is, though we will not see until Section 5 why it is useful. Let us look at the rules in (17); the reader will recall that S and VP are abbreviations, as given in (4) above. Similarly, NP and PP are abbreviations, though I hope that these are familiar to the reader by this point.

(17) a.   S $\rightarrow$ X^2, H[$-$SUBJ]

    b.   NP $\rightarrow$ Det, H^1

    c. N^1 $\rightarrow$ H[30]

    d. N^1 $\rightarrow$ H[35], PP[*of*]

    e.   PP $\rightarrow$ H[38], NP

    f.   VP $\rightarrow$ H[5], NP, NP

The first two rules say that an S-node can consist of any [BAR 2] phrase and a VP (to allow for non-NP 'subjects,' as in *To fight for one's country is noble*), and that an NP can consist of a Determiner and an N^1. The remaining rules differ from these two in that they introduce a *lexical head*, which can be seen from the H[n] notation (a lexical head has both SUBCAT and BAR features). These rules, then, provide the arguments subcategorized for by heads, and are known as *lexical* ID-rules. The non-lexical ID-rules (a) and (b) do not necessarily reflect subcategorization properties of anything, and it is not obvious what generalizations, if any, govern their form.

The rules in (17) will admit the tree in (18) (with some suitable LP-statements).

(18)

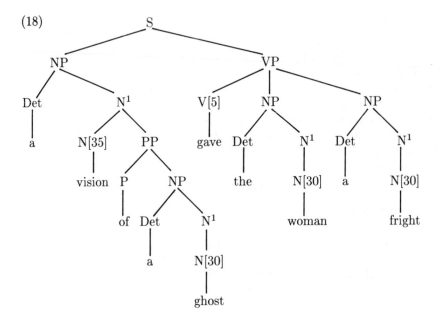

Modifying phrases may be accommodated quite simply, and it is in rules like (19) that we see the full effect of the H notation.

(19)   VP → X^2[+ADV], H

This rule allows an adverbial modifier adjoined to the VP; as the H is fully unspecified, all of the **HEAD** features of the mother will get copied over.[9] The adverbial phrase itself may be any maximal projection—for instance *yesterday* is an NP and *good*, as in *He did it good*, is an AP.

3.2. Metarules

Metarules perform some of the duties in phrase structure grammar that transformations perform in transformational grammar; in a sense, both extend a basic phrase structure grammar in certain ways. Other than this, there are few similarities.

---

[9] I use 'copy' here to give the intuition of the "information flow"; strictly, the GPSG view is that the **HEAD** features on the mother and head daughter are freely instantiated, but are constrained to match.

Let us look at the motivation for metarules. Consider the passive examples in (20); the important parts of these (the bracketed sections) would be admitted by such rules as are shown on the right:

(20) a.   Kim was [kissed].   VP →   H[PAS]

      b.   Sandy was [found in the mine].   VP →   H[PAS], PP

      c.   Lee has been [told that it is over]. VP →   H[PAS], S[FIN]

The feature PAS indicates the presence of passive morphology on the verb. Clearly it would be a mistake to simply list these rules, for they bear a regular relation to the set of rules that admit 'active' VPs, as we can see in (21) (following GKPS, I mark the [PAS] feature on the mother):

(21) a.   VP[PAS] → H[2]   VP →   H[2], NP

      b.   VP[PAS] → H[6], PP   VP →   H[6], NP, PP

      c.   VP[PAS] → H[8], S[FIN] VP →   H[8], NP, S[FIN]

The idea of a metarule is to derive the rules on the left from those on the right. The passive metarule as given in GKPS has the following formulation:

(22)   Passive Metarule

          VP → W, NP

          VP[PAS] → W, (PP[by])

In this metarule, W is a variable over any categories in an ID-rule. The passive feature appears on the VP, but again this is a **HEAD** feature and so the verbal head of the construction will be constrained to be a passive form. The rule says to take any VP-rule that has an NP-daughter, and from that form a new rule with the passive feature indicated on the mother and with the NP missing. Optionally, the new VP-rule may admit a PP daughter; this allows for the agent in a passive to be expressed or not, as in *Dana was arrested/Dana was arrested by the police*.

Note there is no mention of anything becoming a subject in the metarule. This is not necessary for the syntax: the rule effectively intransitivizes verb phrases, and this means that the only NP-position available in a sentence containing such an intransitive verb phrase (as with any intransitive) will be that of the subject. However, the corresponding semantics will change with the Passive Metarule, and will indicate that the NP in the *by*-PP (if there is one) will be interpreted similarly to the syntactic subject in the related active form; the syntactic subject of the passive will likewise have an interpretation corresponding to the interpretation of the object of the active form.

Let us now look at the relation between metarules and transformations. Transformations map trees into new trees, while metarules map rules into new rules. Assuming that the initial trees in a transformational grammar are produced by phrase structure rules, and ignoring empty categories, we can represent the situation in the following way.

(23)

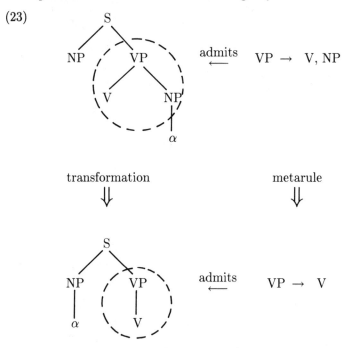

Intuitively, we can either map trees to trees as on the left-hand side of the diagram, or rules to rules as on the right. The former, transformational, way builds sentential structures by phrase structure rules and then transforms them into new structures; the latter uses metarules to expand the set of rules and therefore expand the set of trees admitted. However, the domain over which transformations are defined is much greater than the domain of metarules; potentially the domain of a transformation is an entire tree, while metarules can only apply to rules which admit 'local subtrees,' i.e., subtrees consisting of a mother and some immediately dominated daughter(s). It is impossible, for instance, to define a metarule that mimics the transformational account of 'subject-to-subject raising' (see Chap. 2, Sec. 7) in English, for the metarule cannot mention this much structure.

Another metarule that affects VP-rules is the so-called 'Subject-Aux Inversion' metarule, that allows the grammar to handle the inversion that we find in many English constructions, such as questions (e.g., *Has Robin left?*). The metarule has the following formulation:

(24)   'Subject-Aux Inversion' (SAI) Metarule

$$V^2[-SUBJ] \rightarrow W$$

$$\Downarrow$$

$$V^2[+INV, +SUBJ] \rightarrow W, NP$$

This rule takes any VP-rule and makes it into an S-rule (note that this gives 'flat' S structures, potentially without a VP), adding in the subject NP and the feature INV that indicates the inversion. This is necessary as matrix questions must be inverted, while embedded questions never are (in most dialects at least):

(25) a.   What has Leslie found?

b.   *What Leslie has found?

c.   *Gerry asked what has Leslie found.

d.   Gerry asked what Leslie has found.

The feature INV is also necessary to correctly account for the distribution of the auxiliary verb form *aren't*, which must appear in an inverted sentence if the subject is first person singular (**I aren't leaving*), and *better*, as in *You better leave now*, which can never be inverted. Finally, we can note in connection with (24) that it is perhaps correct to formulate it so as not to apply to S-rules, for the subject of S can be any [BAR 2] category,[10] but not all such categories show up in inverted sentences:

(26) a.   In these hills have been found gold and silver coins.

 b.   *Have in these hills been found silver and gold coins?

 c.   That Kim ate fish bothered Lou.

 d.   *Did that Kim ate fish bother Lou?

These would suggest that it may not be the case that the distribution of subjects is identical in inverted and non-inverted sentences.

Another independent restriction will prevent any metarule applying to an S-rule. This is the 'Lexical Head Constraint,' which states the following condition on metarule application.

(27)   Lexical Head Constraint
Metarules map from lexical ID-rules to lexical ID-rules.

Although I cannot demonstrate the motivation for this constraint in this section, the effect of it is to limit the domain of metarule application to the domain of lexical subcategorization. Thus metarules cannot create rules that arbitrarily change structure without this being sanctioned by some lexical head.

Finally, in connection with the SAI Metarule, it is worth noting that although the metarule applies to any VP-rule, only those which introduce an auxiliary verb will ever be used in the definition of well-formed trees. This is due to a Feature Cooccurrence Restriction (see (37)a below) which only allows INV to be instantiated on nodes that dominate an auxiliary verb. So, for example, while all of the VP-rules listed in (21) above will be input to the metarule, none of the output rules will lead to well-formed trees. Only those VP-rules that introduce auxiliary verbs as the lexical head will be compatible with both the metarule and the Feature Cooccurrence Restriction. (See Sec. 5.1 for more discussion.)

The next metarule for us to consider is the Extraposition Metarule, which covers cases of extraposition such as those illustrated in (28):

---

[10]   There is some debate (among linguists of all persuasions) as to whether the PP *in these hills* is a subject in (26)a/b. I shall assume that it is, though one might take its failure to allow inversion ((26)b) to indicate that in fact it is not a subject. The main point of these examples is to illustrate that it is not necessary (within GPSG) to relate inverted sentences to non-inverted direct counterparts.

(28) a.   That Dana was arrested upset her mother.

  b.   It upset her mother that Dana was arrested.

  c.   That Lee smokes is obvious.

  d.   It is obvious that Lee smokes.

  e.   That Pat found the treasure seems unfair to Kim.

  f.   It seems unfair to Kim that Pat found the treasure.

The name 'extraposition' comes from the transformational analysis which proposed that a transformation 'extraposed' the clause out of subject position and inserted an *it* subject. The metarule for this has the following specification.

(29)   Extraposition Metarule

$$X^2[\text{AGR S}] \rightarrow W$$

$$X^2[\text{AGR NP}[it]] \rightarrow W, S$$

The presence of a sentential subject is encoded in the agreement feature of the verb, so the metarule only applies to rules that introduce as mother a maximal projection that agrees with (i.e., has) a sentential subject. The metarule says that as an alternative, these predicates may take an *it* subject, with a sentential complement. The metarule thus expresses the dependency between the presence of 'dummy' *it* and the presence of an extraposed clause—this dummy only appears with clausal complements (and correspondingly, the other dummy NP in English, *there*, appears with NP arguments, as in *There is a man sick*, and **There is obvious that Lou is shaking*).

Some verbs, like *seem*, can only appear in the extraposed structure when they have a tensed complement; thus we do not have **That Kim can fly seems*. However, this cannot be a general property of such verbs, as they can appear in non-extraposed structures when combined with other predicates; we could not say, for example, that *seem* always requires extraposition of an S[FIN] subject. This is seen in (28)e/f; it is the adjective *unfair* that licenses the sentential subject, and hence we see that adjective phrases must allow extraposition (which is clear from (28)a/b), a property that may then be 'inherited' by VPs. This is why the metarule mentions X^2 phrases, not VPs. When *seem* takes an infinitival complement it inherits the subcategorization properties of that complement; when it is 'bare,' it is introduced by the rule (30), and hence always has an *it* subject.

(30)   VP[AGR *it*] → H[21], S[FIN]

Finally, we come to the Complement Omission Metarule, which allows the complements of [+N] categories (adjectives and nouns) to be omitted; verbs and prepositions obligatorily take their subcategorized arguments, while with nouns and adjectives, arguments are always optional[11] (even for nouns and adjectives derived from verbs). As complements (i.e., subcategorized arguments) appear under the X'-level, and modifiers do not, this is mentioned in the metarule to prevent gratuitous dropping of modifiers. Some relevant data is given in (32).

(31)   Complement Omission Metarule

[+N, BAR 1] → H, *W*

$$\Downarrow$$

[+N, BAR 1] → H

(32) a.   *The enemy destroyed.
     b.   The enemy destroyed the castle.
     c.   the enemy's destruction
     d.   the enemy's destruction of the castle

(33) a.   *Kim respects.
     b.   Kim respects his parents.
     c.   Kim is respectful.
     d.   Kim is respectful to his parents.

---

[11] Exceptions to this, brought to my attention by Tom Wasow, are *fond* and *fondness*.

There are two other metarules given in GKPS, which we will see later in Section 6. This now completes our survey of the basic components of the grammar, with the exception of a brief consideration of the semantics, from which we move to a consideration of the relation between ID-rules and trees.

4. Sketch of Semantics

This will be a good point to give a sketch of the semantics assumed in GPSG, for certain aspects of the semantics are necessary for an understanding of what will follow. What I will present here is a rather crude version of the material in GKPS (Chap. 9).

The semantics adopted in GKPS belongs to a family of closely-related theories of semantics that are usually referred to under the name 'Extended Montague Grammar.' Sentences are assigned a denotation (a meaning) in a model, which corresponds to the way some state of affairs might be. We want our semantics to tell us that in a model where Kim runs that the sentence *Kim runs* is true; of course there may be another model in which Kim does not run, and in that case we would want the sentence to come out false. Rather than dealing directly with model-theoretical objects, which as we will see are things like entities and sets, it is usual to employ an intermediate language of representation, known as *Intensional Logic* (IL).

Following Frege, the denotation of a sentence is taken to be a truth-value, true or false, which are represented by members of the set $\{0, 1\}$; 0 is 'false' and 1 is 'true.' We will take *Kim runs* as our example. What will be the meaning of the noun *Kim*? We can take it to be an *entity*, some kind of thing, and we can represent the denotation of *Kim* by k.

Now what does the VP *runs* mean? We will ignore the tense, and take the denotation of *run* to be the set of things that run. So now we have assigned kinds of meaning to each of the components of our simple sentence. The next step is to decide how those meanings relate to each other. The principle of *compositionality* tells us that the meaning of something is built up out of the meanings of its parts, and practically any linguist will accept this in some form or other. In particular, what we want to say is that the sentence is true iff k is a member of the set of things that run, and false otherwise; this ties everything together. The case where *Kim runs* is true is shown in Figure 3; in that model, *Lee runs* is false.

In general each syntactic category has a unique type of denotation. So for example, the VP *kiss the cook* will denote the set of things that kiss

Universe of Individuals

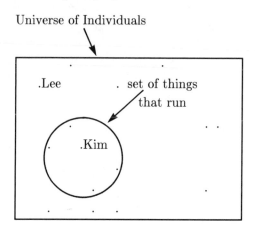

Figure 3

the cook, and the VP *decide that it is time for dessert* will be the set of things that decide that it is time for dessert. However, we do not associate VP-meanings with sets directly. Rather, we associate a VP meaning with the *characteristic function* of a set. The characteristic function of a set tells you, for any given thing, if that thing is in the set or not (true or false). The result of applying the characteristic function of the set of states in the U.S. to 'Oregon' is 1 (true), and 0 if the argument is 'Yorkshire.' Returning to our original example, we have deliberately set up our semantics so that we can view VP-meanings as functions, functions from NP-meanings (entities) to S-meanings (truth-values). The meaning of *runs* is a characteristic function, which when applied to the meaning of the NP *Kim*, will yield a truth-value.

The kind of thing a category denotes is called its *type*. The type of S, represented in GKPS by TYP(S), is symbolized by t; and for NPs that denote entities (not all noun phrases do), TYP(NP) is e. All other types are built up out of these two primitives, truth-values and entities. A VP-meaning is of type $<e, t>$, a function from entities to truth-values. The type of a transitive verb meaning, as a further illustration, will be $<e, <e, t>>$ (a function from entities to a function-from-entities-to-truth-values), while a verb like *tell* will be of type $<t, <e, <e, t>>>$—it takes a sentence and then two NPs as arguments.

In general, we can predict the semantic operation that will combine the meanings of daughter categories in a rule. For example, one typically finds rules of the following sort in the Montague Grammar literature. The prime-notation here is used to represent the meaning of the constituent, and is not related to its usage in X'-Theory.

(34)   S   →   NP, VP; S' = VP'(NP')

This says that syntactically an S consists of an NP and an VP, and that you get the S-meaning by treating the VP-meaning as a function on the NP-meaning.[12] Yet given the semantic types we have assigned, there's not much else you can do with a function from entities to truth-values and an entity, to get out a truth-value. In general, the syntax gives enough clues as to what the modes of semantic combination should be that you don't need to specify them; the operation that interprets the syntax in such a way as to build an appropriate denotation for a mother in a rule is known as *functional realization* (this general approach to semantic interpretation has often been described as "shake'n'bake semantics").

In the discussion of agreement to come below, we will need the semantic notion of *predicative category*, which, for the cases we will discuss, will be a category with a VP-type meaning (VPs 'predicate' some property of their subjects). A predicative category is something whose denotation is of type <TYP(NP), TYP(S)>, that is, something which may be predicated truly or falsely of an entity. For example, besides VPs, adjective phrases and predicate nominals (*proud of his children* in *Kim is proud of his children* and *doctor* in *Lee became a doctor*) are also predicative categories; intuitively, like VPs, they denote sets of entities.

I should also mention the role of grammatical relations like 'subject' and 'object' in GPSG. As in Government-Binding Theory, these are not taken to be primitive notions, but are defined in terms of other primitives of the theory. In GPSG, following Dowty (1982), they are defined in terms of the 'semantic structure,' that is, in the function-argument structure of the semantics. For example, a transitive verb like *find* is a two-place function—it needs two arguments to be complete. The subject is defined as the last argument, i.e., the argument to which the application of the function yields a truth-value. Similarly, the object is the next-to-last argument, and so on for indirect object, etc.

---

[12] There are other logical possibilities; for example, in Montague's best-known work "The Proper Treatment of Quantification in Ordinary English," which appears in Montague (1974), it is the NP-meaning that is the function on the VP-meaning.

I have only sketched here those parts of the semantics that are directly relevant to what I want to say below. Many other phenomena are treated in the semantics; for example, the coverage of the Binding Theory in Government-Binding Theory (at least for overt elements) with respect to the binding properties of pronouns and reflexives will have a semantic account in GPSG, although at present one has not really been developed.[13] These topics have been given analyses within the framework of (Extended) Montague Grammar, and such analyses are certainly compatible with a GPSG syntax. I would guide the reader to GKPS, Chapters 9 and 10, for further discussion and references.

5. Projecting From Rules To Trees

The major part of the burden of syntactic description is borne by the relation between ID-rules and trees. The idea is to characterize a function that 'projects' from rules to trees, as shown in (35). I use the notation $C^\dagger$ to indicate the node in a tree corresponding to a category C in an ID-rule.

(35)   rule   tree

$$C_0 \rightarrow C_1, C_2, C_3 \xrightarrow{\text{projection} \atop \text{function } \phi}$$

$$
\begin{array}{c}
C_0^\dagger \\
\diagup\;|\;\diagdown \\
C_1^\dagger \quad C_3^\dagger \quad C_2^\dagger
\end{array}
$$

The intuition is that the rule 'licenses' the local sub-tree, and that the subtree must include at least the information encoded in the rule, but also may *extend* the rule in various ways. The *projection function* ϕ determines in what ways this 'fleshing out' of information is permissible. For example, from any given VP-rule which does not mention finiteness (the values FIN and INF of the feature VFORM in this system), we would expect to be allowed to have a VP-node in a tree that is specified either as finite or non-finite, and ϕ should sanction this. However, we will want to make sure that the same feature specification that gets put onto the VP also

---

[13] See Pollard and Sag (1983) for an account of reflexives and reciprocals within the closely related 'Head Grammar' framework.

gets put onto the dominating S- and dominated V-nodes in the tree, and ϕ must therefore constrain things accordingly. Clearly we cannot allow a finite ([VFORM FIN]) VP to dominate a non-finite ([VFORM INF]) verb in a tree. We can think of ϕ as composed of various principles that govern what happens with features—in the present example, it would be the Head Feature Convention that governs the distribution of VFORM in the tree.

In this section, we will discuss the various aspects of the grammar which determine that some ϕ is a permissible function for defining a particular local sub-tree with respect to a particular rule. These aspects are: *Feature Cooccurrence Restrictions*, which constrain the class of possible categories in a language (for example, if a category bears a tense feature, then it will be some projection of V); *Feature Specification Defaults*, which specify the 'unmarked' value for a feature (Ss are not inverted unless this is specified via the operation of the SAI metarule; thus INV defaults to $-$); the *Head Feature Convention*, the *Foot Feature Principle*, and the *Control Agreement Principle*, which all determine how features distribute around the tree; and finally the set of *LP-statements*, which determine the order of categories in the tree. (These last four are considered to be principles of Universal Grammar that may be subject to finite variation across languages.) Some particular ϕ will be an *admissible projection*[14] of some rule (or of some category C in a rule) just in case:

- all Feature Cooccurrence Restrictions (FCRs) are true of $\phi(C)$
- $\phi(C)$ is compatible with all Feature Specification Defaults (FSDs)
- ϕ meets the Head Feature Convention, the Foot Feature Principle, and the Control Agreement Principle
- ϕ respects all LP-statements

These switch from being about $\phi(C)$ to being about ϕ as FCRs and FSDs are defined with respect to categories, but the other principles are defined with respect to local subtrees (and hence refer to the function which relates rules to subtrees). I will work through each of these different component parts of the projection in turn.

---

[14] I am glossing over here the distinction in GKPS between a *candidate* projection and an *admissible* one; a candidate projection satisfies the conditions listed with the exception of the defaults. An admissible projection is a candidate projection that is also compatible with all defaults. See GKPS, 99ff for discussion.

5.1. Feature Cooccurrence Restrictions

Feature Cooccurrence Restrictions (FCRs) express certain dependencies between features, and, as categories are sets of feature-value pairs, express certain restrictions on what is a possible category. Some, such as those shown in (36), are presumably universal while others may be language-specific. The identifying number of each FCR is taken from GKPS.

(36) a.   FCR 2:   [VFORM] ⊃ [−N, +V]

   b.   FCR 3:   [NFORM] ⊃ [+N, −V]

   c.   FCR 4:   [PFORM] ⊃ [−N, −V]

   d.   FCR 7:   [BAR 0] ≡ [N]&[V]&[SUBCAT]

   e.   FCR 8:   [BAR 1] ⊃ ~[SUBCAT]

   f.   FCR 9:   [BAR 2] ⊃ ~[SUBCAT]

The first one says that any category with a VFORM feature specification must be a verb; the '⊃' means 'logically implies,' so the FCR says that if a category bears the VFORM feature, then it must also be −N and +V. FCRs 3 and 4 express a similar requirement for nouns and prepositions. The fourth FCR in this list says that any major category with a SUBCAT feature specification is a lexical head ([BAR 0]); '≡' means 'if and only if,' so the FCR says that a category is ([BAR 0]) if and only if it is defined for N *and* V *and* SUBCAT. The last two FCRs say that projections of lexical heads cannot subcategorize, in that they can not ('~') be specified for SUBCAT. Due to FCR 7, we do not need to mention [BAR 0] in lexical ID-rules, for the head bears the SUBCAT feature.

Similarly, the SAI metarule does not mention 'auxiliary,' due to the English-particular FCR shown in (37)a; other possibly non-universal FCRs follow. (Of course, the distinction between universal and language-particular FCRs has no significance when it comes to the matter of the acceptability of a particular tree.)

(37) a.   FCR 1:   [+INV] ⊃ [+AUX, FIN]

   b.   FCR 10:   [+INV, BAR 2] ⊃ [+SUBJ]

   c.   FCR 11:   [+SUBJ] ⊃ [−N, +V, BAR 2]

   d.   FCR 15:   [COMP] ≡ [+SUBJ]

   e.   FCR 17:   [COMP *that*] ⊃ ([FIN] ∨ [BSE])

   f.   FCR 18:   [COMP *for*] ⊃ [INF]

FCR 1 says that if something is inverted, then it is an auxiliary and it is tensed; this expresses the fact that in English, the only things that invert are (tensed, or finite) auxiliary verbs (the non-finite auxiliary verb *to* does not invert).[15] However, in many languages, any verb may invert, so this is definitely specific to English. FCR 10 ensures that only Ss and not VPs bear the INV feature—that is, there is no such thing as an 'inverted VP' in English.

FCR 11 says that only maximal projections of verbs can be [+SUBJ], i.e., that [+SUBJ] is only defined for the category S. FCR 15 says that only Ss have complementizers, and 17 and 18 ensure that the complementizer *that* only appears in a tensed or subjunctive clause ('∨' means 'or'), and *for* in a non-finite clause. The value BSE of the VFORM feature (on a lexical head) indicates a verb in its 'base,' uninflected form; for example, this form appears in tensed clauses where the tense is carried by an auxiliary, or in subjunctive clauses, as seen in (38).

(38) a. Kim might *be* there.

   b. We require that Kim *be* there.

For the sake of completeness, I list here (without comment) the other FCRs that are in GKPS that I will not have cause to refer to later on.

(39) a. FCR 5: [PAST] ⊃ [FIN, −SUBJ]

   b. FCR 12: [AGR] ⊃ [−N, +V]

   c. FCR 13: [FIN, AGR NP] ⊃ [AGR NP[NOM]]

   d. FCR 14: ([+PRD] & [VFORM]) ⊃ ([PAS] ∨ [PRP])

So, in projecting from rule to tree, all FCRs must be respected, i.e., they must be true of the node in the tree (or equivalently, they must be true of ϕ applied to the category in the rule).

5.2. Feature Specification Defaults

Feature Specification Defaults (FSDs) are something that all theories use in some way or other, and although the idea is simple, it turns out to be

---

[15] This FCR ensures that the only output rules from the SAI Metarule ((24) above) which will license well-formed trees will be those with a lexical head which is an auxiliary verb. As such verbs appear sister to VP in the basic ID-rules (see Gazdar, Pullum, and Sag (1982)), the metarule-output rules will contain a VP constituent too.

very tricky to state their operation in any formal way. I will just present here the ideas behind the theory of defaults developed in GKPS.

The FSDs in (40) look like candidates for universal FSDs:

(40) a.   FSD   2:   ~[CONJ]

b.   FSD   3:   ~[NULL]

c.   FSD   4:   ~[NOM]

d.   FSD   7:   [BAR 0] ⊃ ~[PAS]

The first three say that it is marked, i.e., not the usual case, to have a category that is a conjunct, or that is null (phonetically empty), or that bears nominative case. In the special cases where these features do appear, their appearance must be specifically sanctioned by a rule. We can illustrate this with respect to FSD 7, which says that the default for a lexical head is not to be passive; we only want passive verbs to show up when sanctioned by rules created by the Passive Metarule, in which case PAS is explictly mentioned on the rule. If this were not so, we would allow passive verbs to spontaneously appear, and admit things like *Kim was attacked Lee*. In contrast, the PAST feature has no default, and we find past and non-past verbs in any context (roughly speaking).

Let us look at some of the other defaults.

(41) a.   FSD   1:   [−INV]

b.   FSD   5:   [PFORM] ⊃ [BAR 0]

c.   FSD   11:   [+V, BAR 0] ⊃ [AGR NP[NFORM NORM]]

These defaults say that things are not inverted unless specifically forced to be so, that the default for the PFORM feature is for it to appear on lexical heads (prepositions, by FCR 4), and that verbs normally agree with 'normal' NPs: the feature NFORM takes three values, NORM, *it*, and *there*, and the last two must be sanctioned by specific rules. The default is then to NORM, as seen in (42)a below. Along with this, I again complete the list of FSDs given in GKPS, again without further comment.

(42) a.   FSD   8:   [NFORM] ⊃ [NFORM NORM]

b.   FSD   6:   [+ADV] ⊃ [BAR 0]

c.   FSD   9:   [INF, +SUBJ] ⊃ [COMP *for*]

d.   FSD   10:   [+N, −V, BAR 2] ≡ [ACC]

5.3. Head Feature Convention

As I have hinted several times in the preceding sections of this chapter, many of the features proposed in GPSG are **HEAD** features, which means that their distribution in a tree is governed in a certain way that crucially involves the notion of a head, indicated by the H symbol in ID-rules.

Under its simplest formulation, the *Head Feature Convention* (HFC), will say that in any local subtree, the **HEAD** features of the mother are identical to the **HEAD** features of the head daughter. This is expressed in the following way.

(43)   Head Feature Convention
$$\phi(C_0) \mid \textbf{HEAD} = \phi(C_h) \mid \textbf{HEAD}$$

Here C_0 and C_h are the mother and head daughter of a rule, respectively; hence ϕ applied to either of these is the corresponding node in the tree. The vertical line '|' represents function restriction—the domain of the function is restricted in the way indicated by what follows the vertical line. Thus, what (43) says is that the features of the mother restricted to **HEAD** features (i.e., just the **HEAD** features on the mother) are identical to the features of the head daughter restricted to **HEAD** features, as desired. The final formulation of the HFC is somewhat more complicated than this, but we will use this version for present purposes.

As an illustration, we will be allowed, by the HFC, to project the subtree in (45) from the rule in (44).

(44)   VP →   H[1], NP

(45)

$$
\begin{bmatrix}
<N, -> \\
<V, +> \\
<BAR, 2> \\
<VFORM, FIN> \\
<PAST, ->
\end{bmatrix}
$$

$$
\begin{bmatrix}
<SUBCAT, 1> \\
<N, -> \\
<V, +> \\
<BAR, 0> \\
<VFORM, FIN> \\
<PAST, ->
\end{bmatrix}
\qquad
\begin{bmatrix}
<N, +> \\
<V, -> \\
<BAR, 2> \\
<PER, 3> \\
<PLU, +> \\
<CASE, ACC> \\
<NFORM, NORM>
\end{bmatrix}
$$

What goes on with the NP node here is irrelevant for current concerns. On the verbal projection, we have added the features VFORM and PAST to the mother; the other features come from the rule. The HFC tells us that *all* of these features (and their values) must be copied over, and most of them are. Note that the value of BAR differs. It has to be 2 on the mother for this is specified in the rule, but it has to be 0 on the daughter due to FCR 7, which says that major categories with SUBCAT are [BAR 0]. One of the subtleties in a final formulation of the HFC is that it must have this 'defaulty' character—features are only forced to match when it is possible for them to match given other constraints that might apply. Similarly, SUBCAT cannot appear on [BAR 1] or [BAR 2] categories, by FCRs 8 and 9, so this feature is present only on the daughter.

The following example shows a subtree that violates the HFC by having different values for PAST indicated on the mother and on the head daughter.

(46)

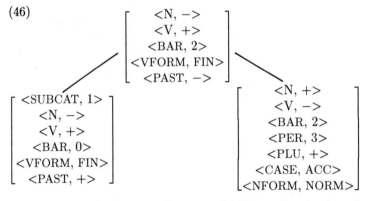

Confusion sometimes arises over the H notation in the rule; why does 'H' not appear in the tree? The answer here is that H is not part of the content of the rule, but rather an instruction about the interpretation of the rule. The daughter H[1] in rule (44) says that there is a [SUBCAT 1] category which *is to be interpreted as* the head of the rule. The H is a metagrammatical symbol; its interpretation can be thought of in the same way as the interpretation of the row of dots in $\{1, 2, \ldots, n\}$: we do not interpret this as the set consisting of four elements, the integers 1 and 2, a row of dots, and some arbitrary number n. Like H, '...' will have a different interpretation depending on context: $\{a, b, \ldots, z\}$ is not interpreted as the set with members a, b, z, and some arbitrary number (23?) of sequential integers.

The HFC, then, largely determines the structure of each X′-projection in a tree. Any arguments and modifiers will have their category specified in the ID-rule that introduces them; of course, their internal structure will again be determined in part by the HFC. The complete list of **HEAD** features presented in GKPS is given in (47).

(47)   Head Features
         {AGR, ADV, AUX, BAR, INV, LOC, N, PAST, PER, PFORM, PLU, PRD, SLASH, SUBCAT, SUBJ, V, VFORM}

We have seen illustrations of most of these; PRD is used to indicate a predicative use of a category—for example, the second complement of *consider* must be a predicative category, and such categories have certain syntactic properties (we will see this in the section below on coordination):

(48) a.   I consider Dr. Jekyll a competent surgeon.

     b.   *I consider Dr. Jekyll Mr. Hyde.

I will postpone discussion of SLASH for the section on unbounded dependencies.

One class of features, then, that distribute around a tree is the class of **HEAD** features; we will see in the next subsection the class of **FOOT** features, which have different properties of distribution. Finally, there are some features which are neither of these types, and they just sit quietly on a node. I list these features in (49) (from GKPS).

(49)   'Non-Propagating' Features
         {CASE, COMP, CONJ, GER, NEG, NFORM, NULL, POSS, RE-MOR, WHMOR}

The feature GER indicates whether something is gerundive or not (we have a gerundive phrase *having been crying* in *Having been crying, Lee looked awful*); the feature POSS indicates the possessive (often called the genitive case in other theories); REMOR indicates whether a pronoun is a reflexive (e.g., *themselves*) or a reciprocal (*each other*), roughly speaking (my use of 'pronoun' is misleading here, but I will not attempt to clarify it more). We will encounter the feature WHMOR (for '*wh*-morphology') in the following subsection.

5.4. Foot Feature Principle

Some features are distributed around a tree without necessarily obeying the Head Feature Convention. For example, it is uncontroversial that the bracketed phrase in (50) somehow 'inherits' a feature of *wh*-ness from the contained relative pronoun *whom*, and that it is this feature that is a criterial part of the syntactic description of the construction. The GPSG analysis of the feature percolation is shown diagrammatically in the tree below, with [+R] indicating the 'relative' feature introduced by the pronoun.

(50)   Kim, [the rumors about whom are totally false], will make a statement later this morning.

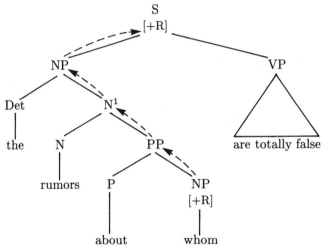

Clearly, in passing up from an NP-node to a PP-node, the feature is not showing the behavior of a **HEAD** feature. Roughly, the idea of the *Foot Feature Principle* is that **FOOT** features will be passed up from *any* daughter in a tree (not just the head), with the upper and lower limits of this propagation determined by prior specification, either in a rule or in a lexical item. For example, we might have the rule in (51) for the non-restrictive relative clause[16] in (50); I will discuss its role in admitting this example immediately below.

---

[16] A plausible but controversial analysis of relative clauses in English is that restrictive relatives (e.g., in *the man who I met*) are sister to N′, while non-restrictives (*the man, who I met*) are sister to NP. Note that H in (51) will be instantiated as NP, by the Head Feature Convention. I offer this rule only as an illustration.

(51)   NP → H, S[+R]

The Foot Feature Principle (FFP) has the following formulation:

(52)   **Foot Feature Principle**

$$\phi(C_0) \mid \textbf{FOOT} \sim C_0 \;=\; \bigsqcup_{1 \leq i \leq n} \phi(C_i) \mid \textbf{FOOT} \sim C_i$$

Recall that $\phi(C_n)$ is the node in the tree corresponding to the member C_n in a rule. This time we are restricting the domain of the principle to **FOOT** features, and the new notation '$\sim C_0$' refers to those features *not* on C_0, which is the mother in the ID-rule. Hence, the first part of the principle can be read as "the features on the mother node restricted to **FOOT** features that were not mentioned on the mother in the rule." What the principle is about then, is those **FOOT** features that have been *instantiated* onto the mother node but not *inherited* onto the mother node from the mother category in the rule. The rest of the principle says that these features instantiated on the mother must be identical to the *unification* (the big square cup—see below) of the **FOOT** features instantiated onto all of the daughters. Note again that we are dealing with instantiation on the daughters and not inheritance (due to the '$\sim C_i$'). The basic idea here is that any **FOOT** feature instantiated on a daughter must be matched by one on the mother, and hence the feature appears to "percolate upwards." The notion of unification roughly corresponds to the idea of set-union,[17] and we can think of it as such; so we have that the (set of) **FOOT** features added onto the mother must be identical to the union of the **FOOT** features added onto the daughters.

In the example and tree (50), none of the nodes that bear the [+R] feature are admitted by rules that mention the feature, with the exception of the S-node. If the feature were to "pass up" through this node, we would have the following subtree:

(53)

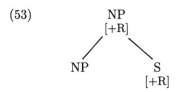

Yet this is exactly the kind of case that the FFP blocks, for the feature has been instantiated on the mother, but not instantiated on any daughters, and so the one is not identical to the other. The daughter bears the feature of course, but in virtue of inheritance. Due to the parallel instantiation on mothers and daughters forced by the FFP, we get the appearance that the feature has actually passed up from the lexical item *whom* to this S-node.

Let us look at some more examples. From the rule in (54), we are licensed by the FFP to admit the subtrees in (55), but not those in (56).

(54)   VP →   H[3], NP, PP

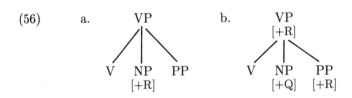

(55)   a.   VP   b.   VP
                   [+R]   [+R]

          V   NP   PP   V   NP   PP
               [+R]   [+R]   [+R]

(56)   a.   VP   b.   VP
                                          [+R]

          V   NP   PP   V   NP   PP
               [+R]   [+Q]   [+R]

In (55)b, although two tokens of the feature have been instantiated on the daughters, the union of these is just the set {[+R]}; hence this is instantiated on the mother. In (56)a no feature has been instantiated on the mother, while one has on one daughter; and in (56)b two different **FOOT** feature specifications have been added to the daughters, but only one of these to the mother. The notation [+Q] , as I will explain presently, indicates the feature that we find in interrogative pronouns, many of which have relative pronoun counterparts.

The **FOOT** feature WH is ultimately the primitive in the grammar that unifies relative and interrogative pronouns. It is a category-valued feature, as can be seen in the sample parts of lexical entries shown in

(57). The feature WHMOR indicates whether the pronoun's morphology is appropriate to a question, a relative clause, or both.

(57) a.   <*what*, NP[WH NP[WHMOR Q]], ... >

b.   <*which*, NP[WH NP[WHMOR Q]], ... >

c.   <*which*, NP[WH NP[WHMOR R]], ... >

d.   <*which*, Det[WH NP[WHMOR Q]], ... >

e.   <*which*, Det[WH NP[WHMOR R]], ... >

The pronoun *what* is only an interrogative pronoun (we do not have **the table what you made* in standard dialects); otherwise, most pronouns of this type can be either relative or interrogative. The entry for *what* says that it is an NP with a WH **FOOT** feature whose value is the category NP with the feature specification appropriate to an interrogative pronoun. The word *which*, on the other hand, can be either an NP or a determiner, and either relative or interrogative:

(58) a.   Which do you prefer?

b.   the tasks which I leave to the housekeeper

c.   Which tasks do you leave to the housekeeper?

d.   Here is my list, to which list Kim has added many more ideas.

The relative use of the determiner *which* is limited to the rather formal sounding non-restrictive relative clauses as in (58)d.

Although I have used the metaphor of a **FOOT** feature "passing up" the tree in this section, for this is useful to understand the basic concept, it is not how the system actually works. I will end this present section with another example to illustrate the system directly.

If we take the question *With what did you catch him?*, we again have a similar propagation. To illustrate the operation of the feature instantiation mechanism, I have split the tree for this into subtrees; each subtree will be admitted by one ID-rule. The dotted line is supposed to indicate how the subtrees link together and is not part of the formal representation of the structure. In this example the lower subtree will have a mother PP with the [+Q] **FOOT** feature; this same category will also be a daughter in the subtree rooted in S. For now we can ignore the structure of *did you catch him*, which in GPSG terms is an S/PP (S-missing-a-PP); such structures are the topic of the section on unbounded dependencies.

(59)

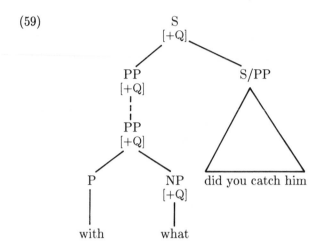

The tree here will be admitted by instantiation of [+Q] on the following rules; I have simplified the structure of PP somewhat in (60)b.

(60) a.   S   → X^2, H/X^2

    b.   PP → H^0, NP

By suitable instantiation, we will admit the subtrees indicated in (59), which will link up, giving the appearance or propagation; something in the grammar will contain the information that S[+Q] is a possible root category (the category of questions). At the "bottom" of the path of [+Q], we will have the category NP[+Q], which may dominate a lexical item like *what*, which, as the reader will recall, is listed as an NP.

I will leave the FFP here, as we will see its operation again (in connection with SLASH) below; GKPS list three **FOOT** features, WH, SLASH (='/'), and RE. The last deals with reflexive and reciprocal pronouns, though I cannot discuss this here (see Pollard and Sag (1983)).

5.5. Control Agreement Principle

The *Control Agreement Principle* (CAP) is part of a theory of agreement that has been the focus of much attention in GPSG. While the 'core' case of agreement is perhaps subject-verb agreement, there are of course many other cases: in some languages, verbs agree with objects, adjectives agree with nouns, and so on. Yet there are also clear constraints—in no language does the subject agree with the object, for example. It is the task of a theory of agreement to predict the existence of just the possibilities that are attested.

The CAP is a 'semantically-based' principle, in that the underlying intuition (due to Ed Keenan—see Keenan (1974)) is that functor categories agree with argument categories. Typically such a functor category is a predicative category, such as a VP, and these categories agree with their *controllers*, such as the subject NP. We thus say that the NP *controls* the VP in virtue of the VP being a predicative category, and the CAP in its crudest form says that controllees agree with their controllers (and not vice versa). This is not to deny a certain symmetry in the agreement relation, but the point is that verbs agree with NPs by showing features that are essentially properties of NPs, such as person, number and gender; we do not find the opposite, say, an NP agreeing with a verb with respect to a 'verbal' feature, such as tense.

The agreement is formally encoded in the AGR feature, which is category-valued, and essentially carries within it a 'copy' of the controller. For example, from the rule in (61) we might admit the tree shown:

(61)   S   →   X², H[−SUBJ]

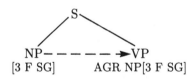

This might be part of the tree ultimately admitting *Joanna feeds herself*, where the treatment of reflexives will interact with the AGR on the VP to ensure that the reflexive will be a [3 F SG] form. Also, as AGR is a **HEAD** feature, agreement will also show up on the head of the VP, and indeed the verb shows its [3 SG] form (verbs in English do not show agreement for gender).

The statement of the CAP is rather complex, and I will not present any of the formal details here; its effect is to ensure that the projection function ϕ for the rule in (61) only meets the CAP just in case the agreement features of the value of the AGR feature on the VP are identical to the agreement features on the NP. As the theory of agreement predicts what agrees with what, it is not necessary to stipulate this agreement, which distinguishes this version of GPSG from its early predecessors and also, for example, from Government-Binding Theory, where the rule coindexing INFL and the subject NP is simply a statement added to the grammar.

In other cases the controller of a predicative category is not directly its subject, though it is a sister; the definition of controller is formulated so as to ensure that the object NP *Susi* is the controller of the embedded VP in (62).

(62)

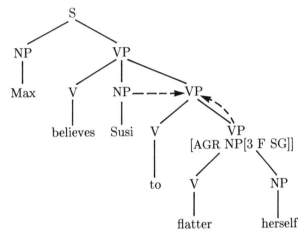

Things are slightly more complex still, as I will outline: in (62), the treatment of reflexive pronouns causes the AGR feature on the lowest VP to have the specification NP[3 F SG]. However, this VP is a predicative category, but it has no controller (no sister NP whose interpretation the interpretation of the VP is predicated of). The CAP says that in such a case the AGR feature passes up to the next node, and so on until a controller is found. This is indicated by the arrows in (62).

This shows what the operation of the CAP does; the reader should consult GKPS for further details. I will turn now to the way GPSG handles the difference between 'raising' verbs like *seem* and *believe* and 'control'[18] verbs like *try* and *persuade*.

---

[18] In the Government-Binding Theory sense of the term. In transformational grammar, such verbs are known as 'Equi-NP Deletion' (or simply 'Equi') verbs.

The examples in (63) will be analysed in part in terms of the syntactic structures shown in (64).

(63) a.   Kim seemed to look puzzled.

    b.   Kim tried to look puzzled.

    c.   Kim believed Dana to love Lee.

    d.   Kim persuaded Dana to love Lee.

(64)

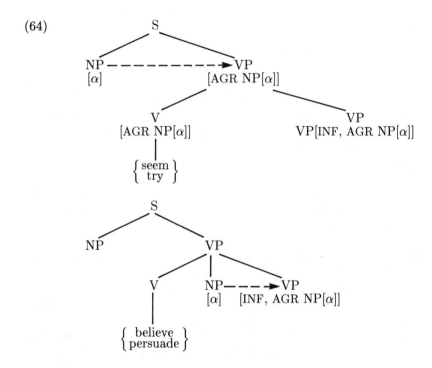

These are the important parts of the structures; with *seem* and *try*, the subject is interpreted as the subject of the lower infinitival VP and controls it (the lower VP has no controller, so the AGR passes up to the higher VP), and with the other verbs it is the object NP that is the controller. Yet there are many differences between the two types of verb; one illustration of this is seen in (65), where the expletive (semantically empty) pronoun *there* cannot appear as an argument of *try* or *persuade*.

(65) a.   There seemed to be a pig in the garden.

b.   *There tried to be a pig in the garden.

c.   Kim believed there to be a pig in the garden.

d.   *Kim persuaded there to be a pig in the garden.

This is handled in the subcategorization for these verbs, that is, in the ID-rules that produce the nodes that immediately dominate them in syntactic structures:

(66) a.   VP →   H[15], VP[INF, +NORM]   *try*

b.   VP →   H[16], VP[INF]   *seem*

The specification [+NORM] is short for AGR NP[NFORM NORM]. The rules in (66) have the property of allowing any kind of NP to be the subject of *seem*,[19] while ensuring, through agreement, that the subject of *try* is [NFORM NORM], i.e., not *it* or *there*. Directly parallel rules are given for *persuade* and *believe*.

The reader may recall that the feature NFORM defaults to NORM, and so the question arises as to how expletive NPs can ever be licensed at all. This brings us back to very complex problem of how exactly the defaults should work, something far beyond the scope of this chapter. However, I will try to explain what the solution to this problem is.

The feature NFORM should default to NORM on the lexical heads admitted by the rules in (66) (by FSD 11—see (41) above); however, it cannot do so when its sister is a VP[INF], for some of these VP[INF]s require a different value, as will be allowed by rule (66)b. For example, the infinitival VP *to be a pig in the garden* might be the complement of *seem*, and it requires a *there* subject. Hence, the default should not apply when the AGR feature on a lexical head (e.g., *seem*) covaries with the AGR feature on the VP[INF]: this latter category lacks a controller, so the AGR feature specification gets passed up to the dominating VP, and by the HFC down to the verb (*seem*). Under such circumstances, the default is stipulated to become inoperative, and this is a property of the set of like structures—so

---

[19] This is a slight simplification of the GKPS rule, which also allows for an optional PP constituent, as in *seem to Lee to be sick.*

any structure with a lexical head verb sister to a VP[INF] complement will have the default inoperative on that lexical head. By the HFC, the inapplicability of the default will also be true of the dominating VP. This will allow *seem* to take *it* and *there* subjects. Of course, nothing will change for *try*, for its [+NORM] specification comes from the rule, which is an absolute specification.

Similarly, when *seem* takes a tensed complement (as introduced by rule (30) above), there is the specification on the lexical head that the agreement is with an *it* subject. Again, FSD 11 will be inoperative, as just outlined; if this were not so, rule (30) would never be able to do any work in the grammar.

5.6. Linear Precedence Statements

Finally we come to the LP-statements, which dictate the order of sisters in a subtree (as the projection function ϕ is applying to rules, the domain of application of any of the principles in this whole section is the individual rule and/or the corresponding local subtree). The following two statements cover much of English.

(67) a. $[SUBCAT] \prec \sim[SUBCAT]$

    b. $[+N] \prec P^2 \prec V^2$

(67)a means that complementizers precede their sister clauses and that any lexical head precedes its arguments; essentially it says that any terminal symbol (i.e., a lexical item) precedes its sisters. This is potentially a very strong claim and if true (more research is necessary to tell) it would seem to pose a problem for other theories of word order, such as the Government-Binding Theory reliance on Case assignment. For example, while the complementizer *for* assigns Case to a subject and can in Government-Binding Theory be made to precede the S containing the subject as a result, the complementizer *that* assigns nothing yet appears in the same position (however, if COMP is the head of S', then these might fall together as English is head-initial). Similarly, (67)a predicts that, in coordinate structures, conjunction words precede their sister conjuncts[20] in English, as in *two men and four women* and not **two men four women*

---

[20] The constituency assigned in coordinate structures is discussed in Section 6.2.

and, which again appears to admit no explanation in Government-Binding Theory terms.

The other LP-statement orders phrasal categories, and not only covers the order of constituents within VP, but also covers cases where PP-modifiers or -arguments in NP and AP follow intermediate projections, as illustrated in (68):

(68)

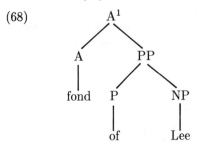

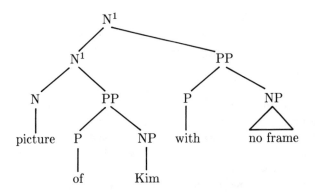

It is clear that LP-statements will be very important in the analysis of cross-linguistic variation, and that LP-statements will indeed vary from language to language.[21] And it is well-known that some languages have a fairly 'fixed' order, while others are rather free. On the other hand, the set of ID-rules is likely to be fairly stable—or more correctly, perhaps, the set of lexical ID-rules, for these express subcategorization properties, and

---

[21] For an analysis of German, see Uszkoreit (1984).

these seem to be quite uniform across languages. The non-lexical ID-rules will vary—many languages, for example, have nothing that corresponds to a complementizer (at least as an independent syntactic unit), and so on. At the phrasal level, some languages seem to lack VP constituent, and one would therefore expect an S-rule that introduces the verb, its subject, and all other arguments as sisters in a 'flat' configuration.

This concludes the review of the components of the rule-to-tree definition. In the final part of this chapter, I will concentrate more on analyses of particular phenomena available within GPSG rather than general properties of the theory.

6. Unbounded Dependencies and Coordination

The phenomenon of 'unbounded dependencies' (I will give examples shortly) was thought for many years to be beyond the scope of a non-transformational grammar; when a phrase structure analysis of such constructions appeared with the earliest versions of GPSG, the theory caught the attention of many linguists, and in particular the interaction of the analysis of unbounded dependencies with the analysis of coordinate structures went beyond the traditional transformational account in its coverage and predictive power. The current formulation of GPSG preserves these earlier insights, while incorporating them in a more general theory of features and principles of Universal Grammar.

6.1. Unbounded Dependencies

Unbounded dependencies appear in many constructions; I just give a few examples here.

(69) a.   Which men does Gerry think are leaving? (question)

b.   the table on which we left the bottle (relative clause)

c.   Pictures like this, the Tate Gallery would never want to buy. (topicalization)

All of these constructions have the property that there is what looks like an 'extra' phrase outside of the main clause, while within that main clause a phrase is correspondingly missing. In (69)a, the VP *are leaving* has no subject, in (b) *leave* is missing a locative argument, and in (c) *buy* has no object. The transformational analysis is to generate the phrase in question within the clause, and then move it to a clause-external position, thereby ensuring a one-to-one match between 'extra' phrases and missing phrases. The relation of dependency between these two positions is potentially unbounded, i.e., a subtree of any arbitrary size can intervene.

The apparent problem for a phrase structure analysis is that it seems that we must add to the grammar extra rules like (70)a, and make all (say) NP constituents optional for the S-internal rules, like (70)b. These might be proposed to handle (69)a.

(70) a.   S   →   NP, S

    b.   S   →   (NP), VP

That is, sentences can have an extra 'displaced' NP, and any NP position is optional. While a lucky coincidence of choice of the right rules will indeed get (69)a, these rules also predict that *Which man did you meet Lee?* and *are happy* are sentences of English; in the first case we have one NP too many, and in the second one too few. Moreover, there is often agreement between something in the domain of the missing constituent and the displaced phrase (cf., (69)a, *Which men does Gerry think is leaving?*). The solution to this problem is to pass information around the tree, between the displaced position and the missing position, such that a correspondence between the two can be maintained. In particular, GPSG proposes the following rule for dealing with many cases of unbounded dependencies.

(71)   S   → X^2, H/X^2

This rule admits a tree with any [BAR 2] category sister to an S carrying the information that it is missing a [BAR 2] category. (The observant reader will note that nothing in the rule ensures that we have the *same* [BAR 2] category in both cases; the rule is not S → α, S/α, where α is a variable over categories. However, the theory of agreement determines this to be an agreement structure, and the general properties of agreement will ensure a match. The fact that the grammar need not stipulate a match in cases similar to this has consequences for the analysis of coordination.) Now the information of the missing constituent is 'carried down' the tree and is ultimately associated with an appropriate null constituent.

It is again perhaps easier from an expository point of view for me to present the operation of the grammar here as if it were bottom-up. So let us look at what happens at the site of the missing constituent. GPSG uses a feature NULL to encode that a constituent is phonologically null (empty). By FCR 19, this triggers the introduction of the **FOOT** feature SLASH, which is a category-valued feature.

(72)   FCR 19:   [+NULL] ⊃ [SLASH]

The empty string e is listed in the lexicon as belonging to the category $\alpha[+\text{NULL}]/\alpha$, and this allows the grammar to license subtrees like (73)a but not (73)b.

(73) a.   NP[NULL, SLASH[NP]]

$$|$$

e

b.   *NP[NULL, SLASH[PP]]

$$|$$

e

(In fact, as α is a variable over categories here, all the features will have to match, except for [NULL], including person, number, and gender features that I have omitted here.) Only in (73)a can the tree terminate at this point; there is nothing wrong with the dominating category in (73)b, just that it cannot dominate e. So the situation is that the specification of NULL triggers the appearance of SLASH, which, being a **FOOT** feature, will start a 'path' going up the tree. As in the cases we saw in the previous section, the SLASH will stop when it gets to a subtree admitted by a rule that mentions SLASH, such as the rule (71).

The feature NULL defaults to being absent; hence it will only ever appear in a tree when sanctioned by a rule. Such rules will be derived by metarule—in fact, by two. The first for us to consider is Slash Termination Metarule 1 (STM1):

(74)   Slash Termination Metarule 1

$$X \to W, X^2$$

$$\Downarrow$$

$$X \to W, X^2[+\text{NULL}]$$

This simply says that any [BAR 2] category can be null. We can now put all the pieces together and see how this will work. From the rule in (75)a we get the new rule in (75)b; when we build a subtree, we must instantiate SLASH to respect FCR 19, and I illustrate this in (76), using the ⋆ to indicate the occurrences of SLASH that have been instantiated (and using '/' for SLASH). The example is an embedded question, as in *Lee wonders which woman you saw*; again I show each subtree, to show how the pieces of the tree fit together.

(75) a.   VP →   H[1], NP

      b.   VP →   H[1], NP[+NULL]

(76)

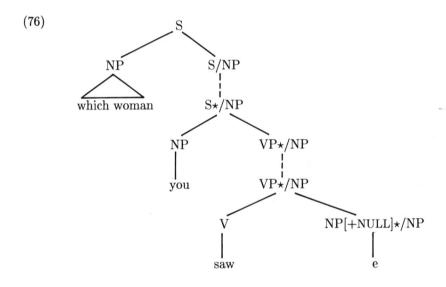

Let us now consider more closely the application of STM1. Essentially, it dictates the distribution of the empty string *e*. (While Government-Binding Theory recognizes four types of empty category, GPSG recognizes only one, which corresponds to *wh*-trace in Government-Binding Theory.) Constraints on the application of this metarule led to the proposal and adoption of the Lexical Head Constraint (LHC), given above in (27), which states that metarules may only apply to lexical ID-rules, those rules that introduce a lexical head as one daughter. Some examples that motivate this are shown below, along with, in each case, the metarule-output rule that would be necessary to sanction the bracketed part of the example.

(77) a.   *Who did Lee say that [_ had arrived]?

  S/NP → NP[+NULL]/NP, VP

 b.   *Kim, the warden gave [_ , who is my brother,] a ticket.

  NP/NP → NP[+NULL]/NP, S[+R]

 c.   *How many did Sandy borrow [_ books]?

  NP/AP → AP[+NULL]/AP, N^1

(78) a.   I wonder who it is [_ that you met]?

  VP/NP → H[44], NP[+NULL]/NP, S[+R]

 b.   Kim, the warden [gave _ a ticket].

  VP/NP → H[5], NP[+NULL]/NP, NP

 c.   How many books did Sandy complain [about _]?

  P^1/NP → H[38], NP[+NULL]/NP

What we notice is that all the good cases have the null category sister to a lexical head, and by imposing the LHC, we can predict the data in (77) and (78). (This is identical in these cases to the part of the ECP in Government-Binding Theory that allows lexical heads to be proper governors, along with the 'strong' definition of government that says you only govern your sisters. The ECP and the LHC were developed independently, and it is striking that they should converge in this way.) No metarule could apply to produce the rules in (77), for the 'source' rules upon which the metarule would operate are non-lexical ID-rules. Hence, the rules given in (77) are not in the grammar of English, and so the examples in (77) are not admissible.

The feature SLASH is categorized not only as a **FOOT** feature, but also as a **HEAD** feature. This has various consequences relating to the distribution of null elements; I will present a simple illustrative example here. It is not generally possible to have a null category inside of an adjunct in English, as seen in the contrast in the examples in (79); the relevant subtrees (in (80)) should both be admissible by the rule (79)c.

(79) a.   Which book did you [buy ‗ after meeting the author]?

   b.   *Which author did you [buy the book after meeting ‗]?

   c.   VP → H, PP

(80) a.

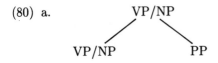

   b.

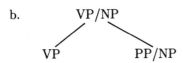

We can predict the difference if we take SLASH to be a **HEAD** feature, for while both subtrees in (80) satisfy the FFP with respect to rule (79)c, only (80)a satisfies the HFC as well. Many other similar cases motivate the dual categorization of SLASH. This requires an additional FCR, to ensure that SLASH does not get down onto a lexical head, for otherwise trees would never terminate.

(81)   FCR 6:   [SUBCAT] ⊃ ~[SLASH]

As the HFC is not an absolute mechanism, it will not override this FCR on lexical heads, but will continue to apply on all projections of lexical heads. The problem that this overcomes is this: if SLASH is a **HEAD** feature, then without FCR 6 we will get nodes labelled V/NP in trees; but these cannot dominate *e*, for no NULL specification is present, and the categories (on either side of the SLASH) do not match. On the other hand, V is a preterminal and cannot dominate any further syntactic structure where we might hope to eliminate the SLASH.[22]

---

[22] In some languages, verbs show special forms when they appear in unbounded dependencies, and this kind of evidence might motivate allowing V/NP as a well-formed category (where the SLASH would 'spell-out' as the special morphology) in such a language. For discussion of relevant cases and issues, see Goldberg (1985) and Zaenen (1983).

The Lexical Head Constraint also has the effect of ruling out NULL subjects, for the subject in English is introduced by a non-lexical ID-rule. This entails that the GPSG analysis of something like *the boy who left* cannot assign the structure shown in (82):

(82)

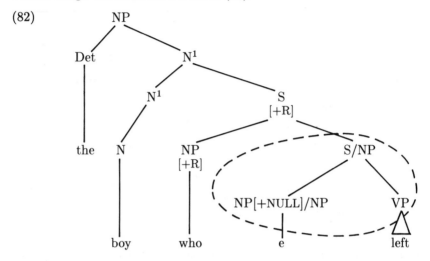

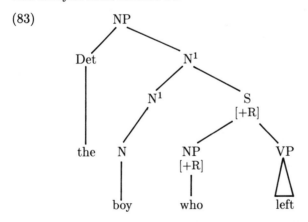

The circled tree in (82) could only be admitted by a rule produced by the application of STM1 to a non-lexical ID-rule (i.e., the rule (17)a above). The analysis must instead be:

(83)

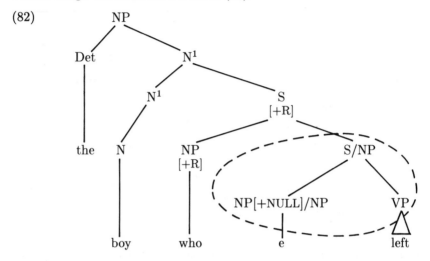

In these cases, there is no displaced phrase, and the relative pronoun appears in the subject position. While this works for simple examples, it does not generalize to cases where the subject really is displaced, as in (69)a above, or in (84):

(84)   the girl who I think has won

Here the verb *think*, which normally takes a sentential complement, appears to have a finite VP as its complement; and this is exactly the structure that GPSG assigns, deriving the required rules via STM2:

(85)   Slash Termination Metarule 2

$$X \rightarrow W, V^2[+\text{SUBJ}, \text{FIN}]$$

$$\Downarrow$$

$$X/NP \rightarrow W, V^2[-\text{SUBJ}]$$

This says that you can take any rule introducing a finite S as one daughter and get back a new rule with a finite VP instead, and with the mother node slashed for NP. Note that this does not introduce NULL, unlike STM1. So from rule (86)a we can get rule (86)b which admits the tree (86)c.

(86) a.   VP → H[40], S[FIN]

     b.   VP/NP → H[40], VP[FIN]

     c.

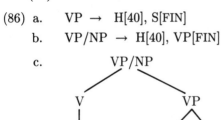

Principles of agreement interact with SLASH to ensure that the lower VP (which is a predicative category lacking a controller) agrees with the displaced NP (which is *who* in (84), which in turn agrees with *girl*). Invoking STM2 again parallels in part the second Government-Binding Theory definition of what counts for proper government, though the details of the analysis are not so similar, for GPSG sticks to the idea that only lexical heads sanction missing structure.

Although STM2 applies to rule (86)a, it will not apply to the following rule, which introduces a complementizer, for the rule is non-lexical.

(87)   S[COMP *that*] → {[SUBCAT *that*]}, S[COMP NIL]

This means that the grammar will never admit subtrees like:

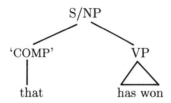

for *that* is not a lexical head ('COMP' here is just an informal way of referring to the {[SUBCAT *that*]} category); in this way, GPSG accounts for the 'COMP-trace' facts shown in (88) (see also Chap. 2, Sec. 8).

(88) a.   Who do you think that Kim saw?

   b.   Who do you think Kim saw?

   c.   *Who do you think that has won?

   d.   Who do you think has won?

Finally, for completeness, I give in (89) the remaining FCRs, though I will not discuss their effects.

(89) a.   FCR 16:   [WH, +SUBJ] ⊃ [COMP NIL]

   b.   FCR 20:   ∼([SLASH]&[WH])

   c.   FCR 21:   [A^1] ⊃ ∼[WH]

   d.   FCR 22:   [VP] ⊃ ∼[WH]

6.2. Coordinate Structures

The traditional wisdom about coordination, which linguists use as a term for both conjunction (with *and* and *but*) and disjunction (with *or*), is that "likes coordinate"; this is generally so—one can coordinate practically any syntactic category with itelf. I will not illustrate the basic facts, but move directly to the more interesting cases whose analysis has influenced the development of GPSG.

The usual analysis for coordinate structures is to posit a rule schema of the form $\alpha \rightarrow \alpha$ *and* α; choosing some value for α (such as NP, A^1, or Det) gives you a particular coordination rule with conjuncts of the same category. Yet such an analysis runs into problems with data like that shown in (90).

(90) a.   Kim is a Republican and proud of it.

b.   Lee is on his way up and looking to take over.

In (a), the coordinated categories are NP and AP, and in (b) we have PP and VP. Clearly this is a problem for the simple analysis, though equally clearly we do not want to give it up completely; for example, all the coordinated phrases in (90) are [BAR 2] categories. In fact, this gives us a clue to the GPSG analysis; the idea is to have what might be considered underspecified categories under certain circumstances. The grammar says that the verb *be* subcategorizes for an X^2 category, and the other principles of the grammar allow this to be compatible with, say, NP and AP. This kind of approach is of course impossible with the coordination schema given above, as the whole point of that is to force categorial identity in all cases.

Consequently, there is a *rule* of coordination, which in its basic form says the following:

(91)   X $\rightarrow$ H, H

This says that the coordination consists of a completely unspecified category as the mother with each daughter being a head; the HFC will force each daughter to match in **HEAD** features with the mother, or almost so (for sometimes the HFC is overriden). Note that this is a rule, and that, other things being equal, could admit a local subtree where each node was just specified as, say, [BAR 1]. In practice, this very rarely happens and much more information must be instantiated to satisfy requirements coming from other parts of the tree.

There are two kinds of coordinate structure in English; one is potentially infinite (*fish, butter, rice, and cake*), and one is binary (*both round and square*). The rules for these are given below; despite what I have said above, they are schemata, for they abstract over the terminal elements (*and* or *or*, etc.). However, with respect to the nature of the syntactic categories that are conjoined, each is a rule.

(92)   Iterating Coordination Schema

   $X \rightarrow H[CONJ \alpha_0], H[CONJ \alpha_1]^+$

   where $\alpha \in \{<and, NIL>, <NIL, and>,$
   $<neither, nor>, <or, NIL>, <NIL, or>\}$

(93)   Binary Coordination Schema

   $X \rightarrow H[CONJ \alpha_0], H[CONJ \alpha_1]$

   where $\alpha \in \{<both, and>, <either, or>, <NIL, but>\}$

For simplicity, let us concentrate on the latter.[23] This allows us to build conjuncts like *both the cat* and *and the mat*; there is good evidence that in English the words like *and* form a constituent with the phrase to their right. If the CONJ value is NIL, there is no conjunction word, as in *came but fell asleep*.

The rules which "spell out" the coordinators are shown in (94).

(94) a. $X[CONJ\ NIL] \rightarrow H$

   b. $X[CONJ\ \alpha] \rightarrow \{[SUBCAT\ \alpha]\}, H$
      where $\alpha \in \{and, both, but, neither, nor, or\}$

Finally, an LP-statement orders the conjuncts according to the value of the CONJ feature.

(95) $[CONJ\ \alpha_0] \prec [CONJ\ \alpha_1]$
      where $\alpha_0 \in \{both, either, neither, NIL\}$
      and $\alpha_1 \in \{and, but, nor, or\}$

---

[23] The '+' notation in (92) indicates a sequence of one or more occurrences of the category.

This now allows subtrees like the following to be admitted:

(96)

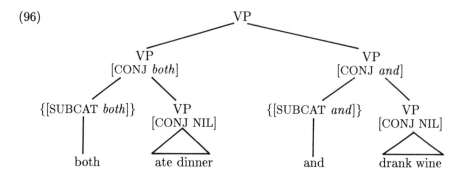

The HFC must also be revised, to allow for the multiple heads that the coordination schemata introduce. Again I present a simplified version of the HFC given in GKPS.

(97)   Head Feature Convention

$$\phi(C_0) \mid \textbf{HEAD} \;=\; \bigcap_{C_i \,\in\, W_H} \phi(C_i) \mid \textbf{HEAD}$$

This says that the **HEAD** features on the mother must be the *intersection* (the big upturned cup) of the **HEAD** features on the head daughters, and it reduces to the HFC as given before (in (43)) in the case where there is just one head. Now let us see how this applies to the cases of coordination of non-identical categories given at the beginning of this section. The verb *be* is introduced by the rule (98).

(98)   VP[+AUX] → H[7], X^2[+PRD]

The verb *be* (which behaves like an auxiliary even in its 'main verb' usage), subcategorizes for any predicative [BAR 2] category. Now the intersection of NP and AP is consistent with this—the intersection is in fact {<N, +>, <BAR, 2>}. Hence the following subtree respects the HFC as stated (ignoring the PRD feature).

(99)

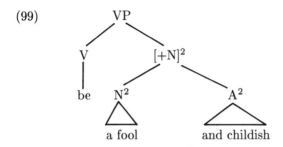

However, in case the mother is more specified, the daughters must be also; we do not get *Kim met a fool and childish as meet subcategorizes for an NP, which would be the mother in the coordinate structure. But the only way for the intersection of each conjunct to be NP is for each conjunct to be at least that highly specified.

Finally we come to the interaction of the analyses of coordination and unbounded dependencies. One general constraint on unbounded dependencies is that, if they go into one conjunct, they must go into all.

(100)a.   the fish that Kim [ate _] [and got sick from _]

b.   the fish that Kim [ate _] [and hopes not to get sick from _]

c.   *the fish that Kim [ate _] [and got sick from chicken]

If there is a missing constituent within one conjunct, there must be one missing somewhere in each; examples (a) and (b) indicate that no further 'parallelism' of structure is necessary. (100)c is bad as this condition, known as the *Coordinate Structure Constraint*, is violated.

These facts follow directly from the analysis of SLASH; being a **FOOT** feature, if it appears on one daughter conjunct, then it must be on the mother too, to satisfy the FFP. Once on the mother, it will now be forced to be on every head, i.e., every conjunct, as SLASH is also a **HEAD** feature. As we have just seen, if the mother is specified for some **HEAD** feature, each conjunct must be.

This account also predicts the data in (101), which do show a kind of 'parallelism' effect.

(101)a.   I know a man who Kim likes _ and Lee hired _ .

b.   I know a man who _ likes Kim and _ adores Lee.

c.   *I know a man who Lee hired _ and _ likes Kim.

d.   I know a man who Kim likes _ and Lee hopes _ will be hired.

The generalization in the data is that parallel non-subject 'gaps' are acceptable, or parallel subject gaps (examples (a) and (b)). However, a mix of the two is not possible. The example (101)d shows that the notions of 'subject' and 'non-subject' are relative to the highest clause in the contruction, for in (d) we have paired object and non-highest-clause subject gaps.

These data are predicted by the analysis of subject displacement as involving a VP constituent, while the non-subject cases involve the category S/NP. Under this analysis, (b) has conjoined VPs, while (a) and (d) have conjoined S/NPs. Let us see why (c) is bad; the relevant part of the structure is shown in (102).

(102)

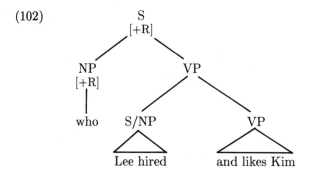

The coordination in (102) violates the FFP as SLASH has been instantiated on the left daughter S but not on the mother; it is impossible to conjoin 'slashed' and 'unslashed' categories for just this reason.

The Coordinate Structure Constraint and the 'parallelism' data are not readily handled within a transformational framework, though it is of course always possible to augment a theory to allow it to cover more data. (In fact, such constraints are somewhat unexpected in a transformational framework, for the idea of movement is to predict a one-to-one correspondence between displaced phrases and missing constituents, but precisely in these cases we have, and must have, a one-to-many correspondence.) Recent analyses of such facts within the Government-Binding Theory framework have indeed introduced additional representations that effectively transmit information through every intervening node between a pre- and post-movement site.

On the other hand, to the extent that there are 'unbounded dependencies' in interpretive phenomena that obey similar constraints to these 'overt' cases, such as with scope of quantifiers and *wh*-phrases, as is claimed by proponents of Government-Binding Theory, there is no way GPSG as presently formulated could account for such correlations. Again, it would be possible to augment the theory by the postulation of **FOOT** features that only have semantic effects to capture such generalizations. However, it has been, and continues to be, a topic of much debate as to just how strong these parallels are.

Where to Look Next

The most complete description of GPSG appears in Gazdar et al. (1985); earlier formulations of the leading ideas can be found in Gazdar (1981), Gazdar (1982), and Gazdar, Pullum, and Sag (1982). The Lexical Head Constraint on metarule application is proposed in Flickinger (1983). Sag et al. (1985) present a much more detailed analysis of coordination than that in Gazdar et al. (1985).

Recently, a related framework known as *Head-driven Phrase Structure Grammar*, or 'HPSG,' has emerged out of the work of Pollard (1984). In this framework, lexical ID-rules as such are eliminated, and subcategorization is stated as a property of lexical heads. This entails that metarules are lexical rules, and arguments for this point of view are given in Pollard (1985). For an overview of this theory, see Sag and Pollard (1986). The analysis of '*wh*-agreement' in Goldberg (1985) is given in terms of this framework. Sag (1986) discusses problems with analysis of linear precedence given in Gazdar et al. (1985), and presents an alternative account in an HPSG formulation.

Chapter 4

Lexical-Functional Grammar

Lexical-Functional Grammar (LFG) was developed initially in the late 1970s by Joan Bresnan and Ron Kaplan; LFG followed *Relational Grammar* in departing from the mainstream of generative grammar by proposing a model of syntax that is not purely structurally-based, or, putting it rather too simply, advocating the view that there is more to syntax than you can express with phrase structure trees.[1] In addition, it differed in being a theory of grammar that was developed with the goal of also serving as the grammatical basis of a computationally precise and psychologically realistic model of human language; many of the theoretical decisions that have been made have been influenced by this aspect of the project (see the introduction to Bresnan (1982)). The most complete description of the formal principles of the theory can be found in Kaplan and Bresnan (1982) (hereafter 'KB').

Lexical-Functional Grammar is the only one of the theories described here that accords the traditional notions of 'subject' and 'object' a distinguished status, in that it alone takes them as primitives (this again is shared with Relational Grammar). The actual theoretical entities are known as *grammatical functions*, and representations which display them are known as *functional structures* (f-structures). The grammatical functions are represented so: SUBJ, OBJ, etc.; and in addition to these the theory recognizes functions that might be less familiar to the reader, like XCOMP, which is an open complement (for example, the participle *laughing* in *She had them laughing in no time*). The name 'function' is chosen not only to indicate the role these objects play in the sentence, such as when we say that *fish* functions as the subject of the predicate *swim* in *Fish swim*,

---

[1] Relational Grammar has been and continues to be a very influential theory of syntax, since its development in the early and mid 1970s; some of the key papers are collected in Perlmutter (1983), and Perlmutter and Rosen (1984).

but is also chosen to indicate the nature of the representation—technically speaking, functional structures are functions, in the mathematical sense, from names to values; so the f-structure for our example will be understood as a function which in this case gives the value *fish* when applied to the name SUBJ. This is analogous (in its mathematical properties) to the Generalized Phrase Structure Grammar idea that categories are functions from features to values, and one can think of SUBJ as the name of a feature (or 'attribute,' as LFG has it).

LFG does not deny that there is a significant aspect of the representation of syntax that is characterized by phrase structure trees, and proposes a level of *constituent structure* (c-structure) that corresponds roughly to the level of PF in Government-Binding Theory and to surface structure in Generalized Phrase Structure Grammar. (Similarly, the level of f-structure corresponds most closely to the level of s-structure in Government-Binding Theory, though the correspondence is weak.)   C-structures have things like NPs and Vs in them, and express properties of word order and phrasal structure, which are taken to be subject to great variation across languages. Most of the invariant grammatical constraints, on things like agreement and anaphora, are functionally-based, i.e., stated on f-structure representations.

The *lexical* part of the name of the theory emphasizes a commitment to characterize processes which alter the 'valence' of predicates in the lexicon (and hence render the c-structure component more 'transparent'); for example, the relation between active and passive constructions is determined solely by a lexical process that relates passive forms of verbs to active forms. In a way, lexical rules do the work of Move-α in Government-Binding Theory and metarules in Generalized Phrase Structure Grammar, but there is no formal correspondence nor parallel empirical coverage in these three mechanisms, so I only mention this in the aid of orienting the reader. Finally, it follows from the fact that there is no transformational component that all lexical items are inserted into c-structures in fully inflected form, as in Generalized Phrase Structure Grammar; similarly the argument for a non-transformational grammar is not that one *can* do it, but that it is an advantage to find other mechanisms to do the work once attributed to transformations.

Figure 4 gives a diagrammatic representation of the organization of the grammar.[2]

---

[2] I indicate the mapping to semantics with a dotted line for the reason that, while a semantic component (e.g., a Montague Grammar-style semantics) is

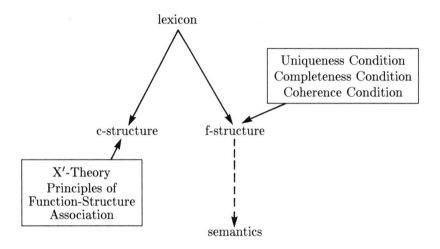

Figure 4.   Lexical-Functional Grammar

While the lexicon and c-structure are the loci of cross-linguistic variation, the level of f-structure is intended to be fairly stable, in the sense that synonymous constructions in different languages might have radically different c-structure representations though very similar f-structures; in general there is no one-to-one correspondence between constituents of a c-structure and constituents of the corresponding f-structure. Indeed, as indicated in Figure 4, while c-structures determine properties of f-structures, there is no direct mapping from c- to f-structures. From a certain point of view, LFG takes the opposite position from Government-Binding Theory as to the nature of the mapping between syntactic levels; while in Government-Binding Theory the idea is that each level differs minimally from the next and is characterized by the same sorts of representations obeying the same sorts of constraints, in LFG the conception is that different levels have different kinds of representations and obey their own constraints. In particular, while the information displayed by an f-structure is *encoded* within the corresponding c-structure, that information is not recoverable solely

---

understood to be part of the LFG system, the semantics do not interact in any strong way with the syntax (unlike, say, in Generalized Phrase Structure Grammar, where the semantics determine certain aspects of syntactic agreement, for example). I will omit any further discussion of the semantics in this chapter.

from the structural relations in the c-structure, in the sense that there is no isomorphic mapping from c-structures to f-structures. For example, it is typical to find that one language will define the subject 'position' to be a privileged structural position, as in English (the NP immediately dominated by S), while another language will mark its subject with particular grammatical case (often Nominative) and allow the subject to appear in any position (for example, in Japanese, it is a rough generalization that subjects are marked with the case-marker *-ga* and that NPs can appear in any order). In the one instance we have structural encoding of the SUBJ function (i.e., the information of subjecthood comes from the particular structural position), and morphological encoding in the other (it is the *ga*-marked NP that is the subject, no matter where it appears in the structure), yet both contribute exactly the same information to an f-structure.

LFG has so far been cautious in proposing universal constraints on cross-linguistic variation, the emphasis having been on characterizing the diversity that we find among languages; presumably from that research patterns of constraints will emerge that will then be incorporated into the theory in an appropriate way. (This is not to claim that LFG has not proposed universal constraints—many will in fact be discussed in this chapter (see, for example, Bresnan's paper "Control and Complementation," in Bresnan (1982) and Levin (1985)); however, the emphasis on making such proposals has not been as great in LFG as it has been, for example, in Government-Binding Theory.)

1. Constituent Structures

Constituent structures (c-structures) are those objects in LFG that characterize phrasal and sentential syntax in the familiar way; however, as c-structures play a restricted role in the theory we can just look briefly at the properties of the structures they describe and then pay more attention to the information they carry about f-structures.

1.1. Phrase Structure

LFG assumes a fairly standard set of phrase structure rules, such as those given in (1) for English (to be revised shortly).

(1) a.   S   →   NP VP
     b.   VP →   V NP

Table 4
X'-Equivalences

X	X'	X''
N	N'	NP
V	V'	VP
A	A'	AP
P	P'	PP
	S	S'

Other languages may have rather less structure than English; for example the Australian language Warlpiri appears to form sentences with little internal constituent structure, and suggests a rule like:

(2)   S   →   X' Aux X'*

Under this rule (proposed in Simpson (1983)), S consists of some constituent, an Auxiliary, and then any number of further consitituents. The point here is that the sequence is generated directly and is not transformed (by an operation known as 'scrambling') from a more configurational structure which might provide information about what is the subject, what is the object, and so on.

Clearly a rule like (2) is not going to be sufficient for Warlpiri; it would allow a sentence to consist of four NPs and an auxiliary verb, yet we can be sure that no sentence of Warlpiri has this form. All of the properties of the lexical items that will be accessed to 'filter out' this overgeneration (such as subcategorization requirements, etc.) are manifested only in the f-structure, and so while our hypothetical string will indeed be given a c-structure of Warlpiri, well-formedness conditions applying at f-structure will rule it out.

Similarly, in English, *Louise sneezed the banana* will have a well-formed c-structure, but will be unacceptable at the level of f-structure, as *the banana* will have no place in the representation, for *sneeze* is intransitive. Section 2.2 covers functional well-formedness in more detail.

Like the other theories, LFG adopts a version of X'-theory, which I summarize in Table 4. (The reader unfamiliar with the ideas of X'-theory should consult Chap. 2, Sec. 1.) This is rather similar to the Government-Binding Theory formulation of the equivalences, except that S and S' are not projections of any lexical category in LFG.

The category S has no head in the X′ sense and is said to be *exocentric*, and this permits it to have a variety of 'functional' heads universally, such as VP, or V in some languages, or even N or A. (It is quite common for languages to express such 'predicative' sentences as *Molly is a doctor* by what is literally 'Molly doctor.')

In respect to the status of S, LFG also differs from Generalized Phrase Structure Grammar, in not taking it to be a projection of V. This latter position is more or less essential in Generalized Phrase Structure Grammar, in order that information pass between the verb and S by the Head Feature Convention; but information flow in LFG is not necessarily determined by such considerations (though it may be, as I describe below), and therefore it is free to leave S exocentric.

1.2. Functional Annotations

As I have mentioned, f-structures are not constructed by directly mapping the c-structure representation into some new phrase-structural representation. Rather, c-structures carry information that is displayed in f-structure, and are annotated with *functional schemata*, which intuitively indicate how the functional information contained on a node in the syntax participates in the f-structure. For example, the S-rule in English is annotated in the following way:

(3)   S   →   NP   VP
                       (↑ SUBJ) =↓   ↑=↓

The up- and down-arrows ("↑" and "↓") refer to the f-structure that corresponds to the c-structure node built by the rule. The "up" refers to the f-structure of the *mother* node and the "down" refers to the f-structure of the node *itself*. The annotations in (3), which are read "up's SUBJ is down" and "up is down" indicate that (a), all the functional information carried by the NP (i.e., the NP's f-structure) goes into the SUBJ part of the mother's f-structure (i.e., the S's f-structure), and (b), all the functional information carried by the VP (the VP's f-structure) is also direct information about the mother's f-structure. Grossly put, the annotations say of the NP that it is the subject, and of the VP that it is the functional head; in a certain sense, "↑=↓" corresponds to the Head Feature Convention in Generalized Phrase Structure Grammar.

Let us see some other rules for English, and then look at a simple example of the relation between a c-structure and an f-structure.

(4)   VP → V   (NP)   (NP)   PP*   (S′)
            (↑ OBJ) =↓ (↑ OBJ2) =↓ (↑ (↓ CASE)) =↓ (↑ COMP) =↓

(5) a.   NP → (Det)   N   (PP)
                          (↑ ADJUNCT) =↓

     b.   PP → P   NP
                          (↑ OBJ) =↓

     c.   S′ → COMP   S
                          ↑=↓

The VP-rule says that the VP can contain a verb, then an NP that is
the OBJ (direct object), then a second object (OBJ2, as in *give the dog a
bone*); these two NPs are optional. Next there can be any number[3] of PPs,
whose function is determined by the annotation '(↑ (↓ CASE)) =↓.' The PP
will be some kind of oblique phrase, as I will explain later. Finally, there
can be an optional S′ constituent, which bears the COMP (complement)
function;[4] this will be for things like *that fruit is cheap* as in *We discovered
that fruit is cheap*.

Note that there is no functional annotation on the V-node; such an
annotation cannot be totally absent, or else the functional information
dominated by that node would never get into the f-structure. Rather, there
is a general convention that all preterminals are associated with '↑=↓,' so
this is not indicated in each rule.

In the NP-rule, then, both the optional Det and the head noun will
be associated with '↑=↓,' so here is another case where the distribution
of '↑=↓' is not parallel to the distribution of X′-heads. The NP may also
contain a PP ADJUNCT; this should probably be Generalized to allow
other cases of adjuncts (or modifiers), such as relative clauses and adjectival
modifiers, as in *the man asleep at the wheel*.

The PP-rule is quite straightforward, and prepositions govern the function OBJ; note there is no confusion between the OBJ of a verb and the OBJ
within a prepositional phrase for in the latter case the OBJ is contained

---

[3] The * notation on the PP node indicates any number of occurrences of that
category from zero up. In some LFG work the attribute CASE in the functional annotation is called PCASE.

[4] The reader should not confuse the function COMP and the c-structure category COMP (for 'complementizer'); the latter appears in rule (5)c. I shall
have no cause to refer to the category COMP in the remainder of this chapter.

within an oblique function corresponding to the whole PP. The rule for S′ is again straightforward (though see Footnote 4).

Functional information (in fact, most of it) is also carried by lexical items, as we see in the simple example entries given in (6). In the tree in (7), the functional annotations appear above the nodes to indicate which objects the up- and down-arrows 'point to.' The value of each PRED ('predicate') within the quotes indicates the semantic content of the item. The notation (↑ PRED) then can be read as "my mother's f-structure has a PRED value which is ...." The mother node will be the preterminal dominating the lexical item in question, and so in this way functional information passes from lexical items onto (f-structures associated with) constituents of the c-structure.

(6) a.   *Louise*   N   (↑ PRED) = 'Louise'

 b.   *Tara*   N   (↑ PRED) = 'Tara'

 c.   *paint*   V   (↑ PRED) = 'paint <(↑ SUBJ)(↑ OBJ)>'

(7)

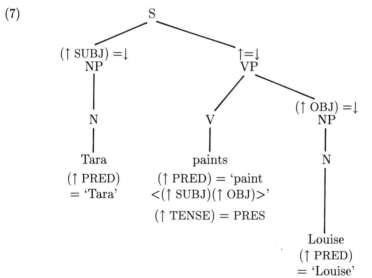

In the entry for the verb, the '<(↑ SUBJ)(↑ OBJ)>' part of the lexical entry indicates that the verb subcategorizes for a SUBJ and an OBJ; this specifies, via the up-arrows, that the mother's f-structure has a SUBJ and an OBJ, though there is no indication as to what the values of those will be (this is what the NPs in a sentence will contribute). The inflection on the verb adds the information that the tense attribute has the value 'present.' The f-structure corresponding to this c-structure is shown in (8).

(8)

$$
\begin{bmatrix}
\text{SUBJ} & [\text{PRED 'Tara'}] \\
\text{OBJ} & [\text{PRED 'Louise'}] \\
\text{TENSE} & \text{PRES} \\
\text{PRED} & \text{'paint} <(\uparrow \text{SUBJ})(\uparrow \text{OBJ})>\text{'}
\end{bmatrix}
$$

Let us work through the way in which this f-structure comes about. The verb carries the information that it has a subject and an object and that the tense is present. In fact, this corresponds to an f-structure, namely:

(9)

$$
\begin{bmatrix}
\text{SUBJ} & [\quad\quad] \\
\text{OBJ} & [\quad\quad] \\
\text{TENSE} & \text{PRES} \\
\text{PRED} & \text{'paint} <(\uparrow \text{SUBJ})(\uparrow \text{OBJ})>\text{'}
\end{bmatrix}
$$

Due to the '$\uparrow=\downarrow$' annotations implicit on the V node and present on VP, this f-structure is also associated with the VP and S nodes.

Within the subject NP, the entry *Tara* carries the information that its mother's f-structure PRED is 'Tara'; hence this is the PRED of the NP. However, the f-structure of the NP is not directly inherited into the f-structure of the S, but rather becomes part of the SUBJ specification within that f-structure. Hence from the subject NP part of the S we get the f-structure shown in (10).

(10)

$$
\begin{bmatrix}
\text{SUBJ} & [\text{PRED 'Tara'}]
\end{bmatrix}
$$

This 'merges' (as I will describe below) with the f-structure information coming from the VP; a similar thing happens with the object NP and we end up with (8).

Clearly there is some relation between the flow of information and the projections of X'-theory; for example, any X'-head will in general be associated with '$\uparrow=\downarrow$,' and any maximal projection that appears in a rule will be associated with '($\uparrow$ G) = $\downarrow$,' where G is a variable over grammatical functions. Hence many of the functional annotations in the rules given above are predictable from more general principles of function-structure association. The nature of these relationships has been the focus of much research in LFG, though the theory allows for cases where there is a divergence, say, between the c-structure (X$'$) head of a structure and the functional head (see e.g., Ishikawa (1985) and Simpson (1983)).

This concludes the basic description of the nature of c-structures; we will return to c-structures at the end of the following section, when we consider in more detail the relation between c- and f-structures.

2. Functional Structures

Functional structures (f-structures) encode information about the various functional relations between parts of sentences, information like what is the subject and what is the predicate. In this section, I will discuss the different kinds of information that we find in f-structures (their 'ontology,' so to speak), the well-formedness conditions that apply to f-structures, and then I will provide more detail about the way c-structures give information about f-structures.

2.1. Properties of F-Structure

Formally, f-structures are just sets of attribute-value (or feature-value) pairs; each thing on the left-hand side of an f-structure is an attribute, and on the right is its corresponding value. Thus the whole functional structure is itself a function, from attributes to values. It is as if we represented the squaring function like this:

(11)
$$
\begin{bmatrix}
1 & 1 \\
2 & 4 \\
3 & 9 \\
\cdots & \cdots
\end{bmatrix}
$$

Attributes may have three kinds of values:

- the value may be an (atomic) *symbol*, as with SG in the specification [NUM SG]

- the value may be a *semantic form*, which is indicated as the value of PRED and enclosed within '...':
  [PRED 'love<($\uparrow$ SUBJ)($\uparrow$ OBJ)>']

- the value may be an *f-structure*, as in

$$
\left[
\begin{array}{ll}
\text{SUBJ} & \left[
\begin{array}{ll}
\text{PRED} & \text{'woman'} \\
\text{DEF} & +
\end{array}
\right]
\end{array}
\right]
$$

Note that in the last example, the values within the inner f-structure are a semantic form and a symbol. Semantic forms provide information necessary for semantic interpretation; for example, presumably 'woman' will be interpreted as denoting the set of women. In addition, semantic forms are *distinct*—no two tokens are the same; we will see the effect of this in Section 2.3.

Certain information that is present in the lexicon or in c-structure does not contribute directly to the construction of an f-structure. While the equations expressed as functional annotations that we have seen so far are *defining* equations, in that they define properties of f-structure, there are also *constraining* equations, which provide well-formedness constraints on f-structures produced by defining equations. We can illustrate this with a simple example. Let us look at the lexical entry for the pronoun *he*.

(12)   *he*   N   ($\uparrow$ PRED) = 'PRO'
                          ($\uparrow$ PERS) = 3
                          ($\uparrow$ NUM) = SG
                          ($\uparrow$ GEN) = MASC
                          ($\uparrow$ CASE) $=_c$ NOM

The first four lines of the lexical entry provide defining equations and describe a simple f-structure. The constraining equation, indicated by the presence of the '$=_c$,' does not provide information directly, but constrains (i.e., checks the appropriateness of) information coming from elsewhere. In the case of (12), unless information that the subject's case is nominative comes from some other part of the c-structure, the f-structure will not be well-formed with respect to this constraining equation; the constraining equation will be violated either if the feature is not specified at all, or if it is specified differently from what the pronoun requires. If we assume that accusative is the unmarked (i.e., general) specification of case in English, then most NP-positions in c-structure will not be specified for case; the constraining equation will correctly prevent *he* from appearing in any of these positions. However, if the case requirement on *he* were a defining equation, then the case attribute would simply be specified in the f-structure to have the value NOM, incorrectly allowing the pronoun to appear. By the constraining equation, *he* will only be allowed (i.e., contribute information about a well-formed f-structure) in just those environments where the case attribute is specified as taking the nominative value.

2.2. Well-Formedness Conditions on F-Structures

There are three main well-formedness conditions imposed on f-structures that 'filter out' most of the overgeneration in c-structure noted above. These are known as the conditions of *Functional Uniqueness* (or *Consistency*), *Completeness*, and *Coherence*. The uniqueness condition ensures that each f-structure is indeed a function, in that each attribute has a unique value (in a given f-structure). Completeness ensures that subcategorization requirements are met, and coherence ensures that every argument is the argument of some predicate; roughly put, completeness ensures that there are not too few arguments for a predicate, and coherence ensures that there are not too many.

I state these conditions in (13)–(15); the last two involve the notion of *governable grammatical function*. For any given language, some function G is a member of the set of governable grammatical functions just in case there is at least one semantic form that subcategorizes for it; that is, G appears within the PRED value of some lexical form. Typically, the governable grammatical functions are SUBJ, OBJ, OBL_{GO}, etc. (OBL_{GO} is the function 'oblique goal,' as in *send flowers to Maria*); things like ADJUNCT are not governable. Hence this is a way of isolating what functions in a given language are associated with arguments.

(13)   Functional Uniqueness
          In a given f-structure, a particular attribute may have at most one value.

(14)   Completeness
An f-structure is *locally complete* if and only if it contains all the governable grammatical functions that its predicate governs. An f-structure is *complete* if and only if it and all its subsidiary f-structures are locally complete.

(15)   Coherence
An f-structure is *locally coherent* if and only if all the governable grammatical functions that it contains are governed by a local predicate. An f-structure is *coherent* if and only if it and all its subsidiary f-structures are locally coherent.

Completeness and coherence are counterparts in a way of the θ-Criterion in Government-Binding Theory. For example, *The girl donated* is incomplete as the verb *donate* governs three functions, SUBJ, OBJ, and OBL$_{GO}$. On the other hand, *The girl donated the school the book* is both incomplete and incoherent; *donate* is missing its OBL$_{GO}$ again, and there is an ungoverned OBJ2 (*the school*), which leads to incoherence. A verb like *give*, which (optionally) governs SUBJ, OBJ, and OBJ2, would then be acceptable if substituted for *donate*.

In contrast to arguments, adjuncts can freely appear (and just as freely fail to do so), and so these are exempt from the conditions outlined here.

2.3. From C-Structures To F-Structures

In this subsection I will provide more of the details of the relation between c- and f-structures. As I have indicated, while f-structures do have certain structural relations of their own, they do not in general stand in any isomorphic structural mapping relation to c-structures. Rather, each piece of c-structure has its own corresponding piece of f-structure, either in virtue of being in a privileged syntactic position (as in the case of English ($\uparrow$ SUBJ) $=\downarrow$), or in virtue of dominating some lexical content. The main business of the algorithm relating c- and f-structures is to put the different pieces together correctly.

The functional annotations on c-structure, which look like equations, are turned into a set of simultaneous equations by a process known as 'instantiation of metavariables'; the metavariables are the up- and down-arrows. Each piece of the c-structure is assigned a number which is a label for the corresponding piece of f-structure, and then these numbers are substituted for the metavariables.

Let us take as an example *She flew to the moon*, and let us assume that *to the Moon* is an (optional) argument of *fly*, rather than a modifier. After instantiation, the top of the example (16) will be as shown in (17).

(16)

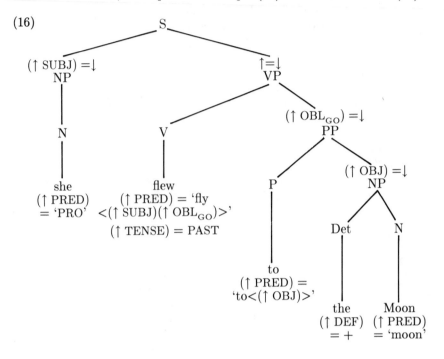

(17)

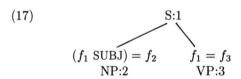

The f-structure corresponding to S is f_1, with component f-structures f_2 and f_3. The f-structure f_1 is formally the minimal object that is the solution of all these simultaneous equations; the set of such equations is known as an *f-description*. At this point, it is necessary to make clear the relation between f-descriptions and f-structures (see also KB, 189ff). F-structures are understood as independently existing objects, objects of which f-descriptions may be true. Hence the annotation '↑=↓' indicates that the f-description of the mother node is satisfied by the same object as the f-description of its own node. In all the functional equations, the '=' means 'is identical to' in the sense that both sides of the equation pick out the same object, i.e., some piece of f-structure. While identity in this sense is stated on objects (i.e., models), the implementation of the LFG system manipulates symbolic expressions, using *unification*. The notion of unification was mentioned in connection with the Foot Feature Principle in Chapter 3; it can be thought of as set union for most purposes, and essentially it makes things identical by 'merging' them together.[5] Unification differs from set union in that it fails if some attribute would be specified for conflicting values. Some illustrative examples are given in (18).

(18) a.   [NUM SG] unifies with [PERS 3] to give

$$\begin{bmatrix} \text{NUM} & \text{SG} \\ \text{PERS} & 3 \end{bmatrix}.$$

     b.   [NUM SG] unifies with [NUM SG] to give [NUM SG].

     c.   [NUM SG] fails to unify with [NUM PL].

The f-structures f_2 and f_3 (from (16) via the instantiation in (17)) are shown below:

(19) f_2 $\begin{bmatrix} \text{PERS} & 3 \\ \text{NUM} & \text{SG} \\ \text{GEN} & \text{FEM} \\ \text{CASE} & \text{NOM} \\ \text{PRED} & \text{'PRO'} \end{bmatrix}$

---

[5] The linguistic relevance of unification was first brought out in work by Martin Kay.

(20)

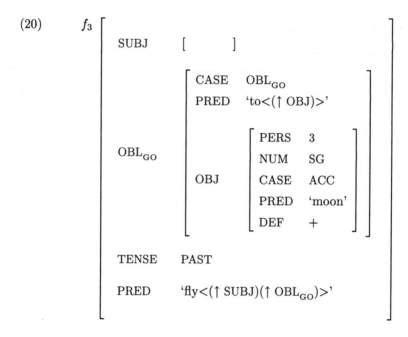

f_3 :

$$\begin{bmatrix} \text{SUBJ} & [\quad] \\[2ex] \text{OBL}_{\text{GO}} & \begin{bmatrix} \text{CASE} & \text{OBL}_{\text{GO}} \\ \text{PRED} & \text{'to}<(\uparrow \text{OBJ})>' \\[2ex] \text{OBJ} & \begin{bmatrix} \text{PERS} & 3 \\ \text{NUM} & \text{SG} \\ \text{CASE} & \text{ACC} \\ \text{PRED} & \text{'moon'} \\ \text{DEF} & + \end{bmatrix} \end{bmatrix} \\[2ex] \text{TENSE} & \text{PAST} \\[2ex] \text{PRED} & \text{'fly}<(\uparrow \text{SUBJ})(\uparrow \text{OBL}_{\text{GO}})>' \end{bmatrix}$$

The structure f_3 is inherited directly as f_1, while f_2 is unified as the value of the SUBJ attribute.

Let us now look at the f-structure of the phrase *to the moon*. This involves the PP-rule given in (5) above.

The CASE notation distinguishes different kinds of oblique phrase, and the names indicate thematic roles[6] (so *put* requires an OBJ and an OBL$_{\text{LOC}}$ (location), while *give* requires OBJ and OBL$_{\text{GO}}$ (goal)). The annotation CASE makes sure that the head of the PP matches the specification on the whole phrase; for example, it ensures that a PP whose f-structure is the value of the OBL$_{\text{GO}}$ function will be headed by the preposition in English that regularly marks 'goal,' namely *to*. I will not go into the details of how the CASE equation is actually solved, but simply refer the interested reader to KB, 198ff.

---

[6] In earlier work in LFG, oblique phrases were distiguished by the morphological form of the preposition, such as TO OBJ or BY OBJ; more recently it has become standard to refer to the thematic role associated with the preposition instead.

The information within the value of OBJ in (20) comes from *the moon*, and is unified in as the object of the preposition. The f-structure corresponding to the NP is formed by unifying the f-structures of the determiner and the noun, as specified by the rule (5)a.

Sometimes, a preposition plays a purely grammatical rather than semantic role. In many languages 'grammatical' prepositions are realized as case-markers; for example, German *ihm* as in *Ich habe ihm ein Buch gegeben* 'I have given a book to him.' The difference in the two types of preposition interacts with the system of anaphoric binding, as discussed in Section 4.3. These two functions that prepositions have can be reflected in the lexical entries of prepositions, and in the entries of predicates that subcategorize for such prepositions. For example, *give* will have (as one possibility) the subcategorization shown in (21)a, and the preposition *to* will have the entry shown in (21)b.

(21) a. *give*   V $(\uparrow \text{PRED}) = \text{'give}<(\uparrow \text{SUBJ})(\uparrow \text{OBJ})$
$(\uparrow \text{OBL}_{GO} \text{ OBJ})>'$

  b. *to*   P $((\uparrow \text{PRED}) = \text{'to}<(\uparrow \text{OBJ})>')$
$(\uparrow \text{CASE}) = \text{OBL}_{GO}$

The entry in (21)a shows *give* subcategorizing directly for the object within the OBL_{GO} argument; in this case the preposition has only a grammatical function. The preposition *to* in (21)b is ambiguous, in that it can have an object, or it can allow its c-structure complement to contribute information about the f-structure directly, in which case the preposition becomes a grammatical marker of some kind, with no PRED attribute. It is the former case that we have in example (16).[7] I leave this now and turn to other features of the information that may come from c-structure (or the lexicon, via lexical insertion).

Note that as semantic forms are distinct, it is not possible to unify them. Even something like [PRED 'PRO'] will not unify with [PRED 'PRO']. This general property, that PREDs can never unify, leads to a very simple account of facts such as the following, from Moroccan Arabic, and Spanish.

In Moroccan Arabic, as in many languages, the object argument of a verb may be realized as an NP, or as a clitic on the verb, but not both.

---

[7] Note that in (16) *to* can be replaced by other prepositions expressing similar semantic relations, such as *towards* or *over*. This is not possible with the OBL_{GO} argument of *give*.

(22) a. šra-t   lbent   lxʷebz
          bought-3sgf the-girl the-bread
          'The girl bought the bread.'

   b. šra-t-u   lbent
          bought-3sgf-3sgm the-girl
          'The girl bought it.'

   c. *šra-t-u   lbent   lxʷebz
          bought-3sgf-3sgm the-girl the-bread
          'The girl bought the bread.'

If we assume that the clitic -*u* introduces a [PRED 'PRO'], to indicate the pronominal object in (22)b, then we can explain (22)c by a failure of unification of the two PRED values, 'bread' and 'PRO.' (Hence, the f-structure will be incoherent, for there will be a PRED 'left over.')

In other languages, the appearance of the clitic does not preclude the appearance of an NP object, as in (certain dialects of) Spanish:

(23) a. Juan lo   vio
          Juan him saw
          'Juan saw him.'

   b. Juan lo   vio a Pedro
          Juan him saw Pedro
          'Juan saw Pedro.'

(We can ignore the *a* in (23)b for our purposes here.) In the Spanish cases, the clitic *can* cooccur with the object NP, which could be handled by making the [PRED 'PRO'] specification optional on the clitic. With this specification optionally absent, (23)a lacks an object PRED, and is incomplete, but (23)b is fine; with this specification present on the clitic, (23)a is good, but in (23)b the failure of unification means that there are two PREDs, violating functional coherence. Hence (23)b is only grammatical if the option is taken of omitting the PRED from the clitic's specification, and conversely for (23)a.[8]

---

[8] On the use of pronominal forms as agreement markers (forms without a PRED), see also Bresnan and Mchombo (1986).

As a final example of how information from different structural sources is represented universally in f-structure, we can consider three different types of language, as illustrated in the c-structures below.

(24) a.

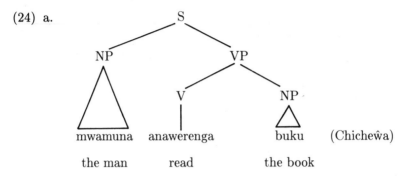

mwamuna   anawerenga   buku   (Chicheŵa)

the man   read   the book

b.

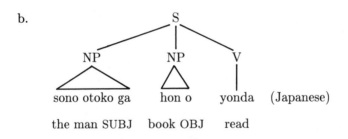

sono otoko ga   hon o   yonda   (Japanese)

the man SUBJ   book OBJ   read

c.

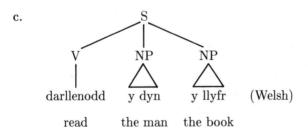

darllenodd   y dyn   y llyfr   (Welsh)

read   the man   the book

In Chicheŵa, the SUBJ function is encoded structurally; the subject is that NP that is sister to the VP, and Chicheŵa differs from English in that the subject may precede *or* follow the VP—hence *anawerenga buku mwamuna* is acceptable also.

In Japanese, the SUBJ function is encoded morphologically by the *ga* case-marker, and so long as the verb remains final, any order of NPs is in principle possible. In our simple example, *hon o sono otoko ga yonda* is also acceptable.

In Welsh, the SUBJ function is encoded positionally, in that the subject must immediately follow the verb, which must be initial in the clause.

However, all of these types of c-structure encoding lead to the same f-structure, namely that in (25).

(25)

$$
\begin{bmatrix}
\text{SUBJ} & \begin{bmatrix} \text{PRED} & \text{`man'} \\ \text{DEF} & + \end{bmatrix} \\[3em]
\text{OBJ} & \begin{bmatrix} \text{PRED} & \text{`book'} \\ \text{DEF} & + \end{bmatrix} \\[2em]
\text{TENSE} & \text{PAST} \\[1em]
\text{PRED} & \text{`read} <(\uparrow \text{SUBJ})(\uparrow \text{OBJ})>\text{'}
\end{bmatrix}
$$

3. The Lexicon

As I have mentioned, the lexicon is the focus of much attention in LFG, and much of the work done by transformations in transformational grammar is done by lexical rules in LFG; for example, the rule of passive is a lexical rule which essentially adds the passive morpheme to a verb and changes its subcategorization, so that the new form is subcategorizing for a SUBJ and an optional OBL_{AG} (Oblique Agent). Note that subcategorization is for grammatical function in LFG, not grammatical category, as in the other theories that I describe here; this will be one of the topics of this section, along with a consideration of the range of subcategorizable grammatical functions, and a discussion of lexical rules.

3.1. Types of Grammatical Function

The grammatical functions fall into different classes in LFG, and this classification interacts with various other parts of the grammar, such as subcategorization, and control (which we will see later). The major distinctions are shown in (26).

(26)

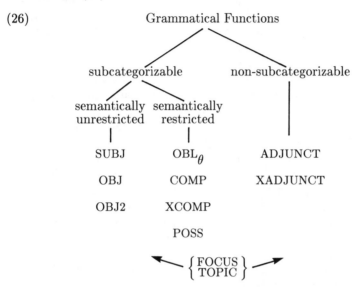

The distinction between the subcategorizable and the non-subcategorizable functions should be quite straightforward; one of the criteria for determining if something is an argument (and hence not an adjunct) is whether it is subcategorized for by some predicate. Recall that COMP is the function assigned to complement clauses; XCOMP is assigned to such complements as infinitival VPs (such as the complement to *try* in *try to kiss Louise*)—see Section 4.1 for more details. The difference between ADJUNCT and XADJUNCT is similarly that the latter has a 'missing' subject, that needs to find an antecedent from elsewhere. The difference is shown in the examples in (27), in which the 'controller' of the XADJUNCT in example (b) is *George*. On the other hand in (a) the ADJUNCT is self-contained.

(27) a.   With George guarding the den, the other boys set off.

b.   Guarding the den, George was scared.

The functions XADJUNCT (open adjunct) and XCOMP (open complement) are known as *open* functions; the rest are *closed*.

The difference between *semantically unrestricted* and *semantically restricted* functions relates to that part of lexical entries that pairs a grammatical predicate with its semantic *predicate-argument* structure. For example, the predicate-argument structure of a verb like *find* will say that *find* denotes a two-place relation between individuals, and that these two individuals will be linked to the thematic roles of Agent and Theme respectively.[9] The unrestricted functions may be linked to any of these argument-types; as an illustration, while subjects are often Agents, they may also be Themes (in a passive construction), or Goals, as in *Max received the prize*, and so on. The unrestricted functions may also realize completely 'non-thematic' arguments, as with the subject of *seem* in *Our goose seems to be cooked*, on the idiomatic interpretation, or with the 'expletive' subjects *it* and *there* as in *It seems that there will be a party*.

The semantically restricted functions are more intimately tied to the semantics, in a sense; for example, the OBL_{GO} function can only be paired with a Goal argument in the predicate-argument structure. The POSS function occurs with the prenominal genitive inside of NP, and is restricted in various ways;[10] for example, we have *the professor's knowledge* but not *chemistry's knowledge* (cf., *knowledge of chemistry*) which suggests that some kind of agency or perhaps sentient feeling is associated with this function (in English, at least). The nature of the semantic restriction on POSS varies with the kind of head noun involved, but the POSS must always be linked to a thematic argument (unlike SUBJ and OBJ). Hence we do not find expletive NPs realizing the POSS function; *it's being obvious that Louise is drunk* and *there's being a party soon* are impossible.

The functions FOCUS and TOPIC are subject to cross-linguistic variation, in that they may be subcategorized for in some languages and not in others; I will not discuss this matter further here.

3.2. Subcategorization

Every form that has a PRED value in its lexical entry is known as a *semantic form*; those that subcategorize for one or more functions are known as

---

[9] For more discussion of these 'thematic roles,' see Chapter 2, Section 3.

[10] These arguments that POSS is a semantically restricted function are due to Rappaport (1983).

lexical forms. For example, if we look at a verb like *seem*, it has the following lexical entry.

(28)   *seem*   V   (↑ PRED) = 'seem<(↑ XCOMP)>(↑ SUBJ)'
                            (↑ SUBJ) = (↑ XCOMP SUBJ)

This entry indicates that *seem* subcategorizes for an XCOMP, which is a (thematic) argument of the predicate (argument-hood is indicated by what is contained within the angle-brackets); thus *seem* also subcategorizes for a non-thematic SUBJ. The equation below the PRED line indicates that the subject of the XCOMP is equal to the subject of *seem*, as I will discuss in detail in the section on Functional Control.

The idea of subcategorizing for functions rather than categories is to allow for a certain category-independence in grammatical processes. For example, it is arguable[11] that in (29), the subject is a PP.

(29)   In this cave dwells a large, ferocious beast.

Given this, then such a PP is expected to undergo subject-to-subject raising (see Chap. 2, Sec. 7) if the rule really makes reference to the *function* of subject, and this appears to be so:

(30)   In this cave seems to dwell a large, ferocious beast.

Thus the LFG analysis is that while the SUBJ function is often realized in English by NP, other maximal projections may be subjects too. This is reflected in the revised S-rule (31).

(31)   S   →   XP   VP
                         (↑ SUBJ) =↓   ↑=↓

Grimshaw (1982) presents other arguments for the functional basis of subcategorization. Other cases of non-NP-subjects were discussed in Chapter 3 (Sec. 3.1); Generalized Phrase Structure Grammar posits an XP position in the syntax too. The facts above are potentially problematic for the Government-Binding Theory account of 'raising' which relies on the Case Filter to force an NP to move to the subject position of *seem* (if it is tensed), for non-NPs should not show the same behavior as they are not subject to the Case Filter.

All lexical forms have a *Predicate-Argument Structure*, each argument of which is linked to a grammatical function. The verb *seem* for example, will have a single argument, that of Proposition, and this will be realized by the XCOMP. The functions outside of the angle-brackets are not linked

---

[11] See e.g., Levin (1985).

to any argument and hence are non-thematic. The *Principle of Function-Argument Biuniqueness* requires that all arguments are paired one-to-one with all (thematic) grammatical functions within any given lexical form.[12] The one allowed exception to this is the case of the null function ∅, which is the function assigned to the Theme argument of a verb like *drink* in *Lou drinks*. The relevant part of the entry for *drink* is shown in (32).

(32)   (↑ PRED) = 'drink< (↑ SUBJ)   ∅   >'
                                    | |
                                  Agent   Theme

This form will be related by a lexical rule to the regular form of *drink*, which pairs the Theme argument with the OBJ function.

Function-argument biuniqueness ensures that each argument is only realized once for each predicate, and hence an example like (33)a will be impossible, for it has two OBL$_{AG}$ arguments. However, we see from example (33)b that this is not a constraint on *by*-phrases *per se*, and indeed so long as the phrases are modifiers, more than one of the same thematic type (Location in (33)c) may appear:

(33) a.   *She was admired by him by the President.

     b.   She was admired by him by the pier/by the hour.

     c.   She was admired by him by the banks of the Ohio by the jetty.

We will return to the topic of the mapping between functions and arguments after the next subsection.

3.3. Some Sample Lexical Entries

To illustrate a few additional points, I present a collection of sample lexical entries that have interesting features.

---

[12] I will not give its definition here; the interested reader may consult Bresnan's paper "The Passive in Lexical Theory," in Bresnan (1982, 163ff), for more details. This principle is rather similar to the θ-Criterion of Government-Binding Theory, in the way it relates semantic arguments and their syntactic realizations.

(34) a.   *a*   Det $(\uparrow$ DEF$) = -$

   b.   *girl*   N $(\uparrow$ PRED$) = $ 'girl'
                          $(\uparrow$ PERS$) = 3$
                          $(\uparrow$ NUM$) = $ SG

   c.   *me*   N $(\uparrow$ PRED$) = $ 'PRO'
                          $(\uparrow$ PERS$) = 1$
                          $(\uparrow$ NUM$) = $ SG
                          $(\uparrow$ CASE$) =_c$ ACC

The example of *a* is quite straightforward; it contributes the information that the containing f-structure is not definite.[13] The noun *girl* is unexceptional too—besides its PRED, it contributes the information that it is 3rd person singular (as opposed to *girls*, which is plural). In example (c) we see the use of a constraining equation, to ensure that *me* only shows up in accusative environments (as opposed to nominative *I*). The equation must constrain and not define, to prevent *me* from accidentally appearing in a position that has no case attribute at all, but would have non-accusative case if it were specified (cf., the discussion of *he* in Sec. 2.1).

Consider next the verb *ask*, which has the entry in (35)a.

(35) a.   *ask*   V $(\uparrow$ PRED$) = $ 'ask$<(\uparrow$ SUBJ$)(\uparrow$ OBJ$)(\uparrow$ COMP$)>$'
                            $\neg[(\uparrow$ SUBJ NUM$) = $ SG $\wedge$ $(\uparrow$ SUBJ PERS$) = 3]$
                            $(\uparrow$ COMP Q$) =_c +$
                            $(\uparrow$ TENSE$) = $ PRES

   b.   *whether* COMP $(\uparrow$ Q$) = +$

The inflectional information in this entry is that the verb is present tense, and cannot have a subject which is both 3rd person and singular.[14] The verb subcategorizes for a subject, object, and complement clause that must be interrogative (the Q attribute), in virtue of the constraining equation. Such an attribute is supplied by *wh*-words and -phrases, including *whether*; this ensures that we get *Betsy asked John whether supper was ready* and not **Betsy asked John that supper was ready*. Again, having a defining rather than constraining equation in (35)a would incorrectly de-

---

[13] The attribute I have labelled DEF is called SPEC (for 'specifier') in KB.

[14] The disjunction in (35)a is clearly missing the generalization that the specification of person and number features is the complement (opposite) of the form *asks*; this matter is taken up in Andrews (1984).

fine lots of complement clauses, which were otherwise unspecified, to have [Q +] in their f-structure.

The lexicon will contain various affixes, which also carry functional information. For example, although I have been presenting fully inflected verb forms, in general these will be derived by regular processes of word-formation which combine base forms and affixes. The verbal affix -*s* will have the following entry:

(36)   -*s*   Af   ($\uparrow$ SUBJ PERS) = SG
                                  ($\uparrow$ SUBJ NUM) = 3
                                  ($\uparrow$ TENSE) = PRES

Such a form, then, regularly contributes the information that the subject of the verb to which it attaches must be 3rd singular, and that the verb carries the information that the clause is present tense.

As another instance of an affix, consider the Spanish 3rd singular present tense affix -*a* (for the appropriate class of verbs). This form may cooccur with (and agree with) an overt subject, or may carry the features of a pronominal subject; so we have *Pedro canta* ('Pedro sings') as well as *canta* ('He/she sings'). Hence the lexical entry for this form might look something like (37).

(37)   -*a*   Af   ($\uparrow$ SUBJ PERS) = SG
                                  ($\uparrow$ SUBJ NUM) = 3

                                  (($\uparrow$ SUBJ PRED) = 'PRO')

                                  ($\uparrow$ TENSE) = PRES

This entry says that the affix contributes the information that there is a 3rd singular subject, within an optional pronominal predicate (this is parallel to the case of the Spanish object clitic, discussed in Sec. 2.3).

3.4. Lexical Rules

A lexical rule takes a lexical item as input and gives back a new lexical item; typically a lexical rule is defined over a whole class of items, for example all transitive verbs, or all adjectives with no more than two syllables. Every theory has lexical rules, but uses them to different degrees. For example, in Generalized Phrase Structure Grammar, the lexical part of passive is the operation that converts a base form of the verb into its participial form; the subcategorization of the verb is changed by the Passive Metarule. In Government-Binding Theory, the lexical passive operation again makes the verb participial, takes away the verb's ability to assign Case, and takes away the external (Agent) θ-role. In LFG, the lexical rule of passive directly changes the subcategorization, while performing the conversion to the participial form also.

Ignoring the morphological change, the rule of passive[15] is the following:

(38)   Passive
         $(SUBJ) \longrightarrow \emptyset/(OBL_{AG})$

         $(OBJ) \longrightarrow (SUBJ)$

This takes the argument associated with the object of the active form and makes it the subject, and either assigns the argument paired with the old subject to the null function or to an Oblique Agent phrase (e.g., *eaten by piranhas*). In this latter case, the input and output entries will be as in (39).

(39) a. $(\uparrow PRED) = $ 'eat$< (\uparrow SUBJ) (\uparrow OBJ) >$'
                                        | |
                                     Agent   Theme

     b. $(\uparrow PRED) = $ 'eat$< (\uparrow OBL_{AG}) (\uparrow SUBJ) >$'
                                        | |
                                     Agent   Theme

Evidence for Passive as a lexical rule comes from the interaction of the passive form with other lexical rules. For example, it seems to be the case that in general any verb with a Theme subject in English can function in its participial form as an adjective; this means that there is a rule that makes new adjectives out of verbs. There are some intransitives that do this, as in *fallen leaf* and *lapsed Catholic*; many passives do too, as in *spared prisoners* and *eaten food*. The fact that the subject must be Theme is seen in the contrast between *a much-given present* and **much-given children*, for *give*

---

[15] This is the formulation given in Bresnan's paper "The Passive in Lexical Theory," in Bresnan (1982). Levin (1985) discusses certain redundant aspects (i.e., aspects predictable on general grounds) of this lexical rule, among others.

has two passives, as it has two subcategorizations. The relation between the two active forms of *give* is shown in (40), and active-passive pairs are given in (41).

(40) $(\uparrow$ PRED$)$ = 'give< $(\uparrow$ SUBJ$)$ $(\uparrow$ OBJ$)$ $(\uparrow$ OBL$_{GO}$$)$ >'

Agent   Theme   Goal

$(\uparrow$ PRED$)$ = 'give< $(\uparrow$ SUBJ$)$ $(\uparrow$ OBJ2$)$ $(\uparrow$ OBJ$)$ >'

(41) a.   Louise gave a present to the children.

   b.   A present was given to the children.

   c.   Louise gave the children a present.

   d.   The children were given a present.

In example (d) the subject is Goal, as the OBJ in the lower entry in (40) is linked to Goal. This shows that the subject of the verbal form must be Theme for it to undergo conversion to an adjective; for while the Goal argument passivizes, as in (d), this verbal form does not undergo conversion (*much-given children*).

The logic of the argument, that Passive must be lexical, should perhaps be made clear. It goes like this: passive forms undergo a rule which only applies to forms with Theme subjects. This shows that the changes induced by passive in subcategorization must be induced in the lexicon, i.e., as a lexical process, in order for such passive forms to be input to the rule. In particular the *give* facts do not admit of a potential counterexplanation— which would be that the adjective conversion rule applies to forms only with a Theme *argument* (this is what Government-Binding Theory passives look like, for the argument that passivizes is the d-structure object, assigned the Theme role)—for (41)d has Theme argument but fails the conversion. Hence, if the generalization is that forms with Theme *subjects* undergo the rule of conversion, and this rule is a lexical rule (which is fairly uncontroversial), then it must be that passive forms have Theme *subjects* as a lexical property. This in turn means that Passive must be a lexical operation.

As a more complex instance of a lexical rule, let us consider the process of causativization in Japanese. The effect of this rule is to add a 'causee' argument to a verb which is morphologically modified by the addition of the -*(s)ase* suffix. This is seen in the examples in (42).

(42) a. Mary ga   aruita.
         Mary SUBJ walk-past
         'Mary walked.'

   b.   John ga   Mary o   aruk-ase-ta.
         John SUBJ Mary OBJ walk-cause-past
         'John made Mary walk.'

(We will not concern ourselves with the particular phonological changes induced in the verb by the past tense suffix and the causative suffix; we will also ignore the rule for causativizing transitive verbs, which is somewhat more complex.) We see from (42) that applying the rule of causative to an intransitive verb makes the argument associated with the SUBJ in (a) appear as the object in (b), and the new 'causee' argument is the SUBJ.

The rule for causativizing an intransitive is given in (43), ignoring the morphological changes induced.

(43)   Causative
        (PRED) $\longrightarrow$ (XCOMP PRED)

   Add: ($\uparrow$ PRED) = 'cause<($\uparrow$ SUBJ)($\uparrow$ OBJ)($\uparrow$ XCOMP)>'

        ($\uparrow$ OBJ) = ($\uparrow$ XCOMP SUBJ)

The effect of causativization is essentially to add one argument, corresponding to the Agent of the causative action. This will be the subject of the new form, and with an intransitive verb the old subject is related to the new object. The lexical rule introduces a new PRED, *cause*, and creates an internal nucleus by making the old PRED the PRED of an XCOMP . The subject of this XCOMP is controlled by the object of the *cause* predicate.[16] The reasons for having this particular analysis are too complex for me to give details here; however the effect is to allow for a simple c-structure as shown in (44) corresponding to a structurally more complex (biclausal) f-structure as shown in (45).

---

[16] This is functional control; see Section 4.1. Roughly, the controlling material is in two places in the f-structure simultaneously.

(44)

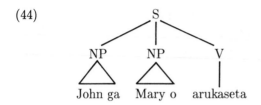

(45)

$$
\begin{bmatrix}
\text{SUBJ} & \begin{bmatrix} \text{PRED} & \text{'John'} \end{bmatrix} \\[2ex]
\text{OBJ} & \begin{bmatrix} \text{PRED} & \text{'Mary'} \end{bmatrix} \\[2ex]
\text{XCOMP} & \begin{bmatrix} \text{SUBJ} & [\quad] \\ \text{PRED} & \text{'walk<(↑ SUBJ)>'} \end{bmatrix} \\[2ex]
\text{PRED} & \text{'cause<(↑ SUBJ)(↑ XCOMP)(↑ XCOMP)>'}
\end{bmatrix}
$$

In (45), *Mary* is both the object in the outer f-structure and subject in the inner one, and there is evidence (from various grammatical processes that pick out subjects and/or objects) that it indeed has the properties of both these functions (the traditional transformational analysis assigns a biclausal structure). On the other hand, there is also evidence with respect to the order of NPs in the causative construction for the simple c-structure (44); the complex f-structure is determined by information from the lexicon, and is not represented directly in the c-structure. As LFG does not directly map between c- and f-structure, it is possible for these two different structures to be assigned to the sentence in question.

4. Control and Binding

The theory of Control (where the Control relation provides the antecedent for a 'missing subject') falls into two parts in LFG, functional control and anaphoric control. Anaphoric control is itself part of a larger theory of anaphoric binding, which includes the binding of overt pronouns and reflexive pronouns. In this section I will discuss each of these topics in some detail.

4.1. Functional Control

Functional Control is the relation that holds between some antecedent and the 'missing subject' in an XCOMP or XADJUNCT. Either of these functions is realized syntactically as any maximal projection of a lexical head in English. Let us concentrate on XCOMP first.

A typical case of XCOMP is the controlled infinitival complement of verbs like *seem* and *try*, as in *Maria seems/tried to work hard*. The control relation between the subject of the verb and the XCOMP's subject is that of functional control in LFG; the relevant parts of the lexical entries are given in (46) and (47).

(46)   *seem*   V   ($\uparrow$ PRED) = 'seem<($\uparrow$ XCOMP)>($\uparrow$ SUBJ)'
           ($\uparrow$ XCOMP SUBJ) = ($\uparrow$ SUBJ)

(47)   *try*   V   ($\uparrow$ PRED) = 'try<($\uparrow$ XCOMP)($\uparrow$ SUBJ)>'
           ($\uparrow$ XCOMP SUBJ) = ($\uparrow$ SUBJ)

Note that functional control covers what in Government-Binding Theory is binding of NP-trace in the former case and obligatory control of PRO in the latter case. In Government-Binding Theory the difference in thematic structure determines which empty category will appear; then the difference in empty categories is used to account for the differences in interpretation between *seem* and *try*. (For example, *try* but not *seem* entails the existence of its subject, so that *A unicorn seems to be approaching* can be true even if there are no unicorns. This is reflected in the non-thematic subject of *seem*.) The only difference in LFG in the subcategorization is that the subject of *try* is thematic (linked to Agent). The semantic interpretation assigned to f-structures is sensitive to this difference in subcategorization, and predicts the correct entailments (see Halvorsen (1983)).

The f-structure of *Louise tries to sleep* is shown in (48).

(48)

$$
\left[
\begin{array}{ll}
\text{SUBJ} & \left[\begin{array}{ll} \text{PRED} & \text{`Louise'} \end{array}\right] \\[4ex]
\text{XCOMP} & \left[\begin{array}{ll} \text{SUBJ} & [\quad\quad] \\ \text{PRED} & \text{`sleep}{<}(\uparrow\text{ SUBJ)}{>}\text{'} \end{array}\right] \\[4ex]
\text{PRED} & \text{`try}{<}(\uparrow\text{ XCOMP)}(\uparrow\text{ SUBJ)}{>}\text{'}
\end{array}
\right]
$$

The curved line here indicates the control relation; intuitively, the controlling material belongs in both places at once.

The relation of functional control is determined by the lexical specification of control in the entry for *try*. Due to the fact that functional control is lexically specified, it will have the following properties: it is local, unique, and obligatory. It is local due to a constraint on the syntax of functional equations, known as *Functional Locality*, which only allows at most two attribute-names to appear in any equation;[17] this means that one can specify ($\uparrow$ XCOMP SUBJ) but not ($\uparrow$ XCOMP XCOMP SUBJ) in a Functional Control equation. Secondly, it is unique as attribute-names must be unique, in order to satisfy Functional Uniqueness. Finally, it is obligatory as it is stated in a lexical entry.

Only the unrestricted grammatical functions SUBJ, OBJ, and OBJ2 are allowed to be functional controllers. I will present now some examples which motivate this restriction.

The verbs *persuade* and *promise* both subcategorize for a SUBJ, OBJ, and XCOMP, but differ in the the control of the XCOMP's subject—it is controlled by the OBJ with *persuade* and by the SUBJ with *promise*:

(49) a.   Herb persuaded Louise to follow.
             (($\uparrow$ XCOMP SUBJ) = ($\uparrow$ OBJ))

     b.   Herb promised Louise to follow.
             (($\uparrow$ XCOMP SUBJ) = ($\uparrow$ SUBJ))

---

[17] In a sense, locality (or 'boundedness') comes from the fact that the equation must be written (without variables) into a lexical entry, and therefore can only have at most a finite number of names in it. The particular restriction of this boundedness to two names comes from Functional Locality.

(Hence, in (49)a, Louise is the one who is to do the following, while it is Herb in (49)b.) Now only (49)a has a passive form; this is known as 'Visser's Generalization.'

(50) a.   Louise was persuaded to follow.

b.   *Louise was promised to follow.

This is correctly predicted as the control equation for *persuade* after the application of the passive rule is the following,

$$(\uparrow \text{XCOMP SUBJ}) = (\uparrow \text{SUBJ})$$

in which the 'old' OBJ is now the SUBJ. However, with *promise* the 'old' SUBJ becomes either $\emptyset$ or OBL_{AG}, neither of which are possible functional controllers, given the restriction on functional controllers noted above. Hence no control equation can be written for the passivized *promise*.

A related fact (known as 'Bach's Generalization') is that one can 'drop' the object of *promise* but not *persuade*:

(51) a.   *Herb persuaded to follow.

b.   Herb promised to follow.

The lexical rule that 'drops' the argument will reassociate an argument linked to the OBJ function with $\emptyset$. With *promise*, this will not affect the control relation, but with *persuade* it will render $\emptyset$ the controller, which again is not permissible.

Linguists consider the verb *promise* to be exceptional, for in general the object will be the controller if an object is present. LFG posits a lexical rule of functional control, which 'fills in' control relations on verbs which are not otherwise marked. As *promise* is exceptional, it will be fully specified independently of this rule, which I give in (52).

(52)   Lexical Rule of Functional Control
        Let L be a lexical form and F_L its grammatical function assignment. If XCOMP $\in F_L$, add to the lexical entry of L:
        $(\uparrow \text{XCOMP SUBJ}) = (\uparrow \text{OBJ2})$ if OBJ2 $\in F_L$; otherwise
        $(\uparrow \text{XCOMP SUBJ}) = (\uparrow \text{OBJ})$ if OBJ $\in F_L$; otherwise
        $(\uparrow \text{XCOMP SUBJ}) = (\uparrow \text{SUBJ})$ if SUBJ $\in F_L$.

There are few instances of OBJ2 controllers in English, though there are many, for example, in Japanese.

Returning to the range of possible functional controllers, the facts in (53) are again predicted by the restriction to semantically unrestricted functions.

(53) a.   I presented it to John dead.

b.   *I presented John with it dead.

This time the XCOMP is the AP *dead*, and the controller of its subject is the OBJ in (53)a. However, *present* has a different subcategorization in which the controlling argument would be an oblique (the object of *with*), and this cannot be a functional controller. Consequently control fails in (53)b, and the structure is incomplete in f-structure, for *dead* has no subject. (Independent thematic restrictions prevent the object *John* in (53)b from being a controller.)

In certain cases there appears to be an oblique controller, as in:

(54)   We spoke of her as cowardly.

Yet in this case we can tell that *her* is the object of a complex verb *speak-of*, for it undergoes passive.

(55)   She was spoken of as cowardly.

The availability of passive shows that *her* in (54) is an OBJ, and therefore it is a possible functional controller.

The control of XADJUNCTs is determined by a rule which annotates a control relation to a c-structure (at least in English). For example, a clause-initial adjectival adjunct is obligatorily controlled by the subject of the clause, as seen in the examples in (56).

(56) a.   Sure of winning, Mary entered the competition yesterday.

b.   *Sure of winning, the competition was entered by Mary yesterday.

c.   *Sure of winning, the thought of the competition excited Mary yesterday.

d.   Sure of winning, Mary was excited by the thought of the competition yesterday.

Here it seems to be the grammatical function of SUBJ that is determining the controller; in (56)b/c the controller is determined to be *the competition*, which is semantically anomalous (and hence my * is perhaps a little inappropriate). To account for these examples, we allow AP to appear S-initially, as in (57).

(57)   S →   (AP)   XP   VP
                   (↑ XADJUNCT) =↓   (↑ SUBJ) =↓   ↑=↓
                   (↑ SUBJ) = (↓ SUBJ)

The annotations here say that the AP is an XADJUNCT and that its subject is (functionally controlled by) the subject of the S.

One important prediction of the LFG system is that there should be instances of identical structural configuration where the functions assigned are different, as it does not accept the view that function can be directly "read off" c-structure. Some examples involving functional control seem to support this view.

The first class of cases to consider involve different subcategorized functions assigned to the same structure.

(58) a.   Susan informed John about the house.

   b.   Susan kept John about the house.

In each of these examples, there is no reason to suppose that the constituent structure (in LFG terms) of the verb phrase is anything but V–NP–PP. However, the two verbs have different subcategorizations, as shown in (59).

(59) a.   *inform*   V   (↑ PRED) = 'inform<(↑ SUBJ)(↑ OBJ)
                                              (↑ OBL$_{TH}$)>'

   b.   *keep*   V (↑ PRED) = 'keep<(↑ SUBJ)(↑ OBJ)
                                          (↑ XCOMP)>'
         (↑ OBJ) = (↑ XCOMP SUBJ)

That is, while *inform* takes an Oblique Theme argument, *keep* takes an XCOMP (controlled by its OBJ), even though both are realized by the same c-structure configuration.

Given this difference, the following contrasts in anaphora can be predicted.

(60) a.   Susan$_i$ informed John about herself$_i$.

   b.   *Susan$_i$ kept John about herself$_i$.

   c.   *Susan$_i$ informed John about her$_i$.

   d.   Susan$_i$ kept John about her$_i$.

Roughly, what determines the distribution of reflexive and regular pronouns in LFG is whether the pronoun is in the same *nucleus* as its antecedent or not, where a nucleus is defined as a PRED and its subcategorized arguments. In (a) but not (b) the reflexive has an antecedent in the same nucleus (for the XCOMP is a nucleus but OBL$_{TH}$ is not); for regular pronouns, the condition is that the pronoun be free of antecedents in its nucleus, so the pattern of grammaticality reverses. I will discuss pronominal binding in more detail below (Sec. 4.3).

In other cases, we have a contrast between a functionally controlled argument and a functionally controlled adjunct (i.e., the difference between XCOMP and XADJUNCT).

(61) a.   Fred struck me as a fool.

  b.   Louise enjoyed sports as a girl.

  c.   I caught Marcia walking the dog.

  d.   I found the money walking the dog.

In examples (a) and (c) the controlled phrase is an XCOMP argument of the verb; in the other examples it is an XADJUNCT. (Example (c) also has a subject-controlled XADJUNCT interpretation for *walking the dog*.) In the adjunct cases, either of the NPs can be a controller; besides the examples given we can have *I enjoy chess as a hobby* and *I found the money lying under the bathmat*. Hence many examples allow for either an XCOMP or an XADJUNCT analysis, with the same controller; the ambiguity between these can sometimes be teased out, as the range of modification is different. So, for example, in *John will serve the meat raw*, *raw* is an XCOMP; XCOMPs are semantically constrained in such a way[18] as to rule out *John will serve the fish tasty*. However, the acceptability of *John will serve the fish, tasty and fragrant with herbs* indicates a second analysis, this time with an XADJUNCT, which is not subject to these semantic constraints.

Now while it is possible to prepose the adjuncts in (61), this is not possible with the arguments (keeping the meaning roughly constant—(62)c is good where the preposed phrase is a subject-controlled adjunct):

---

[18] For instance, the contrast here indicates that the XCOMP must express a physical property of the controller.

(62) a.   *As a fool, Fred struck me.

     b.   As a girl, Louise enjoyed sports.

     c.   *Walking the dog, I caught Marcia.

     d.   Walking the dog, I found the money.

On the other hand, it is possible to form a question out of the argument, but not out of the adjunct.

(63) a.   Which dog did you catch Marcia walking?

     b.   *Which dog did you find the money walking?

These facts suggest that the constraints on preposing and questioning (various kinds of 'long-distance dependency,' to be described below) should be sensitive not to constituent structure, which appears to be the same in either case,[19] but to the functions assigned.

4.2. Anaphoric Control

The domain of *Anaphoric Control* is roughly the domain of optional and arbitrary control in Government-Binding Theory (and was the domain of the transformation of "Super-Equi" in transformational grammar). Some typical examples are given in (64).

(64) a.   Maria thinks that watering the lawn before noon is silly.

     b.   John doesn't know that it is necessary to be obedient to the King.

As before, the controlled position is the subject of a gerund or infinitive (though anaphoric control is more restricted than functional control in that the controlled subject can only be the subject of a VP). In the present cases the controlled position may, but need not, be understood as controlled by the subject of the whole clause. In fact, the missing subject behaves like a pronoun, in that it can have a whole range of possible antecedents; (64)a is perhaps most naturally understood 'generically' (i.e. like *that for one to water the lawn ...*). In other cases, the antecedent may be 'split' as in:

(65)   Louise told Tom that eating together would be more economical.

---

[19]   Though in such cases Government-Binding Theory would propose different structures, on the view that different functions imply different structures.

Here (under one interpretation) *Louise* and *Tom* jointly control the missing subject of *eating*; for some speakers, this example also allows an antecedent that is 'generic,' or is contextually supplied.

The analysis of this data in English involves an optional rule that assigns the following pair of equations to the lexical entry of a verb.

(66) $\{(\uparrow$ SUBJ PRED$) = $ 'PRO',
         $(\uparrow$ FIN$) = -\}$

The application of this rule provides a pronominal subject in f-structure (though note that this pronominal has no c-structure realization) which is then subject to whatever constraints hold on anaphoric control; the f-structure of the relevant part of (64)a (the VP *watering the lawn before noon*) is shown below:

(67)

$$
\begin{bmatrix}
\text{SUBJ} & \begin{bmatrix} \text{PRED} & \text{'PRO'} \end{bmatrix} \\
\\
\text{OBJ} & \begin{bmatrix} \text{PRED} & \text{'lawn'} \\ \text{DEF} & + \end{bmatrix} \\
\\
\text{PRED} & \text{'water}<(\uparrow \text{ SUBJ})(\uparrow \text{ OBJ})>\text{'} \\
\\
\text{ADJUNCT} & \text{"before noon"}
\end{bmatrix}
$$

One interesting case of the difference between functional and anaphoric control lies in the control patterns of nouns derived from verbs. The LFG analysis of such a 'nominalization' process involves the idea that, while verbs may express their arguments via semantically unrestricted functions, nouns can only subcategorize for semantically restricted functions. This means that with a verb like *order*, the function assignment changes as a consequence of nominalization as shown in (68).

(68)   V $(\uparrow$ PRED$) = $ 'order$< \ (\uparrow$ SUBJ$) \quad (\uparrow$ OBJ$) \quad (\uparrow$ XCOMP$) \ >$'
                              $\quad\quad\quad |\quad\quad\quad\quad\quad |\quad\quad\quad\quad\quad\quad |$
                              $\quad\quad$ Agent $\quad\quad$ Goal $\quad$ Proposition
                              $\quad\quad\quad |\quad\quad\quad\quad\quad |\quad\quad\quad\quad\quad\quad |$
         N $(\uparrow$ PRED$) = $ 'order$< \ (\uparrow$ POSS$) \quad (\uparrow$ OBL$_{\text{GO}}) \quad (\uparrow$ COMP$) \ >$'

If all the arguments of the noun are present, we will have the following pair:

(69) a.   Elizabeth ordered the troops to march.

    b.   Elizabeth's order to the troops to march

However, any or all nominal arguments can be missing, so that we can also have things like *the order to march* and *the order*. One interesting difference between the verb and the noun is that the noun can drop its Goal argument, but not the verb.

(70) a.   *Elizabeth ordered to march.

    b.   Elizabeth's order to march.

The reader will recall that verbs of object functional control like *order* cannot drop their objects, for this leaves $\emptyset$ as the functional controller, which is not permissible. However, in the case of the noun, nothing prevents the argument from dropping. This would be predicted if the COMP in the case of the noun were anaphorically controlled.

In fact, this COMP must be so controlled, as there are no candidate functional controllers around; recall that all the arguments of the noun are semantically restricted, but that only semantically unrestricted functions may be functional controllers. Similarly, one can have (71)b but not (71)a.

(71) a.   *We were promised by the King to abdicate.

    b.   the promise by the King to abdicate

The former example is bad as the OBL$_{AG}$ phrase cannot be a functional controller, though it can be an anaphoric controller, in (71)b.

Returning to the example of *order*, we can also "fill in" the controlled subject of the nominal complement, but not of the verb:

(72) a.   *The Queen ordered the general for the troops to leave.

    b.   the Queen's order to the general for the troops to leave

This would again follow if the verb is specified as requiring functional control, but not the noun; in (72)a, there is nothing to be functionally controlled.

4.3. Anaphoric Binding

The topic of *anaphoric binding* covers the binding of overt pronouns and reflexives, in contrast to anaphoric control, which is concerned with the (possibly different) binding of pronouns that have no c-structure representation. There are two properties that are taken to be important in determining the appropriate antecedent for a pronominal,[20] and these are encoded as features, namely:

- [sb]: whether or not the antecedent for the pronominal is a subject
- [ncl]: whether or not the antecedent for the pronominal is in the same nucleus

These are binary-valued features, and the basic English facts in (73) are handled by the assignment of binding specifications in (74).

(73) a.   Mary$_i$ defended herself$_i$.

b.   *Mary$_i$ defended her$_i$.

c.   *Mary$_i$ hopes that Max hires herself$_i$.

d.   Mary$_i$ hopes that Max hires her$_i$.

(74)   Reflexive pronouns in English are [+ncl] and non-reflexive pronouns are [−ncl].

The interpretation of the binding feature specifications are in fact a little more complex than one might initially suspect. In the case of [sb], the idea is that if a pronominal is [+sb] then that means its antecedent must be a grammatical subject (somewhere in the sentence); if a pronominal is [−sb], then its antecedent must not be a grammatical subject. I will discuss [sb], and some additional aspects of its interpretation, in connection with the Norwegian data below.

The interpretation of the feature [ncl] introduces a slight asymmetry; the interpretation is given in (75).

(75)   Pronominals that are [+ncl] must find an antecedent within the minimal nucleus containing the pronominal and a SUBJective function.
Pronominals that are [−ncl] must not find an antecedent within the minimal nucleus.

---

[20] For the remainder of this chapter I will use the term 'pronoun' to refer to non-reflexive pronouns, and 'pronominal' to refer to both pronouns and reflexive pronouns.

A SUBJective function is either SUBJ or POSS (these are notionally the 'subjects' within S and NP respectively). The reader will recall that a *nucleus* is the f-structure domain of a PRED and its subcategorized arguments. For example, the noun *story* subcategorizes for an oblique argument in the examples below, and so creates a nucleus, but that nucleus contains no SUBJective function.

(76) a.   Mary$_i$ liked [the story about herself$_i$].

b.   Mary$_i$ liked [the story about her$_i$].

In these examples either a reflexive or a pronoun is grammatical; the bracketed domain corresponds to an f-structure nucleus, within which the regular pronoun is free of an antecedent (in (b)), and in (a) the reflexive is able to find an antecedent outside of this nucleus too, as the inner nucleus contains no SUBJective function. If we add such a function, we have:

(77) a.   *Mary$_i$ liked [Louise's story about herself$_i$].

b.   Mary$_i$ liked [Louise's story about her$_i$].

A similar effect shows up with PPs whose head is a 'semantic' preposition, i.e., a preposition with some semantic content, rather than purely grammatical content as with, say, *to* in *send a book to Max*. The contrast in the examples in (78) stems from this this difference.

(78) a.   Mary$_i$ sent the book to herself$_i$.

b.   *Mary$_i$ sent the book to her$_i$.

c.   Mary$_i$ pulled the blanket around herself$_i$.

d.   Mary$_i$ pulled the blanket around her$_i$.

In these examples an inner nucleus is formed only by the PRED *around*, which subcategorizes for an OBJ argument, and the interpretation assigned to [ncl] again allows for either pronominal form to appear in examples (c/d). Example (b) is bad as the minimal nucleus is the whole clause, but the pronoun is bound within this domain. In the following discussion I will just use the term 'nucleus,' but understand it to be qualified with the SUBJectivity condition.

The interaction of the features [sb] and [ncl] can be illustrated by the following facts of Norwegian, which has four pronominal NPs that we can

consider here. The analysis of these in terms of the binding features is
given in (79).

(79) a.   *seg selv*   [+sb, +ncl] 'self'

b.   *seg*   [+sb, −ncl] 'self'

c.   *ham selv*   [−sb, +ncl] 'himself'

d.   *ham*   [−ncl]   'him'

In addition to the interpretation of these features given so far, there is
another factor that is relevant, and must be brought into the theory. This
is known as the *Finite Domain Parameter*, and it specifies the domain in
which [sb] is interpreted; if it is positively stated, as it is in Norwegian, it
requires that a [+sb] pronominal be bound by a subject *within the minimal
tensed (finite) domain* containing the pronominal. Similarly, a [−sb] form
must be free of a subject, but only within that minimal domain.

Let us look at some examples involving each of these pronominal forms.
With *seg selv*, we have the following distribution.

(80) a.   Ola$_i$ snakket om   seg selv$_i$.

Ola talked   about self

'Ola talked about himself.'

b.   *Vi fortalte Ola$_i$ om   seg selv$_i$.

We told   Ola about self

c.   *Ola$_i$ vet   at   vi snakket om   seg selv$_i$.

Ola knows that we talked   about self

d.   *Ola$_i$ bad   oss snakke om   seg selv$_i$.

Ola asked us   to-talk about self

The form *seg selv* must be bound to a subject within its nucleus; in
(80)d, the main verb takes an XCOMP argument, whose subject is controlled by the object *oss*. Hence this is the only possible antecedent for *seg
selv*, but as the person and number features of *oss* and *seg selv* conflict,
the example is ungrammatical.

Looking now at *seg*, we have a different pattern; *seg* must again take
a subject antecedent, but in this case that subject must be outside of the
local nucleus of *seg*, and due to the Finite Domain Parameter, that subject
must also be within the minimal finite domain. This distinguishes examples
(c) and (d) below.

(81) a.   *Ola$_i$ snakket om   seg$_i$.
            Ola talked   about self

      b.   *Vi fortalte Ola$_i$ om   seg$_i$.
            We told   Ola about self

      c.   *Ola$_i$ vet   at   vi snakket om   seg$_i$.
            Ola knows that we talked   about self

      d.   Ola$_i$ bad   oss snakke om   seg$_i$.
            Ola asked   us to-talk about self
            'Ola asked us to talk about him.'

In (c) the pronominal is bound by a subject outside of its minimal finite domain, and so the example is bad. In (d) the embedded clause is non-finite, and this allows *seg* to take the matrix subject as antecedent. The generalization about *seg*, then, is that it must be free in its nucleus and bound to a subject within the minimal tensed clause; hence it will only appear inside of infinitival clauses, and may in principle be arbitrarily far away from its antecedent, so long as only non-finite clauses intervene.

Moving now to *ham selv*, this must be bound by a non-subject within its nucleus:

(82) a.   *Ola$_i$ snakket om   ham selv$_i$.
            Ola talked   about himself

      b.   Vi fortalte Ola$_i$ om   ham selv$_i$.
            We told   Ola about himself
            'We told Ola about himself.'

      c.   *Ola$_i$ vet   at   vi snakket om   ham selv$_i$.
            Ola knows that we talked   about himself

      d.   *Ola$_i$ bad   oss snakke om   ham selv$_i$.
            Ola asked   us to-talk about himself

Finally, *ham* must be free in its nucleus; as it is not specified for [sb], questions of finiteness do not arise, and so both (83)c and (83)d are acceptable.

(83) a.   *Ola$_i$ snakket om   ham$_i$.
     Ola   talked   about him

    b.   *Vi fortalte Ola$_i$ om   ham$_i$.
      We told   Ola   about him

    c.   Ola$_i$ vet   at   vi snakket om   ham$_i$.
      Ola   knows that we talked   about him
      'Ola knows that we talked about him.'

    d.   Ola$_i$ bad   oss snakke om   ham$_i$.
      Ola   asked us to-talk about him
      'Ola asked us to talk about him.'

An important relation in f-structure that is relevant to anaphoric binding is the relation of *f-command*, which is the corresponding notion in this theory to the notion of c-command in Government-Binding Theory. The idea is that the antecedent of a pronominal must be 'superordinate' in some sense; in LFG, the pronominal must be contained in all the f-structures containing the antecedent. As f-structures have a rather different structural configuration from c-structures, the two notions f- and c-command have rather different extensions.

The definition of f-command is given in (84).

(84)   **F-Command**
       An antecedent A *f-commands* a pronominal P iff
       (a) A does not contain P, and
       (b) every nucleus that contains A contains P.

Clause (a) need not concern us here, though strictly speaking it is important as we do not want f-command to hold between some piece of structure and another piece that is contained within the first.

The idea of f-command can be simply demonstrated with reflexives; with non-reflexive pronouns, the facts are rather more complicated, and we will therefore avoid them. The contrast in (86) follows from the condition in (85).

(85)   A reflexive pronoun must be f-commanded by its antecedent.

(86) a.   Louise$_i$ dressed herself$_i$.

    b.   *Louise$_i$'s mother dressed herself$_i$.

If we look at the f-structure for (86)b, we can see why the indicated anaphora fails.

(87)

$$
\begin{bmatrix}
\text{SUBJ} & \begin{bmatrix} \text{POSS} & [\text{PRED 'Louise'}] \\ \text{PRED} & \text{'mother}<(\uparrow \text{ POSS})>\text{'} \end{bmatrix} \\[3em]
\text{OBJ} & \begin{bmatrix} \text{PRED} & \text{'PRO'} \\ \text{REFL} & + \end{bmatrix} \\[2em]
\text{PRED} & \text{'dress}<(\uparrow \text{ SUBJ})(\uparrow \text{ OBJ})>\text{'}
\end{bmatrix}
$$

Here *Louise* fails to f-command the object, for one of the f-structure nuclei containing it does not contain the object (namely the f-structure that is the value of the SUBJ attribute). The f-command condition correctly predicts, of course, that the whole SUBJ 'Louise's mother' is a potential antecedent for the reflexive pronoun.

We will return to the topic of anaphoric binding in the next section. The full system developed in Bresnan et al. (forthcoming) includes a third feature, [log], for the notion of *logophoricity*, which I have not touched on here. The application of this 3-feature system to Japanese is discussed in Kameyama (1984) and in more detail in Kameyama (1985).

5. Long-distance Dependencies and Coordination

In this section I will present two areas of LFG that postdate KB; in the case of coordination, the research (by Bresnan, Kaplan, and Peterson) extends the KB framework, and in the case of long-distance dependencies, the analysis presented here (based on work by Kaplan and Zaenen) is different from that given in KB.

5.1. Long-distance Dependencies

In a *long-distance dependency* (also known as an 'unbounded dependency'), there exists a relation between two positions in syntactic structure, a relation that may stretch over a potentially unbounded portion of tree. A simple illustration is given in (88).

(88)   Which woman did Max say _ has declared herself President?

The phrase *which woman* appears initially, though there is a sense in which it 'belongs' in the position indicated by the ' _ ,' and we have clear syntactic evidence of this from the verb form *has*, which is 3rd singular, and from the reflexive *herself*, which we know independently cannot have an antecedent as 'far away' as the surface position of *which woman*.

The transformational analysis of such constructions is to have a level of structure in which the phrase *which woman* is indeed in the position indicated by the ' _ ,' and then to map via a transformation into a new structure with the surface order of constituents as in (88). In the Government-Binding Theory formulation of this operation, the movement leaves behind an empty category which bears agreement features and is used to ensure the correct form of the verb and the reflexive, etc. As LFG only acknowledges one level of phrase-structure representation (i.e., c-structure), such an analysis is not available.

The idea of the LFG analysis is to use the mechanism of functional control to allow the 'displaced phrase' (i.e., *which woman*) to belong in the f-structure counterparts of *both* places simultaneously. This account differs from the Government-Binding Theory account in that what appears in the place of the ' _ ' at the relevant level of structure is the whole displaced constituent in LFG, in contrast to an empty category bearing only the agreement features of the head of the displaced phrase, in the Government-Binding Theory formulation.

The functions FOCUS and TOPIC are assigned to such displaced phrases, though I will not go into details here about exactly how one decides which of the two is assigned in a particular construction.[21] In a question like (a) below, the italicized phrase is FOCUS; in (b) and (c), a topicalization and a relative clause, it is TOPIC.

(89) a.   *Which picture* do you like _ best?

     b.   *Fresno*, they tell me is nice in winter.

     c.   *the woman* to whom you are responsible

For the purposes of illustration, let us take as an example the topicalization *Maria, Max loves*. If we add to our grammar the rule in (90), and

---

[21] For discussion, see Bresnan and Mchombo (1986, 1987).

allow c-structure nodes to be optional[22] (e.g., the object of *loves*), we will get the f-structure in (91).

(90)   S′ →   XP   S

$\left\{ \begin{array}{l} (\uparrow \text{TOPIC}) = \downarrow \\ (\uparrow \text{FOCUS}) = \downarrow \end{array} \right\}$ $\uparrow = \downarrow$

(91)

$$\left[\begin{array}{ll} \text{TOPIC} & \left[\begin{array}{ll} \text{PRED} & \text{'Maria'} \end{array} \right] \\ \\ \text{SUBJ} & \left[\begin{array}{ll} \text{PRED} & \text{'Max'} \end{array} \right] \\ \\ \text{OBJ} & \left[\quad \right] \\ \\ \text{PRED} & \text{'love}{<}(\uparrow \text{SUBJ})(\uparrow \text{OBJ}){>}\text{'} \end{array} \right]$$

As it stands, this f-structure is incomplete as there is no value for OBJ. Clearly what is needed is an extra link that identifies the TOPIC value with the OBJ value. Equally clearly, we must integrate the TOPIC function, or else we would allow the grammar to admit things like *Maria, Max *loves Cindy*, which does lead to a complete f-structure given the system as described so far; again, intuitively, what we want in this last case is for the f-structure to be *incoherent*, in that the TOPIC function is not integrated in any way into the rest of the clause. We therefore add two more parts to the account; to rule (90), we add a functional control equation that links (in the example in question) the TOPIC value to the OBJ value, and secondly we extend the *Coherence Condition* to cover TOPIC and FOCUS.[23]

I state this *Extended Coherence Condition* first.

---

[22] The analysis of long-distance dependencies developed by Kaplan and Za-enen does not acknowledge the existence of any kind of empty category; c-structure nodes are optional, rather than being obligatory but being allowed to dominate no lexical material.

[23] This extension was proposed by Fassi Fehri; see Fassi Fehri (to appear).

(92)   Extended Coherence

An f-structure is *locally coherent* if and only if all the governable grammatical functions that it contains are governed by a local predicate. In addition, the functions TOPIC and FOCUS must be linked to predicate-argument structure either by being functionally identified with subcategorized functions or by anaphorically binding subcategorized functions. An f-structure is *coherent* if and only if it and all its subsidiary f-structures are locally coherent.

Here 'functionally identified with' means 'being in the relation of functional control to'; the clause about 'anaphorically binding' need not concern us here: it has to do with those cases where the position indicated by the ' _ ' in the examples above is not a 'missing' constituent in c-structure, but rather some kind of pronominal form.

Let us now consider how to specify the functional control relation. Clearly it would be far too restrictive to specify in the rule (90) something like ($\uparrow$ TOPIC) = ($\uparrow$ OBJ), for the relation is potentially unbounded; rather, we should say that the TOPIC function is linked to *some* other function, and generalizing maximally, we have the rule in (93).

(93)   S$'$ $\rightarrow$ XP   S

$$\left\{ \begin{array}{l} (\uparrow \text{ TOPIC}) = \downarrow \\ (\uparrow \text{ FOCUS}) = \downarrow \end{array} \right\} \quad \uparrow = \downarrow$$

$$(\uparrow \ldots) = \downarrow$$

The notation '...' is taken to range over arbitrary sequences of function names (such as COMP COMP SUBJ, etc.); any restrictions (such as island constraints) on where the ' _ ' may appear will be restrictions on the possible combinations within such sequences, and the uniqueness, completeness, and coherence conditions will ensure that the only good f-structures are those where the function picked out by '...' will have no value coming from anywhere else in the c-structure (i.e., will be a 'missing' constituent in the c-structure). Actually, the '($\uparrow$ ...) =$\downarrow$' annotation builds in the Extended Coherence Condition, in that it requires that FOCUS or TOPIC are identified with some grammatical function; (92) is effectively a hypothesis about this identification. Kaplan and Zaenen (1986) introduce a regular language to describe these paths through the f-structure; for English something like '{COMP $\vee$ XCOMP}* COMP' is a reasonable first approximation: the path can go through any number (including zero) of COMPs or XCOMPs (or mixtures of both) and ends with any grammatical function *except* COMP.

More formally, the '...' represents the relation of *inclusion* in f-structure. The definition of inclusion is given in (94).

(94)   Inclusion

f *includes* g iff there exists an a such that $(f\ a) = g$
or $(f\ a)$ includes g.

This says that some f-structure f includes another f-structure g just in case either g is the value of some attribute (function name) a in f, or g is included within the f-structure that is the value of some a within f. More simply put, it says that g is included in f just in case g is a value somewhere within f.

Our example now has the following c- and f-structure representations:

(95)

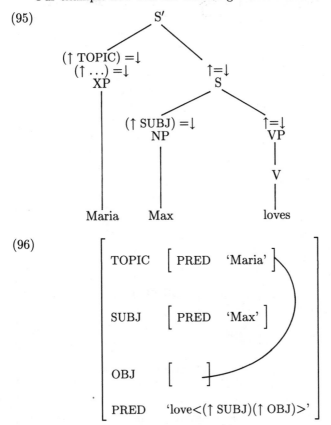

(96)

This particular analysis of long-distance dependencies interacts in an interesting way with the analysis of anaphoric binding, and supports the idea that, in some way, the displaced phrase belongs in two places at the same time.

Many speakers find examples like (97) ambiguous, in that either NP may be the antecedent for the reflexive pronoun.

(97)   Which picture of himself does Max think Larry prefers?

These have been a puzzle for many years in the transformational framework, in that the most natural principles that one would advance for the binding of reflexives fail to predict that *Max* is a possible antecedent. Within the LFG framework, this is indeed a prediction that is made, given the f-command condition on anaphoric binding and the rather 'flat' f-structure configuration that we have just seen (in (96)). The f-structure of the present example has the following form, omitting all but relevant information.

(98)

$$
\left[
\begin{array}{ll}
\text{FOCUS} & \left[
\begin{array}{ll}
\text{OBL}_{\text{TH}} & \left[
\begin{array}{ll}
\text{PRED} & \text{'PRO'} \\
\text{REFL} & +
\end{array}
\right] \\
\text{PRED} & \text{'picture}<(\uparrow \text{OBL}_{\text{TH}})>\text{'}
\end{array}
\right] \\
\\
\text{SUBJ} & \left[\begin{array}{ll}\text{PRED} & \text{'Max'}\end{array}\right] \\
\\
\text{COMP} & \left[
\begin{array}{ll}
\text{SUBJ} & [\text{PRED 'Larry'}] \\
\text{OBJ} & [\quad] \\
\text{PRED} & \text{'prefer}<(\uparrow \text{SUBJ})(\uparrow \text{OBJ})>\text{'}
\end{array}
\right] \\
\\
\text{PRED} & \text{'think}<(\uparrow \text{SUBJ})(\uparrow \text{COMP})>\text{'}
\end{array}
\right]
$$

The reader will recall that a reflexive pronoun must be f-commanded by its antecedent, which must also be within the minimal nucleus containing a

SUBJective function. In (98), the reflexive pronoun (the value of the OBL_{TH} attribute) is f-commanded in its position within the FOCUS function by *Max*, and is also f-commanded in its OBJ position by *Larry*; hence either is a potential antecedent. In particular, *Max* may be an antecedent due to the 'flat' f-structure, in which the subcategorized functions of the clause are at the same level as the FOCUS function.

However, if the displaced phrase is an XCOMP, with a controlled subject, then only the controller of that subject will be a potential antecedent. The example (97) contrasts with (99) in this regard.

(99)   How proud of himself does Max think Larry is?

Only *Larry* is a possible antecedent here, as we can see from the f-structure.

(100)

$$
\begin{bmatrix}
\text{FOCUS} & \begin{bmatrix} \text{SUBJ} & [\quad] \\[2mm] OBL_{TH} & \begin{bmatrix} \text{PRED} & \text{'PRO'} \\ \text{REFL} & + \end{bmatrix} \\[4mm] \text{PRED} & \text{'proud}<(\uparrow \text{SUBJ})(\uparrow OBL_{TH})>\text{'} \end{bmatrix} \\[10mm]
\text{SUBJ} & \begin{bmatrix} \text{PRED} & \text{'Max'} \end{bmatrix} \\[6mm]
\text{COMP} & \begin{bmatrix} \text{SUBJ} & [\text{PRED 'Larry'}] \\ \text{XCOMP} & [\quad] \\ \text{PRED} & \text{'be}<(\uparrow \text{XCOMP})>(\uparrow \text{SUBJ})\text{'} \end{bmatrix} \\[6mm]
\text{PRED} & \text{'think}<(\uparrow \text{SUBJ})(\uparrow \text{COMP})>\text{'}
\end{bmatrix}
$$

Here the displaced AP is an XCOMP; the verb *be* subcategorizes for an XCOMP and a non-thematic SUBJ which functionally controls the SUBJ of the XCOMP. This means that now the minimal nucleus containing the reflexive also contains a SUBJective function, and so the only possible antecedent for the reflexive pronoun is that SUBJ, whose predicate is 'Larry,' in virtue of the control relation specified by *be*.

5.2. Coordination

As the reader might suspect, the role of functional structure is again important in the LFG account of coordination. While the more common conception in generative grammar is that 'likes coordinate,' where 'like' means identity of syntactic category, in LFG the identity is with functions, in f-structure.

For instance, examples like the following show that identity at the syntactic (categorial) level is not the correct generalization about what can coordinate with what.

(101)a.   We consider him honest and a likely candidate for the next election.

b.   Maria was asleep and causing a stoppage in the traffic.

The categories of the conjuncts in these examples are AP and NP in the first example, and AP and VP in the second. The Generalized Phrase Structure Grammar solution to this problem is to redefine the way coordination works so that identity is not forced in all cases (see Chap. 3, Sec. 6.2). In LFG, the idea is that there *is* identity in these structures, but identity of function, not of category; in these examples, the function is XCOMP, which may be realized by any maximal projection of a lexical category.

Before getting to the analysis, we must first consider what coordinated f-structures will look like. Rather than single objects, f-structures will now be allowed to be sets; for example, in *Tom and Herb argued*, the value of the SUBJ function will be a set, with two members, which are the f-structures determined by *Tom* and *Herb* respectively. Ultimately, it will be necessary to say what it means for an attribute to have a set as its value, but we can wait for a while before doing this.

The rule of coordination in its simplest form is shown in (102).

(102)   C   →   C   Conj   C
                       $\downarrow \in \uparrow$ $\downarrow \in \uparrow$

The *Conj* category is for the conjoining word, *and*, *but*, and so on; I will not say much more about this in the remainder of the discussion. In the rule, 'C' ranges over syntactic categories but is not interpreted as a variable;

the rule might generate a tree with an N dominating a VP and a A′ (though one might want to impose more constraints, such as that the bar-levels of all categories be identical). However, such a tree will be filtered out by the f-structure well-formedness conditions (assuming that these different categories cannot realize the same grammatical functions). Certain cases of categorial mismatch will be allowed, such as in the examples in (101), for the functions are the same.

The annotations '↓ ∈ ↑' on the categories in the rule indicate that the f-structure of each such category is an element of the f-structure of the mother—that is, that the mother's f-structure is a set.

The interpretation of a set of f-structures is as follows:

(103)　　If some f-structure f is a set, then the value of an attribute a in f is v (that is, $(f\ a) = v$) iff for every $g \in f$, $(g\ a)$ includes the information in v.

Using an example to illustrate (103), it says that in a set, the value of the attribute OBJ is [PRED 'Max'] only if the value of OBJ includes the information [PRED 'Max'] in each member of the set.[24]

Let us now look at a simple example, *Louise danced and drank vodka.* The f-structure for (104) is shown in (105).

(104)

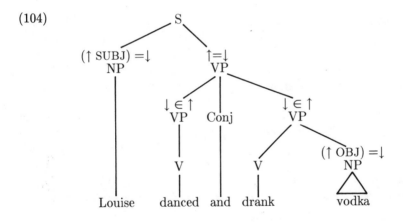

---

[24] The definition in (103) gives much the same results as the statement of the Head Feature Convention for coordinate structures in Generalized Phrase Structure Grammar. In either definition, some attribute (or feature) only has a value if each member of the set has that value, though this is stated

(105)

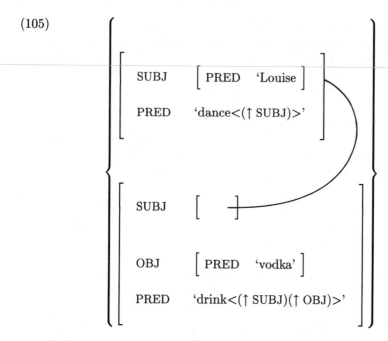

As each verb dictates the basic form of its f-structure, coordinated Vs or VPs lead to the set appearing at the outer level. The subject, *Louise*, is the subject of the coordinated VP, which means that in f-structure it 'distributes' to all the elements of the set representing the conjunction. Given the definition of a value above, it is then the case that the value of SUBJ in (105) is [PRED 'Louise'].

If we consider now the case where we coordinate verbs, we can explain the contrast in (106). In example (a) below, transitive verbs are coordinated and the object *vodka* will distribute to be the value of OBJ for each verb. In example (b), the verb *dance* does not subcategorize for OBJ, but OBJ will distribute to both conjuncts; this makes the nucleus of *dance* incoherent, for it has an OBJ that is not subcategorized by the verb.

---

on f-structures in one case and on surface structures in the other. Moreover, the expression 'includes the information in' allows different information to appear in each conjunct—the value of the attribute being effectively the intersection of the values of that attribute in each conjunct, a conception again similar to that found in Generalized Phrase Structure Grammar.

(106)a.   Louise made and drank vodka.

    b.   *Louise made and danced vodka.

One of the motivating reasons for the change in the treatment of long-distance dependencies from that in KB is the interaction of long-distance dependency constructions with coordination, in particular the phenomenon that was handled in transformational grammar by the *Coordinate Structure Constraint*.[25] The basic facts are shown in (107).

(107)a.   That woman, I interviewed _ and Max hired _ .

    b.   *That woman, I interviewed _ and Max hired a former doctor.

The generalization is that whenever there is a dependency into one conjunct in a coordinate structure, it must be into each conjunct. The treatment this receives is essentially no different from the case considered above of the coordinated transitive and intransitive verbs. For instance, if the FOCUS is functionally identified with some attribute in some member of set of f-structures, then such an identification must take place into each member of the set. This does not happen in (107)b, and so the whole f-structure set has no value for '$(\uparrow \ldots) = \downarrow$' (cf., rule (93)), and the FOCUS is not integrated properly. The f-structure of (107)b is shown in (108)(See p. 190). In this way, the Coordinate Structure Constraint need not be stipulated as an independent condition, for its effect follows as a consequence of the interaction of the analyses of coordination and long-distance dependencies.[26]

LFG currently has not developed an account of the 'COMP-trace' facts of long-distance dependencies (see Chap. 2, Sec. 8, and Chap. 3, Sec. 6.1), nor of the 'parallelism' facts discussed in Chapter 3, Section 6.2. In addition, there is no obvious way to extend its treatment of long-distance dependencies to interpretive phenomena, such as constraints on scope, as discussed in Chapter 2, Sections 5.4 and 8; as noted in Chapter 3, there is some controversy over the convergence in constraints on syntactic and interpretive long-distance phenomena.

---

[25] See also Chapter 3, Section 6.2.

[26] My presentation is somewhat simplified here; see Kaplan and Zaenen (1986) for more details of this interaction.

(108)

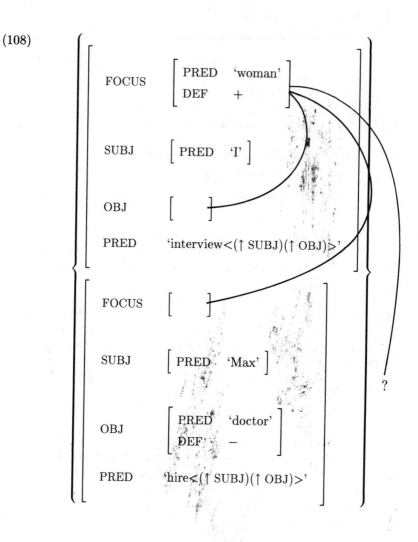

Where to Look Next

The standard source for LFG is the collection of papers in Bresnan (1982), which presents a wide variety of aspects of the theory; see also Levin, Rappaport, and Zaenen (1983), and Iida, Wechsler, and Zec (to appear). The integration of semantic structures into the LFG system is described in Halvorsen (1983).

The Moroccan Arabic data in Section 2.3 is from Wager (1983); the analysis of Japanese causatives in Section 3.4 is drawn from Ishikawa (1985). Levin (1985) presents a study of general principles of function-argument association. On control, see Bresnan, "Control and Complementation" (in Bresnan (1982)), Mohanan (1983) and Simpson and Bresnan (1983); the account of nominalization and its interaction with control (Sec. 4.2) is given in Rappaport (1983).

The basics of the account of anaphoric binding can be found in Kameyama (1984) and in more detail in Kameyama (1985); the Norwegian data is drawn from Bresnan, Halvorsen, and Maling (forthcoming). The discussion in Section 5 is based on the analyses sketched in Saiki (1985); the account of long-distance dependencies is given in more detail in Kaplan and Zaenen (1986). The discussion of the interaction of long-distance dependencies and anaphoric binding is based on material from class lectures given by Joan Bresnan. Fassi Fehri (to appear) presents an account of various aspects of these phenomena based on data from Arabic. On coordination, see Bresnan, Kaplan, and Peterson (1986).

Chapter 5

Postscript

by Thomas Wasow

The preceding chapters have presented an enormous amount of information about the assumptions, mechanisms, and results of three contemporary theories of syntax. To the newcomer, this may seem overwhelming. The purpose of this postscript is to provide a somewhat more global perspective, bringing out some of the important similarities and differences among the theories.[1] Since one important similarity is that they share a common ancestry, I will begin with a few remarks on the recent history of theoretical syntax.

For this purpose, it is useful to note the unique position occupied by Noam Chomsky in the field of theoretical linguistics. Probably no other academic discipline has been so dominated by one individual in recent times. Virtually every innovation that has occurred in this field over the past quarter century has been either an elaboration of or a reaction to some suggestion of Chomsky's. On at least three occasions, Chomsky has revolutionized the way in which syntactic theorizing has been pursued. A brief summary of these changes will be helpful in contrasting the theories covered in this monograph.

---

[1] It should be emphasized that, like much else in syntax, the issue of how much real difference there is among contemporary grammatical theories (and where the differences lie) is quite controversial. By and large, those with the strongest commitment to one theory tend to see greater differences between it and the others than those of us who are less committed. This postscript, then, must be taken as my own personal perspective on the current state of the field. A number of people (including some close colleagues) have taken exception to some of the claims made below.

Three Phases

Chomsky's early work, best exemplified by *Syntactic Structures,* was primarily concerned with establishing the need for generative grammars. At the time, linguists (in America, at least) focussed their attention on methods of data collection and analysis. The goal was to develop precise and objective procedures for classifying corpora of utterances. Chomsky argued that linguists should be concerned primarily with theory construction rather than methodology. He pointed out that languages are infinite and argued that this fact should be of central importance in linguistics. Rather than worrying about the taxonomy of finite corpora, Chomsky proposed that linguists should be writing grammars for infinite languages and testing them against the intuitions of native speakers.

This phase of Chomsky's work was also characterized by a high degree of formal explicitness and an interest in the mathematical properties of grammar formalisms. Chomsky (1959) developed a hierarchy of grammar types (now known as the Chomsky Hierarchy), and proved a number of theorems about what kinds of sets of strings each grammar type could and couldn't generate. These mathematical results, it was claimed, could be used to demonstrate conclusively the inadequacy of certain theories of syntax, on the grounds that natural languages exhibited constructions provably beyond the generative capacity of formalized versions of the theories in question. In the place of the discredited formalisms, Chomsky put forward his theory of transformational grammar. Advocating "the method of rigorously stating a proposed theory and applying it strictly to linguistic material with no attempt to avoid unacceptable conclusions by ad hoc adjustments or loose formulation" (Chomsky, 1957, 5), he presented his analyses in the form of explicit rules for generating a substantial fragment of English.

The emphasis, in short, was largely on what was later to be called "observational adequacy": generating the correct set of strings for a natural language. Meaning was deemed to be outside of the realm of linguistics, and psychological considerations played no role in syntactic theorizing. While some attention was paid to making analyses simple and elegant, top priority was given to developing a theory capable of generating all and only those strings that are well-formed sentences. The major result of this period was the claim that observational adequacy could be achieved with a transformational grammar, but not with a phrase structure grammar.

In the mid-1960's, Chomsky's focus changed dramatically. The so-called 'Standard Theory' of Chomsky (1965) (following earlier work by Fodor, Katz, and Postal) included a semantic component and was explicitly linked to questions of how knowledge of language was represented in the mind. Language was viewed as a system of connections between meanings and sounds, and the job of the linguist was to discover the rules that speakers employ in associating meanings with sounds.

The Standard Theory identified two distinguished levels of representation for sentences: deep and surface structures. Deep structures served as the basis for semantic interpretation, and surface structures as the basis for phonological interpretation. The two levels were related to one another by transformations. Hence, transformations played the central role in connecting meanings with sounds.[2] It was claimed that the same transformational rules needed to distinguish sentences from non-sentences would also serve this connecting function between sounds and meanings. Moreover, it was expected that they would turn out to be "psychologically real," in the sense that they could be shown to play a role in human sentence-processing.[3]

The focus of attention, then, was what Chomsky (1964) called "descriptive adequacy": modeling the ability of speakers to relate meanings and sounds. Interest in the mathematical properties of the theory was subordinated to concern with semantic and psychological questions; consequently, standards of explicitness and rigor were relaxed. The principal result claimed for this period was that descriptive adequacy could be achieved with a transformational grammar of a certain form.[4]

---

[2] This most extreme version of this view was what was called "Generative Semantics," which held that deep structures could be identified with representations of meaning (see Newmeyer (1980, Chaps. 4 and 5) for an overview and references). While Chomsky opposed Generative Semantics, he did at one time endorse the idea that transformations provided the primary link between meaning and sound.

[3] For a survey of literature on this question, see Fodor, Bever, and Garrett (1974).

[4] Some clarification is in order here, for in introducing the distinctions among levels of adequacy for a linguistic theory, Chomsky argued that standard transformational grammar attained (at least on some points) the highest level, namely "explanatory adequacy." Thus, my association of the Standard Theory with concern for descriptive adequacy appears to be in direct conflict with what Chomsky himself asserted at the time. I contend, how-

The widespread acceptance of the Standard Theory lasted only a few years. Beginning with the bitter battle over Generative Semantics in the late sixties, generative grammar became fragmented and factionalized. Until the late seventies, most syntactic research was carried on within some revised and/or extended form of the Standard Theory, though radically different approaches also began to gain visibility.

A common theme in the most important work of this period was the need to constrain the power of transformational grammar. The Standard Theory was so rich in descriptive devices that its ability to provide analyses of particular constructions began to seem rather unremarkable. This intuition was substantiated by Peters and Ritchie (1973), who proved that standard transformational grammars had the power of Turing machines—that is, that they could be used to formalize any procedure that was in principle formalizable. Further, linguists began to take seriously Chomsky's earlier claim that there was a higher level of adequacy than descriptive adequacy to aspire to. A theory would attain "explanatory adequacy" if it provided a means for inferring a grammar on the basis of the facts of the language. In other words, explanatory adequacy is concerned with learnability: it says that syntactic theory should only permit grammars that could be learned on the basis of the primary data available to real language learners. Such a theory could not have the descriptive power of existing versions of generative grammar, which all permitted infinitely many different analyses of any phenomenon.

The third phase of Chomsky's work is dominated by the quest for explanatory adequacy. His books and papers consistently assert that the fundamental question linguistics needs to answer is how language can be learned. The most striking fact about language, he says, is the gap between the small and arbitrary corpora children are exposed to and the unbounded ability people have to produce and understand utterances. This "argument from the poverty of the stimulus" indicates that the innate human language faculty narrowly constrains the class of possible hypotheses available to the child about the structure of the language being learned. Then even a small amount of data about a language may provide the learner with

---

ever, that the overwhelming bulk of the research of the time was concerned with generating the right strings and assigning to them structures which were semantically or psychologically plausible. Little more than lip service was paid to explanatory adequacy, that is, to the goal of establishing a highly constrained theory of universal grammar.

enough information to identify the language uniquely. Thus, this line of reasoning leads to a picture in which as much as possible is factored out of the grammars of particular languages and put into the theory of grammar— or "universal grammar," as it is sometimes called.

It is difficult to pinpoint when this third phase began. As noted in Footnote 3, Chomsky advocated the goal of explanatory adequacy during his second phase. However, the concern with learnability actually did not become a serious motivating force in syntactic analyses until the mid seventies. Government-Binding Theory (GB), introduced by Chomsky (1981), represents the culmination of this tendency. GB research seeks to reduce the grammars of particular languages to settings for a small number of parameters, leaving the remainder to a rich set of universal principles. Because of the focus on universals, the GB literature differs from earlier transformational work in devoting considerable attention to cross-language comparisons. Only in this way can the parameters of language variation be identified and tested.

With the concentration on learnability and universal grammar, many details in the analyses of particular constructions began to receive less attention. Likewise, concern for explicitness and formalization diminished. Indeed, there seems to be quite a general trade-off between theoretical elegance and attention to empirical detail. As Chomsky has sought to attain higher and higher levels of adequacy in his theories, he has concerned himself less and less with analyzing the specifics of particular constructions. Thus, although the discussion of levels of adequacy in the literature claims that attainment of any level presupposes attainment of the lower levels, in actual practice, there has been a cost attached each time the sights have been raised.

The Place of GPSG and LFG

The preceding section described a monotonic course of development in syntactic theorizing over the past thirty years, with formal rigor and attention to grammatical details gradually giving way to an emphasis on universal grammar and larger theoretical questions. Generalized Phrase Structure Grammar (GPSG) and Lexical-Functional Grammar (LFG) can be viewed as attempts to preserve certain attractive features of the earlier phases of generative grammar. More specifically, I will argue that GPSG represents a return to a serious concern for observational adequacy, while LFG's emphasis is on descriptive adequacy. I hasten to add, however, that this is an oversimplification, as both GPSG and LFG do address the question of universals in substantive ways. Nevertheless, I think it is fair to characterize the emphases of the theories in this way, and that it is useful to do so, in trying to fit them into a larger picture.

Like Chomsky's early work, the GPSG literature exhibits a keen interest in the mathematical properties of grammar formalisms. More specifically, Gazdar and others (see especially Pullum and Gazdar (1982)) have revived interest among linguists in questions of "weak generative capacity"—that is, of the sets of strings generable by various types of grammars. In order to investigate such questions, it is necessary that the grammars in question be formulated with considerable precision. Thus, work in GPSG resembles the transformational literature of twenty-five years earlier in its formal rigor. Likewise, GPSG papers typically present explicit grammar fragments, which are evaluated on the basis of the acceptability of the strings they generate.

One striking dissimilarity, however, between GPSG and Chomsky's early theory is the role of semantics. Whereas *Syntactic Structures* excluded the study of meaning from the domain of linguistics, GPSG's semantic analyses are such an integral part of the theory as to be inseparable from the syntactic proposals. More than anything else, this reflects the fact that the intervening decades saw the development of a rigorous formal approach to natural language semantics (Montague Grammar). Unlike the work on meaning by transformationalists in the sixties, no psychological significance has been attached to the semantics of GPSG.

More generally, like the *Syntactic Structures* theory, GPSG has not been tied to any psychological claims, and its proponents have generally been agnostic on the question of the proper relationship between theories of grammar and models of language users.[5] Moreover, though GPSG differs from early transformational grammar in that it makes far stronger claims about universal grammar, its proponents do not invoke the problem of language acquisition as the reason for putting forward such claims. Rather, the motivation appears to stem from general methodological considerations, viz., that universal claims are preferable to existential ones. Thus, even with regard to the quest for linguistic universals, GPSG has been largely free from psychological claims.

LFG, in contrast, has its origin in the concern for the role of grammatical theory in models of processing. Ronald Kaplan, one of the developers of LFG, was trained as a psychologist, and began his career doing ex-

---

[5] There are a few exceptions, e.g., Crain and Fodor (1985).

perimental work on human sentence processing. In an important paper marking the transition from transformational grammar to LFG, Bresnan (1978) argued for the innovations she proposed on the grounds that they were psychologically "realistic." The focus on LFG as a basis for modeling how people process language has been maintained, especially in work by Marilyn Ford. Further, Pinker (1984) has argued that LFG can provide natural explanations for many facts about language acquisition. In short, LFG resembles the work of the Standard Theory period in its emphasis on descriptive adequacy.

LFG and standard transformational grammar are also alike in positing two distinguished levels of grammatical representation, one which is used as the basis for semantic interpretation and one which is used as the basis for phonological interpretation. Of course, the f-structures of LFG do not look like the deep structures of the Standard Theory, but their roles in the two theories are quite similar. Specifically, deep structures and f-structures are the loci of grammatical information and constraints which depend on the predicate-argument relations in sentences. Especially important among these are subcategorization and control relations.

A crucial difference between LFG and transformational grammar is the place of grammatical functions (or "grammatical relations," as they are sometimes called) like 'subject' and 'object' in the two theories. Chomsky (1965) argued that insofar as grammatical functions played a role in linguistic descriptions, they could be defined in terms of configurations in phrase structure trees. For example, he proposed that a subject is an NP directly dominated by S. LFG, in contrast, takes grammatical functions to be primitives of the theory, in terms of which a great many rules and conditions are stated.

In this, LFG is like the theory of Relational Grammar developed by David Perlmutter, Paul Postal, and others over the past dozen years or so. During that period, a large body of literature has been produced, analyzing syntactic phenomena (especially those having to do with the internal structure of clauses) in an impressively wide variety of languagues. Though it is rarely acknowledged, the influence of Relational Grammar on all contemporary work in syntactic theory would be hard to overestimate. Of the theories discussed in this monograph, only LFG adopts the central tenet of Relational Grammar (namely, that grammatical functions are primitive), but proponents of all three have devoted considerable energy to describing phenomena and capturing generalizations first discovered by relational grammarians. Noteworthy examples are Burzio (1981), Dowty (1982), and Bresnan (1982, passim).

I return now to the main theme of this section. The three theories represented in this monograph correspond—at least in what they choose to emphasize—to the three stages of Chomsky's work described in the previous section. The correspondence is not, of course, perfect. However, the styles of doing linguistics, the kind of questions asked, and the criteria for evaluating analyses do match fairly well. It is important to understand that I am not accusing GPSG or LFG of arrested development. As I pointed out above, each stage in Chomsky's work has had its strengths and weaknesses. As the focus changed from observational to descriptive to explanatory adequacy, standards of explicitness, rigor, and attention to empirical detail declined. This is natural, for the larger the questions addressed, the harder it is to give complete answers. Like Chomsky's three stages, the theories under consideration constitute different choices regarding this trade-off.

Some Points of Convergence

In spite of the considerable differences in emphasis, formalism, and substance, there are some respects in which the theories under discussion are surprisingly similar. In this section, I will describe some that have struck me; there may well be others. These points of convergence are of special interest because they indicate areas where linguists may have attained some real new insight transcending the more superficial differences among theories.

Perhaps the most obvious similarity is the reduced role of transformations in the these theories. Their common ancestor, standard transformational grammar, encoded most relationships among the elements of sentences by positing levels of representation at which the related elements were identical or adjacent; it then turned these abstract representations into the actual sentences by means of transformational rules. For example, the Standard Theory posited a transformation of 'Equi-NP Deletion' to remove the subject of a subordinate clause when it was identical with an NP in the main clause; so, the fact that *Pat* is the 'understood' subject of *leave* in *Pat wants to leave* would be encoded by deriving it from *Pat wants Pat to leave* by deletion under identity. None of the theories considered in this monograph adopts this kind of analysis.

More generally, alternative devices for encoding grammatical relationships have supplanted transformations almost everywhere. GPSG and LFG have no transformations, and GB has only one (Move-α). Moreover, most of the real work accomplished by Move-α is a function of the coindexing that is required between the moved element and the pre-movement position. Indeed, Chomsky (1982, 33) goes so far as to say, "It is immaterial ... whether Move-α is regarded as a rule forming s-structure from d-structure, or whether it is regarded as a property of s-structures that are 'base-generated' ... It is in fact far from clear that there is a distinction apart from terminology between these two formulations."

The reduced status of transformations in contemporary linguistic theories can be traced back to the observation that a great many of the transformations in the Standard Theory produced outputs that were structurally identical to base-generated trees. For example, a passive sentence like *The dog was chased by the cat* appears to have the same constituent structure as an active sentence like *The dog was racing by the house.* This fact led Emonds (1976) to develop a theory in which a large class of transformations was required to be 'structure preserving.' This idea is manifested, in a more general form, in the Projection Principle of GB. It also served as an important motivation for eliminating the transformational component altogether in GPSG and LFG. If deep structures and surface structures were isomorphic, it was reasoned, then why relate them by means of rules with the power to alter structure?

There is considerable diversity in the mechanisms proposed in the different theories to do what had formerly been done with transformations. Even here, however, I think that there are significant commonalities. This is most evident in the treatment of unbounded dependencies. In standard transformational grammar, these were handled by means of rules that moved (or deleted) elements across arbitrarily large stretches of a sentence. Contemporary theories, on the other hand, adopt analyses in which the relationship between 'fillers'[6] and 'gaps' is mediated by intervening elements. In GB, this is accomplished by means of 'successive cyclic' movement: *wh*-elements are moved through the COMP nodes of intervening clauses, and the resulting coindexed traces form a chain connecting the surface position of the *wh*-element with its d-structure position. In GPSG, the SLASH feature is passed up the tree along a path of nodes connecting the gap with its filler. In the current LFG analysis, fillers and gaps are connected by means of a sequence of grammatical functions, summarized by the nota-

---

[6] Referred to in the chapters above as 'displaced phrases.'

tion '(↑ ...),' though in this case the path through the f-structure is stated as one expression, not as a series of links.

While the formal mechanisms are different in these three theories, they share the property of effectively reducing unbounded dependencies to sequences of local dependencies, thereby taking the same position on what had been a controversial issue in the transformational literature of the early seventies. The differences among these analyses are slight in comparison with the difference between any of them and any treatment that posits no licensing relation between filler and gap. While clear empirical evidence has been found for the existence of elements sensitive to the presence of unbounded dependencies (see Zaenen (1983)), I know of no direct argument to choose among coindexing, feature passing, and sequences of functions.

Similarly, the three theories agree, roughly speaking, that the gaps in these constructions must, in some sense, be licensed by a lexical element in its clause. In GB, this requirement is embodied in the Empty Category Principle.[7] In GPSG, it follows from the Lexical Head Constraint that the Slash Termination Metarules can only introduce gaps as sisters to lexical heads. Finally, since unbounded dependencies in LFG are handled by means of sequences of grammatical functions, a gap must be identified in terms of the grammatical function it plays with respect to some lexical predicate.[8] In short, not only must fillers and gaps be connected by some chain of intermediate elements, but the gap itself must stand in a special relationship with a lexical head close to it.

These somewhat technical similarities reflect what I believe is a more fundamental insight, namely that unbounded dependencies are permitted only under rather limited circumstances. Standard transformational grammar treated movement or deletion over arbitrary stretches as the norm, specifying certain configurations as 'islands' blocking such operations; contemporary theories, in contrast, treat dependencies between widely separated elements as the exception, requiring special mechanisms to license them.

---

[7] The ECP also permits gaps to be licensed through coindexing, but, as Sells notes, these are in a sense not the "core" cases of the ECP.

[8] An earlier LFG treatment of unbounded dependencies required that for each gap there be a 'lexical signature' (Kaplan and Bresnan (1982, 246ff)). This requirement was even closer to the ECP and the effects of the Lexical Head Constraint than the current LFG treatment.

Another basic idea embodied in these three theories is that clause structure is largely predictable from the semantics of predicates. That is, if you know what a verb (or a predicative adjective or noun) means, you can tell a great deal about what else will occur in a clause it heads. Grammar rules are needed only to state certain language-wide generalizations about how the pieces of sentences are put together and to deal with apparent exceptions to the normal patterns. Most of what was stipulated in the grammars of earlier theories is taken to be a function of lexical semantics.

This idea is clearest in GB. The θ-Criterion says (oversimplifying somewhat) that the meaning of a predicate determines what grammatical arguments it will have. The Projection Principle guarantees that the structure determined by the lexical head's meaning cannot be altered in essential ways. The problem of acquiring a language, then, reduces largely to learning the meanings of words. There is more to it, of course, such as discovering the basic order of constituents, determining what the bounding nodes are, and learning which verbs trigger S′-deletion (such as *seem* and *believe* in English), and so on. In the canonical cases, however, sentence structure is a projection of the semantics of words.

In LFG, the Principle of Function-Argument Biuniqueness ensures that grammatical functions will be paired with thematic roles. The Completeness and Coherence conditions, in turn, see to it that every grammatical function is filled by exactly one constituent in the f-structure. Hence, aside from exceptional predicates permitting non-thematic functions, clause structure is essentially determined by the thematic roles required by the predicate. Again, a certain amount of idiosyncratic information must be stipulated, but far less than in earlier theories.

The version of GPSG presented in Chapter 3 does not really embody this idea of clause structure as a projection of lexical semantics. The closest thing to it is "shake'n'bake semantics": the lexical type of a predicate determines the number and type of arguments that it will combine with; any sentence in which a predicate cooccurred with the wrong number or types of arguments would be uninterpretable. But the alert reader will recall that subcategorization is handled in the syntax, so that a sentence whose verb has the wrong number or category of sister constituents will be ungrammatical, not just semantically anomalous. That is, the lexical meaning of a predicate determines how the semantics of the pieces of a clause should be composed, but it does not determine what those pieces will be.

In recent modifications of GPSG, however, this has been changed. In particular, Pollard's (1984, 1985) work on Head-driven Phrase Structure Grammar involves specifying subcategorization information in lexical entries, rather than in ID-rules. This permits the subcategorization to be linked rather directly to the lexical semantics, while at the same time allowing the ID-rules to be extremely general schemata. Thus, in the most recent incarnations of GPSG, it resembles GB and LFG in deriving canonical clause structure largely from lexical semantics.

Conclusion

It is interesting that contemporary syntactic theories seem to be converging on the idea that sentence structure is generally predictable from word meanings, for this seems to be close to the naive view of a great many non-linguists. The layperson generally equates languages with collections of words, assuming, for example, that learning a new language consists of learning its vocabulary. It might seem unimpressive, then, that linguists are finally coming around to this common-sense view. I contend, quite the contrary, that this is rather remarkable, for the conventional wisdom appears, on closer inspection, to be hopelessly simplistic.

Consider, for example, what happens when one takes a sentence of one language and translates each word into some unrelated language; in general, such word-for-word translations are not only not sentences of the second language, they are not even comprehensible to its speakers. Further, most linguists can produce numerous examples of synonyms or near synonyms that exhibit significant syntactic differences. For example, *likely* takes an infinitival complement (as in *Pat is likely to win*), but *probable* does not (hence, **Pat is probable to win*); and *have,* in the sense of possession, cannot appear in the passive voice, unlike other verbs of possession (hence, *Too many TV stations are owned/*had by fundamentalists*). Thus, the naive view appears at first to be too naive to be taken very seriously; and it was not, as indicated by the emphasis on the study of rule systems in earlier stages of generative grammar.

What has happened to change this is that syntacticians have identified the ways in which languages deviate from the naive view. They have isolated certain kinds of grammatical information that are not predictable from lexical semantics, and have developed theories to permit them to be expressed compactly. The surprising thing (to linguists) has been how little needs to be stipulated beyond lexical meaning. Languages differ (within certain specifiable limits) in constituent and word ordering, in where unbounded dependencies will be permitted, in which constituents can be omitted, in which words have syntactic idiosyncracies, and in a few other ways. They do not, as an earlier generation of linguists maintained, differ without limit. Indeed, the naive view that word meanings determine sentence structure turns out not to be a bad first approximation, though it leaves the most challenging problems in the study of syntax still to be accounted for.

In short, there is evidence here of real progress. Current theories of syntax have focussed on a few key types of phenomena, namely those that aren't fully explainable in terms of what the words in the sentences mean. These are the loci both of cross-language variation and of the most interesting linguistic universals. There is significant disagreement about what the relevant generalizations are and how they should be formulated, but there is even more significant agreement about what the important phenomena are.

Finally, it should be emphasized that all of the theories presented here, as well as the relationships among them, are in the process of fairly rapid change. It is safe to say that most of what appears in this work will be rendered obsolete within a few years. However, if my assessment that genuine progress is taking place is correct, then some familiarity with the current state of these syntactic theories should be useful to the specialist and interested non-specialist alike.

List of Abbreviations

AP	Adjective Phrase
C	variable over syntactic categories
CAP	Control Agreement Principle
COMP	Complementizer node
Det	Determiner node
ECP	Empty Category Principle
FCR	Feature Cooccurrence Restriction
FFP	Foot Feature Principle
FSD	Feature Specification Default
GB	Government-Binding Theory
GKPS	Gazdar, Klein, Pullum, and Sag (1985)
GPSG	Generalized Phrase Structure Grammar
H	head (in an ID-rule)
HFC	Head Feature Convention
ID-rule	Immediate Dominance rule
INFL	Inflection node
KB	Kaplan and Bresnan (1982)
LF	logical form
LFG	Lexical-Functional Grammar
LGB	Chomsky (1981)
LHC	Lexical Head Constraint
LP-statement	Linear Precedence statement
NP	Noun Phrase
PF	phonetic form
PP	Prepositional Phrase
PS-rule	Phrase Structure rule
QR	Quantifier Raising
S	Sentence
SAI	Subject-Auxiliary Inversion
STM	Slash Termination Metarule
TG	Transformational Grammar
UG	Universal Grammar
VP	Verb Phrase
XP	maximal projection of any major category

References

Andrews, Avery. 1984. Lexical Insertion and the Elsewhere Principle in LFG. Ms., Australian National University.

Baltin, Mark. 1982. A Landing Site Theory of Movement Rules, *Linguistic Inquiry* 13:1–38.

Bresnan, Joan. 1978. A Realistic Transformational Grammar. In M. Halle, J. Bresnan, and G. Miller (Eds.), *Linguistic Theory and Psychological Reality*. Cambridge, Mass.: MIT Press, 1–59.

Bresnan, Joan. (Ed.). 1982. *The Mental Representation of Grammatical Relations*. Cambridge, Mass.: MIT Press.

Bresnan, Joan, Per-Kristian Halvorsen, and Joan Maling. Forthcoming. Logophoricity and Bound Anaphors. CSLI, Stanford University.

Bresnan, Joan, Ronald Kaplan, and Peter Peterson. 1986. Coordination and the Flow of Information Through Phrase Structure. Ms., CSLI, Stanford University.

Bresnan, Joan and Sam Mchombo. 1986. Grammatical and Anaphoric Agreement. In A. Farley, P. Farley, and K.-E. McCullough (Eds.), *Papers from the Parasession on Pragmatics and Grammatical Theory at the 22nd Regional Meeting*. Chicago Linguistics Society, Chicago, 278–297.

Bresnan, Joan and Sam Mchombo. 1987. Topic, Pronoun, and Agreement in Chicheŵa. To appear in *Language*.

Burzio, Luigi. 1981. *Intransitive Verbs and Italian Auxiliaries*. Doctoral dissertation, MIT.

Chomsky, Noam. 1957. *Syntactic Structures*. The Hague: Mouton.

Chomsky, Noam. 1959. On Certain Formal Properties of Grammars, *Information and Control* 2:137–167.

Chomsky, Noam. 1964. *Current Issues in Linguistic Theory*. The Hague: Mouton.

Chomsky, Noam. 1965. *Aspects of the Theory of Syntax*. Cambridge, Mass.: MIT Press.

Chomsky, Noam. 1981. *Lectures on Government and Binding*. Dordrecht: Foris.

Chomsky, Noam. 1982. *Some Concepts and Consequences of the Theory of Government and Binding*. Cambridge, Mass.: MIT Press.

Chomsky, Noam. 1986a. *Knowledge of Language: Its Nature, Origins, And Use*. New York: Praeger.

Chomsky, Noam. 1986b. *Barriers*. Cambridge, Mass.: MIT Press.

Crain, Stephen and Janet D. Fodor. 1985. How Can Grammars Help Parsers? In D. Dowty, L. Karttunen, and A. Zwicky (Eds.), *Natural Language Parsing: Psychological, Computational, and Theoretical Perspectives*. New York: Cambridge University Press, 94–128.

Dowty, David. 1982. Grammatical Relations and Montague Grammar. In P. Jacobson and G. K. Pullum (Eds.), *The Nature of Syntactic Representation*. Dordrecht: Reidel, 79–130.

Emonds, Joseph. 1976. *A Transformational Approach to English Syntax*. New York: Academic Press.

Fassi Fehri, Abdelkader. To appear. Agreement in Arabic, Binding, and Coherence. In M. Barlow and C. A. Ferguson (Eds.), *Agreement in Natural Language: Approaches, Theories, Descriptions*. CSLI, Stanford University.

Flickinger, Daniel. 1983. Lexical Heads and Phrasal Gaps. In M. Barlow, D. Flickinger, and M. Wescoat (Eds.), *Proceedings of WCCFL 2*. Stanford Linguistics Association, 89–101.

Fodor, Jerry A., Thomas Bever, and Merrill Garrett. 1974. *The Psychology of Language*. New York: McGraw-Hill.

Gazdar, Gerald. 1981. Unbounded Dependencies and Coordinate Structure, *Linguistic Inquiry* 12:155–184.

Gazdar, Gerald. 1982. Phrase Structure Grammar. In P. Jacobson and G. K. Pullum (Eds.), *The Nature of Syntactic Representation*. Dordrecht: Reidel, 131–186.

Gazdar, Gerald, Ewan Klein, Geoffrey K. Pullum, and Ivan Sag. 1985. *Generalized Phrase Structure Grammar*. Cambridge, Mass.: Harvard University Press.

Gazdar, Gerald and Geoffrey K. Pullum. 1981. Subcategorization, Constituent Order, and the Notion *Head*. In M. Moortgat, H. van der Hulst, and T. Hoekstra (Eds.), *The Scope of Lexical Rules*. Dordrecht: Foris, 107–123.

Gazdar, Gerald, Geoffrey K. Pullum, and Ivan Sag: 1982. Auxiliaries and Related Phenomena in a Restrictive Theory of Grammar, *Language* 58:591–638.

Goldberg, Jeffrey. 1985. Lexical Operations and Unbounded Dependencies. In W. Eilfort, P. Kroeber, and K. Peterson (Eds.), *Papers from the 21st Regional Meeting*. Chicago Linguistics Society, 122–132.

Grimshaw, Jane. 1982. Subcategorization and Grammatical Relations. In A. Zaenen (Ed.), *Subjects and Other Subjects: Proceedings of the Harvard Conference on the Representation of Grammatical Relations*. Bloomington: Indiana University Linguistics Club, 35–55.

Gruber, Jeffrey. 1965. *Studies in Lexical Relations*. Doctoral dissertation, MIT.

Halvorsen, Per-Kristian. 1983. Semantics for Lexical-Functional Grammar, *Linguistic Inquiry* 14:567–615.

Hornstein, Norbert. 1984. *Logic as Grammar*. Cambridge, Mass.: MIT Press.

Huang, C.-T. James. 1982. *Logical Relations in Chinese and the Theory of Grammar*. Doctoral dissertation, MIT.

Iida, Masayo, Stephen Wechsler, and Draga Zec. (Eds.). To appear. *Studies in Grammatical Theory and Discourse Structure, Volume I: Interactions of Morphology, Syntax, and Discourse*. CSLI: Stanford University.

Ishikawa, Akira. 1985. *Complex Predicates and Lexical Operations in Japanese*. Doctoral dissertation, Stanford University.

Jackendoff, Ray. 1972. *Semantic Interpretation in Generative Grammar*. Cambridge, Mass.: MIT Press.

Jaeggli, Osvaldo. 1984. Subject Extraction and the Null Subject Parameter. In C. Jones and P. Sells (Eds.), *Proceedings of NELS* 14. Graduate Linguistic Student Association, University of Massachusetts at Amherst, 132–153.

Kameyama, Megumi. 1984. Subjective/Logophoric Bound Anaphor *Zibun*. In J. Drogo, V. Mishra, and D. Testen (Eds.), *Papers from the 20th Regional Meeting*. Chicago Linguistics Society, Chicago, 228–238.

Kameyama, Megumi. 1985. *Zero Anaphora: The Case of Japanese*. Doctoral dissertation, Stanford University.

Kaplan, Ronald and Joan Bresnan. 1982. Lexical-Functional Grammar: A Formal System for Grammatical Representation. In Bresnan (Ed.), 173–281.

Kaplan, Ronald and Annie Zaenen. 1986. Long-Distance Dependencies and Constituent Structure. Ms., Xerox-PARC.

Kayne, Richie. 1984. *Connectedness and Binary Branching*. Dordrecht: Foris.

Keenan, Edward L. 1974. The Functional Principle: Generalizing the Notion of *Subject Of*. In M. La Galy, R. Fox, and A. Bruck (Eds.), *Papers from the 10th Regional Meeting*. Chicago Linguistics Society, Chicago, 298–309.

Koopman, Hilda. 1984. *The Syntax of Verbs: from Verb Movement Rules in the Kru Languages to Universal Grammar*. Dordrecht: Foris.

Lasnik, Howard and Mamoru Saito. 1984. On the Nature of Proper Government, *Linguistic Inquiry* 15:235–289.

Levin, Lori. 1985. *Operations on Lexical Forms: Unaccusative Rules in Germanic Languages*. Doctoral dissertation, MIT.

Levin, Lori, Malka Rappaport, and Annie Zaenen. (Eds.). 1983. *Papers in Lexical-Functional Grammar*. Bloomington: Indiana University Linguistics Club.

Manzini, Maria Rita. 1983. On Control and Control Theory, *Linguistic Inquiry* 14:421–446.

May, Robert. 1985. *Logical Form: Its Structure and Derivation*. Cambridge, Mass.: MIT Press.

Mohanan, K. P. 1983. Functional and Anaphoric Control, *Linguistic Inquiry* 14:641–674.

Montague, Richard. 1974. *Formal Philosophy: Selected Papers of Richard Montague*, R. Thomason (Ed.). New Haven: Yale University Press.

Newmeyer, Frederick. 1980. *Linguistic Theory in America: The First Quarter-Century of Transformational Generative Grammar*. New York: Academic Press.

Newmeyer, Frederick. 1983. *Grammatical Theory: Its Limits and Its Possibilities*. Chicago: University of Chicago Press.

Nishigauchi, Taisuke. 1984. Japanese LF: Subjacency vs. ECP. To appear in *Seoul Papers On Formal Grammar Theory*.

Nishigauchi, Taisuke. To appear. *Quantification in Syntax*. Doctoral dissertation, University of Massachusetts at Amherst.

Perlmutter, David. (Ed.). 1983. *Studies in Relational Grammar 1*. Chicago: University of Chicago Press.

Perlmutter, David and Carol Rosen. (Eds.). 1984. *Studies in Relational Grammar 2*. Chicago: University of Chicago Press.

Pesetsky, David. 1982. *Paths and Categories*. Doctoral dissertation, MIT.

Peters, Stanley and Robert Ritchie. 1973. On the Generative Power of Transformational Grammars, *Information and Control* 18:483–501.

Pinker, Steven. 1984. *Language Learnability and Language Development*. Cambridge, Mass.: Harvard University Press.

Pollard, Carl. 1984. *Generalized Phrase Structure Grammars, Head Grammars, and Natural Language*. Doctoral dissertation, Stanford University. To appear, Cambridge: Cambridge University Press.

Pollard, Carl. 1985. Phrase Structure Grammar Without Metarules. In J. Goldberg, S. Mackaye, and M. Wescoat (Eds.), *Proceedings of WCCFL 4*. Stanford Linguistics Association, 246–261.

Pollard, Carl and Ivan Sag. 1983. Reflexives and Reciprocals in English: An Alternative to the Binding Theory. In M. Barlow, D. Flickinger, and M. Wescoat (Eds.), *Proceedings of WCCFL 2*. Stanford Linguistics Association, 189–203.

Pullum, Geoffrey K. and Gerald Gazdar. 1982. Natural Languages and Context-free Languages, *Linguistics and Philosophy* 4:471–504.

Rappaport, Malka. 1983. On the Nature of Derived Nominals. In Levin et al., 113–142.

Reinhart, Tanya. 1983. *Anaphora and Semantic Interpretation*. London: Croom Helm.

van Riemsdijk, Henk and Edwin Williams. 1986. *Introduction to the Theory of Grammar*. Cambridge, Mass.: MIT Press.

Rizzi, Luigi. 1982. *Issues in Italian Syntax*. Dordrecht: Foris.

Rizzi, Luigi. 1986. Null Objects in Italian and the Theory of *pro*, *Linguistic Inquiry* 17:501–557.

Safir, Kenneth. 1985. *Syntactic Chains*. New York: Cambridge University Press.

Sag, Ivan. 1986. Grammatical Hierarchy and Linear Precedence. CSLI Report No. 60, Stanford University. Also to appear in G. Huck and A. Ojeda (Eds.), *Discontinuous Constituency (Syntax and Semantics Vol. 20)*. New York: Academic Press.

Sag, Ivan, Gerald Gazdar, Thomas Wasow, and Steven Weisler. 1985. Coordination and How to Distinguish Categories, *Natural Language and Linguistic Theory* 3:117–171.

Sag, Ivan and Carl Pollard. 1986. Head-Driven Phrase Structure Grammar: An Informal Synopsis. To appear as a CSLI Report, Stanford University.

Saiki, Mariko. 1985. On the Coordination of Gapped Constituents in Japanese. In W. Eilfort, P. Kroeber, and K. Peterson (Eds.), *Papers from the 21st Regional Meeting*. Chicago Linguistics Society, Chicago, 371–387.

Simpson, Jane. 1983. *Aspects of Warlpiri Morphology and Syntax*. Doctoral dissertation, MIT.

Simpson, Jane and Joan Bresnan. 1983. Control and Obviation in Warlpiri, *Natural Language and Linguistic Theory* 1:49–64.

Sproat, Richard. 1985. Welsh Syntax and VSO Structure, *Natural Language and Linguistic Theory* 3:173–216.

Stowell, Timothy. 1981. *Origins of Phrase Structure*. Doctoral dissertation, MIT.

Travis, Lisa. 1984. *Parameters and Effects of Word Order Variation*. Doctoral dissertation, MIT.

Uszkoreit, Hans. 1984. *Word Order and Constituent Structure in German.* Doctoral dissertation, University of Texas at Austin.

Wager, Jan. 1983. *Complementation in Moroccan Arabic.* Doctoral dissertation, MIT.

Williams, Edwin. 1981. Argument Structure and Morphology, *Linguistic Review* 1:81–114.

Williams, Edwin. 1984. Grammatical Relations, *Linguistic Inquiry* 15:639–673.

Zaenen, Annie. 1983. On Syntactic Binding, *Linguistic Inquiry* 14:469–504.

Index of Names

Andrews, Avery, 159.

Baltin, Mark, 46.
Bever, Thomas, 195.
Bresnan, Joan, 135, 138, 158, 161, 179, 191, 199–200, 202.
Burzio, Luigi, 200.

Chomsky, Noam, 2–5, 15, 19–20, 26–27, 30, 32–34, 36–37, 41–42, 45, 53, 55, 61, 68, 76, 193, 195–201.
Crain, Stephen, 198.

Dowty, David, 99, 200.

Emonds, Joseph, 201.

Fassi Fehri, Abdelkader, 181, 191.
Flickinger, Daniel, 133.
Fodor, Janet D., 198.
Fodor, Jerry A., 195.
Ford, Marilyn, 199.

Garrett, Merrill, 195.
Gazdar, Gerald, 77, 86, 103, 133, 198.
Goldberg, Jeffrey, 49, 124, 133.
Grimshaw, Jane, 157.
Gruber, Jeffrey, 35.

Halvorsen, Per-Kristian, 165, 191.
Hornstein, Norbert, 76.
Huang, James, 47, 76.

Iida, Masayo, 191.
Ishikawa, Akira, 144, 191.

Jackendoff, Ray, 35.
Jaeggli, Osvaldo, 67.

Kameyama, Megumi, 179, 191.
Kaplan, Ronald, 135, 179, 181–182, 189, 191, 198, 202.
Katz, Jerrold, 195.
Kay, Martin, 149.
Kayne, Richie, 32, 49, 55, 65, 76.
Keenan, Edward L., 113.
Koopman, Hilda, 76.

Lasnik, Howard, 64.
Levin, Lori, 138, 157, 161, 191.

Maling, Joan, 191.
Manzini, Maria Rita, 76.
May, Robert, 76.
Mohanan, K. P., 191.
Montague, Richard, 99.

Newmeyer, Frederick, 16–17, 195.
Nishigauchi, Taisuke, 76.

Perlmutter, David, 135, 199.
Pesetsky, David, 32, 49.
Peters, Stanley, 196.
Peterson, Peter, 179, 191.
Pinker, Steven, 199.
Pollard, Carl, 78, 100, 112, 133, 204.

Postal, Paul, 61, 195, 199.
Pullum, Geoffrey K., 86, 103, 133,
    198.

Rappaport, Malka, 156, 191.
Reinhart, Tanya, 38–39.
van Riemsdijk, Henk, 76.
Ritchie, Robert, 196.
Rizzi, Luigi, 48, 50, 65–67, 72, 76.
Rosen, Carol, 135.

Safir, Kenneth, 67, 72.
Sag, Ivan, 84, 100, 103, 112, 133.
Saiki, Mariko, 191.
Saito, Mamoru, 64.
Simpson, Jane, 139, 144, 191.
Stowell, Timothy, 30, 42, 54–55,
    57, 76.

Travis, Lisa, 76.

Uszkoreit, Hans, 118.

Wager, Jan, 191.
Wasow, Thomas, 96.
Wechsler, Stephen, 191.
Williams, Edwin, 35, 76.

Zaenen, Annie, 49, 124, 179, 181–
    182, 189, 191, 202.
Zec, Draga, 191.

Index of Subjects

A-Binding, 69, 72–73.
A-Free, 72–73.
A-Movement, 57–58.
A-Position, 44–45, 57, 62, 69.
Ā-Binding, 62, 64, 69, 72–73.
Ā-Movement, 47, 57.
Ā-Position, 44–45, 57, 64.
Adjacency, 54–56, 61.
Adjunction, 46–47, 66.
Admissible Projection, 101.
Affix, 13, 160.
AGR (feature), 84, 88, 95, 104,
    113–116.
AGR (in INFL), 45–46.
Anaphoric Binding, 151, 165, 174–
    179, 182, 184, 191.
Anaphoric Control, 165, 171–174.
Argument, 28, 31–32, 35–38, 40,
    44, 54, 56, 58, 60, 71, 89, 96,
    107, 113, 117–118, 147, 151,
    157, 161, 169, 170, 173, 175.
    See also External Argument,
    Internal Argument.
Argument Structure, 35–36.
Atom-Valued Feature, 83.
Attribute, 136, 141, 143–146, 149–
    151, 159, 166, 179, 183, 185–
    187, 189.
Auxiliary (Aux), 20, 94, 102–103,
    139.
Auxiliary Reduction, 20.

Bach's Generalization, 167.

BAR, 82–84, 86, 88–89, 96, 102,
    104–106.
[BAR 2], 120, 122, 128, 130. *See
    also* Maximal Projection.
Barrier, 40–41, 75.
Binding Theory, 34, 42, 45, 58–59,
    67–74, 100.
Bounding Node, 48–50, 52, 203.

C-Command, 38–42, 64, 66–67,
    71–72, 87, 178.
C-Selection (Categorial-Selection),
    32, 36.
C-Structure, 136–140, 142, 144,
    146–147, 153–154, 163, 168–169,
    172, 174, 178, 180–181, 183.
Candidate Projection, 101.
Case (Case Theory), 28, 42–43,
    52–61, 64, 73, 117, 161.
Case Filter, 53, 55, 57, 73, 157.
Category-Valued Feature, 84, 110.
Causativization, 162–163.
Chain, 43, 53, 57, 75.
Characteristic Function, 98.
Clitic, 152.
Closed Function, 156.
Coherence Condition, 146–147,
    152, 181–182, 203. *See also* Ex-
    tended Coherence Condition.
Coindexing, 44–45, 68.
COMP-Trace Effects, 65–66, 127,
    189.
Complementary Distribution, 68.

Complementizer, 30, 49, 61–64, 82–83, 88, 103, 117, 119, 127, 141.

Completeness Condition, 146–147, 182, 203.

Compositionality, 97.

Consistency Condition, 146. *See also* Functional Uniqueness.

Constituent, 9, 11, 119.

Constraining Equation, 145, 159.

Control, 68, 73–76, 114, 165, 191, 199.

Control Agreement Principle, 101, 112–117.

Controllee, 113–116.

Coordinate Structure Constraint, 131–132, 189.

Coordination, 82, 107, 117, 120, 127–132, 179, 186–191.

D-Structure, 19–23, 31–34, 36–38, 42–45, 48, 51–52, 56, 201.

Deep Structure, 16, 19, 195, 199, 201.

Defining Equation, 145, 159.

Descriptive Adequacy, 195, 197, 199–200.

Directionality of Case and θ-Role Assignment, 56.

Ditransitive Verb, 55–56.

Empty Category, 34, 42–44, 52–53, 62–65, 67–68, 70–73, 92, 122, 165, 180. *See also* NP-Trace, Trace, *wh*-Trace.

Empty Category Principle (ECP), 42, 62–66, 70, 123, 202.

Equi-NP Deletion, 114, 200.

Exceptional Case Marking, 60.

Exocentric, 140.

Explanatory Adequacy, 195–196, 200.

Extended Coherence Condition, 181.

Extended Projection Principle, 34, 37, 43.

External Argument, 36, 43, 55, 58.

Extraposition, 95.

Extraposition Metarule, 94.

F-Command, 178–179, 184–185.

F-Description, 148–149.

F-Structure, 135–151, 153–154, 160, 163–165, 172, 175, 178–181, 183–184, 186–199.

Feature Cooccurrence Restriction (FCR), 94, 101–104, 106, 121–122, 124, 127.

Feature Specification Default (FSD), 101, 103–104, 116–117, 121.

Features, 80–84.

Finite Domain Parameter, 176.

FOCUS, 156, 180–182, 185, 189.

FOOT Feature, 107–112, 121, 123, 131, 133.

Foot Feature Principle (FFP), 101, 107–112, 124, 131–132, 149.

Function-Argument Biuniqueness, 158, 203.

Functional Control, 163–171, 173, 180–182, 185.

Functional Locality, 166.

Functional Realization, 99.

Functional Schemata, 140.

Functional Uniqueness, 146, 166, 182. *See also* Consistency Condition.

Generalized Phrase Structure Grammar (GPSG), 15, 26, 32, 52, 60, 78–133, 136–137, 140–141, 157, 160, 186–188, 197–198, 200–204.

Generative Grammar, 3, 194, 196.

Generative Semantics, 195–196.

Governable Grammatical Function, 146.

Governing Category, 69–73.

Government, 38–42, 53, 55, 60–65, 71, 73, 75, 80, 87, 123. *See also* Proper Government.

Government-Binding Theory (GB), 19–76, 78, 80–81, 87–88, 99–100, 114, 117–118, 122–123, 126, 132–133, 136–139, 147, 157–158, 161–162, 165, 171, 178, 180, 197, 201–204.

Grammatical Relations, 99, 199.

Head, 27–28, 30–32, 35–38, 40, 44, 62, 64–66, 81, 86–87, 89, 91, 102, 104, 117, 123, 140, 144, 165.

HEAD Feature, 86, 90–91, 105, 107–108, 113, 123–124, 128, 130–131.

Head Feature Convention (HFC), 86, 101, 105–108, 116–117, 124, 128, 130, 140, 187.

Head Grammar, 100.

Head-Driven Phrase Structure Grammar (HPSG), 133, 204.

ID-Rule, 79, 88–91, 94, 97, 107, 109, 111, 116, 118, 204. *See also* Lexical ID-Rule, Non-Lexical ID-Rule.

ID/LP Format, 84–86.

Inclusion, 183.

INF, 117.

Infinitive, 30, 46, 53, 73, 96, 165, 177.

INFL, 20, 26, 30, 41, 45, 47, 53, 56, 62–63, 70, 73, 81, 114.

Inherited Features, 109.

Instantiated Features, 109–112, 132.

Instantiation of Metavariables, 147.

Intensional Logic, 97.

Internal Argument, 36, 38, 42, 58.

Intransitive Verb, 14, 58, 91, 163, 189.

INV, 93–94, 101–104.

Island Constraints, 48, 182, 202.

Labelled Bracketing, 11.

Landing Sites, 38, 46–47.

Lexical Form, 157.

Lexical Head Constraint (LHC), 94, 122–123, 125, 133, 202.

Lexical ID-Rule, 89, 118, 122, 133.

Lexical Rule, 133, 136, 154, 158, 160–164, 167.

Lexical-Functional Grammar (LFG), 52, 60, 76, 88, 135–191, 197–204.

Lexicon, 13–15, 137, 154–164.

Licensing, 34, 62.

Linear Precedence Statements (LP-Statements), 89, 101, 117–119, 129.

Logical Form (LF), 19–20, 23–24, 33, 42, 46–47, 51–53, 57, 62, 64–65, 76. *See also* Quantifier, Quantifier Raising, Wide Scope.

Long-Distance Dependency, 171, 179–186, 189–191. *See also* Unbounded Dependency.

Major Category, 83.
Maximal Projection, 28, 30–32, 38–41, 52, 59, 61, 64, 82, 84, 90, 95, 103, 143, 157, 165, 182, 186. *See also* [BAR 2].
Metarule, 89–97, 122–123, 133, 136, 161.
Minor Category, 83, 88.
Model-Theoretic Semantics, 78.
Modifier, 28, 107, 118, 141.
Montague Grammar, 78, 97, 99–100, 136, 198.
Morphology, 13, 43, 87, 91, 111, 124.
Mother, 11, 86, 90–91, 93, 95, 99, 105–106, 109–111, 126, 128, 130–132, 140, 142–143, 149, 187.
Move-α, 21–23, 25–26, 37, 42–46, 48, 55, 136, 201.

NFORM, 104, 107, 116.
Node-Admissibility Conditions, 79.
Nominalization, 191.
Non-Lexical ID-rule, 119, 123, 125.
NP-Movement, 42–44, 47, 55, 58–59, 61.
NP-Trace, 43, 70, 165.
Nucleus (F-Structure), 170, 174–178, 184, 186, 188.
NULL, 107, 121, 125–126.

Observational Adequacy, 194, 197, 200.
Open Function, 156.

Parameter, 26, 46, 48, 50, 54, 56, 65, 71, 197.
Passive, 16, 21–22, 33–34, 37, 43–45, 55–56, 58, 61, 88, 91, 104, 154, 160–162, 167–168, 201.
Passive Metarule, 92.
Phonetic Form (PF), 19–21, 53, 58, 81, 136.
Phonology, 13.
Phrase Structure Rule (PS-rule), 11–13, 15, 20, 31, 76–80, 84–85, 87, 92, 138, 140, 157, 186.
Predicate-Argument Structure, 156–157, 182.
Predicative Category, 99, 113–114, 126.
Preterminal Symbol, 13, 141–142.
PRO, 68, 73–76, 165.
pro, 71–72, 76.
Projection Function, 100–101, 113, 117.
Projection Principle, 33–34, 37, 42–43, 46, 201, 203.
Pronoun, 67–73, 75, 100, 107, 116, 165, 170, 174–175, 178.
Proper Government, 62–66, 70, 73, 123, 127.

Quantifier, 23–24, 46, 65, 133.
Quantifier Raising, 46–47, 57.

R-Expression, 67, 69, 72.
Raising to Object, 59, 88, 114.
Raising to Subject (Subject-to-Subject Raising), 16, 58, 75, 93, 114, 157.
Recursion, 2, 12.

Reflexive (Reflexive Pronoun), 67–68, 70, 100, 107, 112–113, 165, 170, 174–175, 178–180, 184–186.
Relational Grammar, 135, 199.
Rule R, 20, 26.
Rule-to-Tree Definition, 79–80.

S-Selection (Semantic-Selection), 36.
S-Structure, 19–21, 23, 33–34, 42–43, 45–46, 52–53, 55–56, 59, 62, 64, 67, 136, 201.
S'-Deletion, 58–61, 70, 203.
Scope, 23–24, 46, 133, 189.
Semantic Form, 145, 156.
Semantically Restricted Function, 156, 172–173.
Semantically Unrestricted Function, 156, 166, 168, 172–173.
Semantics, 97–100.
Sister, 11, 28, 32, 40–41, 87–88, 103, 108, 114, 117, 123.
SLASH, 112, 121–122, 124, 126, 131–132, 201.
Slash Termination Metarules, 121–122, 125–127, 202.
Specifier, 28, 30.
Strong Crossover, 72.
SUBCAT, 87–89, 102, 105–106, 117, 124, 127, 129–130.
Subcategorization, 14–15, 31–38, 41, 60, 80–81, 84, 86–89, 94, 102, 116, 118, 131, 133, 139, 142, 146, 151, 154–159, 161–162, 165, 168–169, 175, 182, 188, 199, 203–204.
Subjacency, 48–52, 76.
Subject-Verb Agreement, 20, 45–46, 84, 88, 112.

SUBJective Function, 174–175, 185–186.
Superiority, 64.
Surface Structure, 16, 19, 195, 201.

Terminal Symbol, 13, 117.
that-Trace Effects. See COMP-Trace Effects.
θ-Criterion, 36–38, 43–44, 53, 59, 76, 147, 158, 203.
θ-Marking, 37–38, 53, 60.
θ-Position, 44, 58.
θ-Role (Thematic Role), 35–38, 42–44, 55–60, 75–76, 84, 150, 161, 203.
θ-Theory, 35–38.
$\bar{\theta}$-Position, 44, 46, 58.
TOPIC, 156, 180–182.
Trace, 42, 55, 62. See also Empty Category.
Transformational Grammar (TG), 15–16, 19–22, 31, 33, 46, 59, 66, 78, 90, 92, 154, 171, 189, 194, 196, 198–202.
Transformations, 15–16, 33, 42, 48, 58–59, 72, 92, 119–120, 132, 195.
Transitive Verb, 14, 43, 87, 99, 189.
TYP, 98–99.

Unbounded Dependency, 111, 119–127, 131–132, 179, 201–202. See also Long-Distance Dependency.
Unification, 109, 149–152.
Universal Grammar (UG), 22–27, 80, 101, 119, 197.

Variable, 44, 72. See also wh-Trace.

Visser's Generalization, 167.

Wh-Feature, 52.
wh-Movement, 42, 44, 47, 57, 77.
wh-Phrase, 16, 46–49, 51, 57, 64,
    72, 133, 159.
wh-Trace, 44, 72, 122.
Wide Scope, 23, 66.

X′-Theory, 27–32, 38, 40, 44, 81–
    83, 86–87, 96, 99, 107, 139–141,
    143–144.

CSLI Publications

Reports

Titles distributed by CSLI may be ordered directly from CSLI Publications, Ventura Hall, Stanford University, Stanford, California 94305-4115 or by phone (415)723-1712, (415)723-1839. Orders can also be placed by e-mail (pubs@csli.stanford.edu) or FAX (415)723-0758. All orders must be prepaid by check or Visa or MasterCard (include card name, number, and expiration date). For shipping and handling, add $2 for first book and $0.50 for each additional book; $1.50 for first report and $0.25 for each additional report. California residents add 7.25% sales tax. For overseas shipping, add $3 for first book and $1 for each additional book; $2 for first report and $0.50 for each additional report. All payments must be made in U.S. currency.

The Situation in Logic–I Jon Barwise CSLI842 ($2.00)

Coordination and How to Distinguish Categories Ivan Sag, Gerald Gazdar, Thomas Wasow, and Steven Weisler CSLI843 ($3.50)

Belief and Incompleteness Kurt Konolige CSLI844 ($4.50)

Equality, Types, Modules and Generics for Logic Programming Joseph Goguen and José Meseguer CSLI845 ($2.50)

Lessons from Bolzano Johan van Benthem CSLI846 ($1.50)

Self-propagating Search: A Unified Theory of Memory Pentti Kanerva CSLI847 ($9.00)

Reflection and Semantics in LISP Brian Cantwell Smith CSLI848 ($2.50)

The Implementation of Procedurally Reflective Languages Jim des Rivières and Brian Cantwell Smith CSLI849 ($3.00)

Parameterized Programming Joseph Goguen CSLI8410 ($3.50)

Shifting Situations and Shaken Attitudes Jon Barwise and John Perry CSLI8413 ($4.50)

Completeness of Many-Sorted Equational Logic Joseph Goguen and José Meseguer CSLI8415 ($2.50)

Moving the Semantic Fulcrum Terry Winograd CSLI8417 ($1.50)

On the Mathematical Properties of Linguistic Theories C. Raymond Perrault CSLI8418 ($3.00)

A Simple and Efficient Implementation of Higher-order Functions in LISP Michael P. Georgeff and Stephen F.Bodnar CSLI8419 ($4.50)

On the Axiomatization of "if-then-else" Irène Guessarian and José Meseguer CSLI8520 ($3.00)

The Situation in Logic–II: Conditionals and Conditional Information Jon Barwise CSLI8421 ($3.00)

Principles of OBJ2 Kokichi Futatsugi, Joseph A. Goguen, Jean-Pierre Jouannaud, and José Meseguer CSLI8522 ($2.00)

Querying Logical Databases Moshe Vardi CSLI8523 ($1.50)

Computationally Relevant Properties of Natural Languages and Their Grammar Gerald Gazdar and Geoff Pullum CSLI8524 ($3.50)

An Internal Semantics for Modal Logic: Preliminary Report Ronald Fagin and Moshe Vardi CSLI8525 ($2.00)

The Situation in Logic–III: Situations, Sets and the Axiom of Foundation Jon Barwise CSLI8526 ($2.50)

Semantic Automata Johan van Benthem CSLI8527 ($2.50)

Restrictive and Non-Restrictive Modification Peter Sells CSLI8528 ($3.00)

Institutions: Abstract Model Theory for Computer Science J. A. Goguen and R. M. Burstall CSLI8530 ($4.50)

A Formal Theory of Knowledge and Action Robert C. Moore CSLI8531 ($5.50)

Finite State Morphology: A Review of Koskenniemi (1983) Gerald Gazdar CSLI8532 ($1.50)

The Role of Logic in Artificial Intelligence Robert C. Moore CSLI8533 ($2.00)

Applicability of Indexed Grammars to Natural Languages Gerald Gazdar CSLI8534 ($2.00)

Commonsense Summer: Final Report Jerry R. Hobbs, et al CSLI8535 ($12.00)

Limits of Correctness in Computers Brian Cantwell Smith CSLI8536 ($2.50)

On the Coherence and Structure of Discourse Jerry R. Hobbs CSLI8537 ($3.00)

The Coherence of Incoherent Discourse Jerry R. Hobbs and Michael H. Agar CSLI8538 ($2.50)

A Complete, Type-free "Second-order" Logic and Its Philosophical Foundations Christopher Menzel CSLI8640 ($4.50)

Possible-world Semantics for Autoepistemic Logic Robert C. Moore CSLI8541 ($2.00)

Deduction with Many-Sorted Rewrite José Meseguer and Joseph A. Goguen CSLI8542 ($1.50)

On Some Formal Properties of Metarules Hans Uszkoreit and Stanley Peters CSLI8543 ($1.50)

Language, Mind, and Information John Perry CSLI8544 ($2.00)

Constraints on Order Hans Uszkoreit CSLI8646 ($3.00)

Linear Precedence in Discontinuous Constituents: Complex Fronting in German Hans Uszkoreit CSLI8647 ($2.50)

A Compilation of Papers on Unification-Based Grammar Formalisms, Parts I and II Stuart M. Shieber, Fernando C.N. Pereira, Lauri Karttunen, and Martin Kay CSLI8648 ($10.00)

An Algorithm for Generating Quantifier Scopings Jerry R. Hobbs and Stuart M. Shieber CSLI8649 ($2.50)

Verbs of Change, Causation, and Time Dorit Abusch CSLI8650 ($2.00)

Noun-Phrase Interpretation Mats Rooth CSLI8651 ($2.00)

Noun Phrases, Generalized Quantifiers and Anaphora Jon Barwise CSLI8652 ($2.50)

Circumstantial Attitudes and Benevolent Cognition John Perry CSLI8653 ($1.50)

A Study in the Foundations of Programming Methodology: Specifications, Institutions, Charters and Parchments Joseph A. Goguen and R. M. Burstall CSLI8654 ($2.50)

Intentionality, Information, and Matter Ivan Blair CSLI8656 ($3.00)

Computer Aids for Comparative Dictionaries Mark Johnson CSLI8658 ($2.00)

A Sheaf-Theoretic Model of Concurrency Luís F. Monteiro and Fernando C. N. Pereira CSLI8662 ($3.00)

Discourse, Anaphora and Parsing Mark Johnson and Ewan Klein CSLI8663 ($2.00)

Tarski on Truth and Logical Consequence John Etchemendy CSLI8664 ($3.50)

The LFG Treatment of Discontinuity and the Double Infinitive Construction in Dutch Mark Johnson CSLI8665 ($2.50)

Categorial Unification Grammars Hans Uszkoreit CSLI8666 ($2.50)

Generalized Quantifiers and Plurals Godehard Link CSLI8667 ($2.00)

Radical Lexicalism Lauri Karttunen CSLI8668 ($2.50)

What is Intention? Michael E. Bratman CSLI8669 ($2.00)

Understanding Computers and Cognition: Four Reviews and a Response Mark Stefik, Editor CSLI8770 ($3.50)

The Correspondence Continuum Brian Cantwell Smith CSLI8771 ($4.00)

The Role of Propositional Objects of Belief in Action David J. Israel CSLI8772 ($2.50)

Two Replies Jon Barwise CSLI8774 ($3.00)

Semantics of Clocks Brian Cantwell Smith CSLI8775 ($2.50)

HPSG: An Informal Synopsis Carl Pollard and Ivan A. Sag CSLI8779 ($4.50)

The Situated Processing of Situated Language Susan Stucky CSLI8780 ($1.50)

Muir: A Tool for Language Design Terry Winograd CSLI8781 ($2.50)

Final Algebras, Cosemicomputable Algebras, and Degrees of Unsolvability Lawrence S. Moss, José Meseguer, and Joseph A. Goguen CSLI8782 ($3.00)

The Synthesis of Digital Machines with Provable Epistemic Properties Stanley J. Rosenschein and Leslie Pack Kaelbling CSLI8783 ($3.50)

An Architecture for Intelligent Reactive Systems Leslie Pack Kaelbling CSLI8785 ($2.00)

Order-Sorted Unification José Meseguer, Joseph A. Goguen, and Gert Smolka CSLI8786 ($2.50)

Modular Algebraic Specification of Some Basic Geometrical Constructions Joseph A. Goguen CSLI8787 ($2.50)

Persistence, Intention and Commitment Phil Cohen and Hector Levesque CSLI8788 ($3.50)

Rational Interaction as the Basis for Communication Phil Cohen and Hector Levesque CSLI8789 ($4.00)

Models and Equality for Logical Programming Joseph A. Goguen and José Meseguer CSLI8791 ($3.00)

Order-Sorted Algebra Solves the Constructor-Selector, Mulitple Representation and Coercion Problems Joseph A. Goguen and José Meseguer CSLI8792 ($2.00)

Extensions and Foundations for Object-Oriented Programming Joseph A. Goguen and José Meseguer CSLI8793 ($3.50)

L3 Reference Manual: Version 2.19 William Poser CSLI8794 ($2.50)

Change, Process and Events Carol E. Cleland CSLI8895 ($4.00)

One, None, a Hundred Thousand Specification Languages Joseph A. Goguen CSLI8796 ($2.00)

Constituent Coordination in HPSG Derek Proudian and David Goddeau CSLI8797 ($1.50)

A Language/Action Perspective on the Design of Cooperative Work Terry Winograd CSLI8798 ($2.50)

Implicature and Definite Reference Jerry R. Hobbs CSLI8799 ($1.50)

Thinking Machines: Can There be? Are we? Terry Winograd CSLI87100 ($2.50)

Situation Semantics and Semantic Interpretation in Constraint-based Grammars Per-Kristian Halvorsen CSLI87101 ($1.50)

Category Structures Gerald Gazdar, Geoffrey K. Pullum, Robert Carpenter, Ewan Klein, Thomas E. Hukari, Robert D. Levine CSLI87102 ($3.00)

Cognitive Theories of Emotion Ronald Alan Nash CSLI87103 ($2.50)

Toward an Architecture for Resource-bounded Agents Martha E. Pollack, David J. Israel, and Michael E. Bratman CSLI87104 ($2.00)

On the Relation Between Default and Autoepistemic Logic Kurt Konolige CSLI87105 ($3.00)

Three Responses to Situation Theory Terry Winograd CSLI87106 ($2.50)

Tools for Morphological Analysis Mary Dalrymple, Ronald M. Kaplan, Lauri Karttunen, Kimmo Koskenniemi, Sami Shaio, Michael Wescoat CSLI87108 ($10.00)

Fourth Year Report of the Situated Language Research Program CSLI87111 (free)

Bare Plurals, Naked Relatives, and Their Kin Dietmar Zaefferer CSLI87112 ($2.50)

Events and "Logical Form" Stephen Neale CSLI88113 ($2.00)

Backwards Anaphora and Discourse Structure: Some Considerations Peter Sells CSLI87114 ($2.50)

Toward a Linking Theory of Relation Changing Rules in LFG Lori Levin CSLI87115 ($4.00)

Fuzzy Logic L. A. Zadeh CSLI88116 ($2.50)

Dispositional Logic and Commonsense Reasoning L. A. Zadeh CSLI88117 ($2.00)

Intention and Personal Policies Michael Bratman CSLI88118 ($2.00)

Unification and Agreement Michael Barlow CSLI88120 ($2.50)

Extended Categorial Grammar Suson Yoo and Kiyong Lee CSLI88121 ($4.00)

Unaccusative Verbs in Dutch and the Syntax-Semantics Interface Annie Zaenen CSLI88123 ($3.00)

What Is Unification? A Categorical View of Substitution, Equation and Solution Joseph A. Goguen CSLI88124 ($3.50)

Types and Tokens in Linguistics Sylvain Bromberger CSLI88125 ($3.00)

Determination, Uniformity, and Relevance: Normative Criteria for Generalization and Reasoning by Analogy Todd Davies CSLI88126 ($4.50)

Modal Subordination and Pronominal Anaphora in Discourse Craige Roberts CSLI88127 ($4.50)

The Prince and the Phone Booth: Reporting Puzzling Beliefs Mark Crimmins and John Perry CSLI88128 ($3.50)

Set Values for Unification-Based Grammar Formalisms and Logic Programming William Rounds CSLI88129 ($4.00)

Fifth Year Report of the Situated Language Research Program CSLI88130 (free)

Locative Inversion in Chicheŵa: A Case Study of Factorization in Grammar Joan Bresnan and Jonni M. Kanerva CSLI88131 ($5.00)

An Information-Based Theory of Agreement Carl Pollard and Ivan A. Sag CSLI88132 ($4.00)

Relating Models of Polymorphism José Meseguer CSLI88133 ($4.50)

Psychology, Semantics, and Mental Events under Descriptions Peter Ludlow CSLI89135 ($3.50)

Mathematical Proofs of Computer System Correctness Jon Barwise CSLI89136 ($3.50)

The X-bar Theory of Phrase Structure András Kornai and Geoffrey K. Pullum CSLI89137 ($4.00)

Discourse Structure and Performance Efficiency in Interactive and Noninteractive Spoken Modalities Sharon L. Oviatt and Philip R. Cohen CSLI90138 ($5.50)

The Contributing Influence of Speech and Interaction on Some Aspects of Human Discourse Sharon L. Oviatt and Philip R. Cohen CSLI90139 ($3.50)

The Connectionist Construction of Concepts Adrian Cussins CSLI90140 ($6.00)

Lecture Notes

The titles in this series are distributed by the University of Chicago Press and may be purchased in academic or university bookstores or ordered directly from the distributor at 11030 South Langely Avenue, Chicago, Illinois 60628 or by phone 1-800-621-2736, (312)568-1550. For overseas orders, see information below.

A Manual of Intensional Logic Johan van Benthem, second edition, revised and expanded. Lecture Notes No. 1

Emotion and Focus Helen Fay Nissenbaum. Lecture Notes No. 2

Lectures on Contemporary Syntactic Theories Peter Sells. Lecture Notes No. 3

An Introduction to Unification-Based Approaches to Grammar Stuart M. Shieber. Lecture Notes No. 4

The Semantics of Destructive Lisp Ian A. Mason. Lecture Notes No. 5

An Essay on Facts Ken Olson. Lecture Notes No. 6

Logics of Time and Computation Robert Goldblatt. Lecture Notes No. 7

Word Order and Constituent Structure in German Hans Uszkoreit. Lecture Notes No. 8

Color and Color Perception: A Study in Anthropocentric Realism David Russel Hilbert. Lecture Notes No. 9

Prolog and Natural-Language Analysis Fernando C. N. Pereira and Stuart M. Shieber. Lecture Notes No. 10

Working Papers in Grammatical Theory and Discourse Structure: Interactions of Morphology, Syntax, and Discourse M. Iida, S. Wechsler, and D. Zec (Eds.) with an Introduction by Joan Bresnan. Lecture Notes No. 11

Natural Language Processing in the 1980s: A Bibliography Gerald Gazdar, Alex Franz, Karen Osborne, and Roger Evans. Lecture Notes No. 12

Information-Based Syntax and Semantics Carl Pollard and Ivan Sag. Lecture Notes No. 13

Non-Well-Founded Sets Peter Aczel. Lecture Notes No. 14

Partiality, Truth and Persistence Tore Langholm. Lecture Notes No. 15

Attribute-Value Logic and the Theory of Grammar Mark Johnson. Lecture Notes No. 16

The Situation in Logic Jon Barwise. Lecture Notes No. 17

Other Books from CSLI Distributed by the University of Chicago Press

Agreement in Natural Language: Approaches, Theories, Descriptions Michael Barlow and Charles A. Ferguson (Eds.) — ()

Papers from the Second International Workshop on Japanese Syntax William J. Poser (Ed.) — ()

The Proceedings of the Seventh West Coast Conference on Formal Linguistics (WCCFL 7) — ()

The Proceedings of the Eighth West Coast Conference on Formal Linguistics (WCCFL 8) — ()

Books Distributed by CSLI

Titles distributed by CSLI may be ordered directly from CSLI Publications, Ventura Hall, Stanford University, Stanford, California 94305-4115.

The Proceedings of the Third West Coast Conference on Formal Linguistics (WCCFL 3) — ($9.00)

The Proceedings of the Fourth West Coast Conference on Formal Linguistics (WCCFL 4) — ($10.00)

The Proceedings of the Fifth West Coast Conference on Formal Linguistics (WCCFL 5) — ($9.00)

The Proceedings of the Sixth West Coast Conference on Formal Linguistics (WCCFL 6) — ($12.00)

This book was typeset with TEX on Turing, CSLI's principal computer, by the author and Emma Pease in Computer Modern Roman type, designed by Donald Knuth with his digital-font designing program, METAFONT. The cover design is by Nancy Etchemendy, the book design by Dikran Karagueuzian. TEX, which was also created by Knuth, is a trademark of the American Mathematical Society.